TEENAGE RAMPAGE

Other books in the Virgin True Crime series

TEENAGE RAMPAGE

The Worldwide Youth Crime Explosion

Antonio Mendoza

First published in 2002 by

Virgin Books
Thames Wharf Studios
Rainville Rd
London W6 9HA

ISBN 0 7535 0715 3

Typesetting by TW Typesetting, Plymouth, Devon

Printed and bound by Mackays of Chatham PLC

CONTENTS

school and everyone knows someone that has killed or been killed. Born out of this subculture of poverty, death and violence are the Sicarios, teenage assassins armed and ready to blow someone away.

15. ANARCHY IN THE UK

The Youth Crime Phenomenon – As crack cocaine and the proliferation of deadly weapons in Britain becomes increasingly commonplace, the UK's disenfranchised and alienated youth carries out drug turf wars, chilling teen-on-teen homicides, armed mobile phone jackings and gangster-style executions. The numbers don't lie. Crime is up, the perpetrators are getting younger, and their ruthlessness is unmatched. Welcome to the twenty-first century, where ultraviolence rules and life itself becomes increasingly worthless.

ACKNOWLEDGMENTS

Dedication: To my mother, for her unconditional love. And to all the victims of the senseless violence chronicled in these pages.

Acknowledgments: I want to thank my editor Kerri Sharp for her patience over the protracted delivery of this manuscript. I also want to thank my wife Deirdre Mendoza, for proofreading most of the book and assisting with chapters Angel of Death and Anarchy in the UK; Stephen Siciliano, for co-writing The Colombian Sicarios; Gregory Miller, for researching The Vampire Clan, and Jaime Glantz.

Some parts of this book have previously appeared, in different forms, in The Internet Crime Archives (www.mayhem.net), in the sections called Intermittent Explosive Disorder, Cults R' Us, and The Mass Murderer Hit List.

1. SCHOOLYARD KILLERS

LOCK AND LOAD

You're always angry. You're tired of always being picked on. You're tired of all the bullies. You wish they wouldn't call you 'freak' or 'fag' or 'creep'. You wish they wouldn't make fun of the way you dress, of your hair, of your awkwardness, of your geeky body.

You wish your mother would understand why no one likes you, but she won't understand anymore. Not after you stabbed her in the shower. She was such a pain, always depressed and badgering you. Looks like she won't mind if you use her car this morning. She can have it back after you're done.

You put on your camouflage outfit, then drape two ammunition belts across your chest, Rambo style. On top of it, you put on a black trench coat. You put on sunglasses. You're the Terminator, ready to get the job done.

You're driving to school with an arsenal in the trunk. You've brought the pipe bombs you've been making in anticipation of this day. No one ever listened to you, but today they will. All the times you said you would come to school and blow everyone up. They should have listened, but now it's too late.

All your life no one cared about you, but today you're a rock god. People will write books about you. There'll be internet chat rooms dedicated to your thoughts. Other kids who have been bullied will mutter, 'Way to go, asshole, chalk this one up for the freaks.' You're like the geek Jesus, crying for all the other geeks.

You imagine it will be like the 'Jeremy' video, or a scene from *Basketball Diaries*, or like playing 'Doom'. And at the end a cop will blow your head off, or you'll do it yourself. Doesn't matter as long as you're dead. Knowing that you will die makes it all that much easier.

You put your headphones on and crank Rammstein up to 10. Fuck, it's cool. You can taste the fear on your lips. You can feel the adrenaline pumping through your veins. You take a minute to collect your thoughts. You march into the school's commons with your black duster flapping and your mind focused on drawing blood. Under the coat, your hands are holding a TEC-9 semi-automatic and a pump action shotgun. It's time for lock and load.

You see the first flash and it all starts happening in a blur. You barely hear the screaming. You go into automatic. Bodies are strewn all over the floor. You reload. There's one of your friends. What an idiot. You told him not to show up. Fuck him, you shoot him dead on the spot.

You did it. You have one bullet left. You back into a closet. Outside you hear the SWAT team getting into position. You hope you got a bigger body count than Columbine. Now you're a superstar. You put the muzzle of the shotgun in your mouth and bang! Your head is splattered all over the wall. You're another teen rampager who has settled the score.

TEEN ALIENATION

'I just don't like Mondays. This livens up the day. I have to go now. I shot a pig, I think, and I want to shoot some more.' – Brenda Spencer

In 1979, when sixteen-year-old Brenda Spencer started shooting at children at the Cleveland Elementary School, teen rampagers were a freakish anomaly. More than two decades later, the schoolyard massacre has metastasized into something horrifyingly commonplace. Throughout the United States, the once hallowed school grounds have become the killing fields for the bullied and the disenfranchised.

Experts agree that teen alienation has reached epidemic proportions, especially in rural and semi-rural areas. And it's not just other people's kids pulling the trigger. Teen rampagers, like Dylan Klebold, Kip Kinkel or Barry Loukaitis, all come from relatively stable, middle-class suburban homes. In some cases, these violent teens come from broken families, though dysfunction does not seem prevalent in their pre-rampage day-to-day living.

Alienated teens once chose suicide as a way out. Now school rampages – with guns and bombs and high body counts – are the preferred option. In the time it takes to unload a TEC-9 semi-automatic into a crowded cafeteria, these children go from being pathetic nobodies to becoming America's Most Wanted media stars.

In the United States, Dylan Klebold's and Eric Harris's assault on Columbine High that left fifteen dead is seen as the deadliest example of the deep malaise affecting the middle-class youth. In Europe, the recent assault by Robert Stein-haeuser in Erfurt's Gutenberg Gymnasium that left sixteen dead is by far the bloodiest and most horrifying manifestation of this deadly trend.

'There are at least thirteen children killed every day by weapons in this country. No other country has this syn-drome,' said Dianne Feinstein, a Democratic congresswoman representing California. 'This is a gun-happy culture.'

Between 1994 and 1998, there have been 173 violent deaths in US schools. Surprisingly, a large portion of these deaths happen in white, middle-class, 'heartland-type' school districts, not urban, inner-city areas where violence and gang culture are the norm.

Paradoxically, this rise of school violence has happened at a time when overall violent crime in the United States has been on the decline. Colin Moore, a leading New York defense lawyer, told the BBC World Service: 'It could very well be that what we have been doing in the United States is solving the crime in the inner-city areas, in the predominantly black and Hispanic areas, only to have ignored the whole question of law enforcement in the white suburban areas.'

Just like the war on drugs. As it focused on the inner city, there was a marked rise of addiction in suburban homes. Alienated white teens have discovered something inner-city kids have always taken for granted: guns and violence will buy them the respect from their peers that they will otherwise never know.

IMPULSE CONTROL

'I'm going to kill you all. You've been giving us shit for years . . . You're fucking going to pay for all the shit . . . We don't give a shit because we're going to die doing it.' – Eric Harris

Is there a pattern to the mayhem? The phenomenon of children shooting their classmates and teachers can be seen, in part, as the result of pent-up rage, a growing sense of hopelessness, obsessive planning and easy access to weapons. 'These are not impulsive acts,' says J Reid Meloy, a forensic psychologist and expert on sociopathic behavior. 'There's a planning and a purpose, and an emotional detachment that's very long-term.'

In a recent study, the US Secret Service looked at 41 children involved in 37 school shootings spanning over two decades. The study, titled 'The Safe School Initiative', was conducted by the Secret Service National Threat Assessment Center in collaboration with the US Department of Justice in Washington and the National Institute of Justice. It concluded that, though it could not give a single profile of a school shooter, in most rampage attacks the shooter planned the attack over a period of time and invariably told more than one person what they were planning.

Of the killers studied, some lived with both parents in 'ideal, all-American homes', some were children of divorce, some were adopted, and some lived in foster homes. A few were loners, but most had close friends. Few had disciplinary records. Some were honor roll students and were in Advanced Placement courses, some were failing out of school. Few showed a change in friendships or interest. In short, most were normal teenagers coping however they could with the social pressures stemming from the hierarchical system of the typical American high school.

Aaron R Kipnis, the author of the 1999 book *Angry Young Men: How Parents, Teachers, and Counselors Can Help 'Bad Boys' Become Good Men*, says that schools unwillingly condone bullying, teasing and cliques by labeling and dividing students according to their academic and athletic abilities, leaving some students – particularly non-athletic boys – institutionally marginalized.

'The fact that schools issue varsity sweaters with letters to the top athletes, and not the top physics students, underscores this idea that physical prowess and athletic achievement is really what's most important. Anything else is geeky, nerdy, kooky, or uncool.' Conversely, many school rampagers who were bullied, threatened and physically attacked for being nerdy and uncool, initially set out to hunt down abusive jocks.

COMMON TRAITS

'Tomorrow you will find out if you live or die.' – Mitchell Johnson

According to the Secret Service findings, school rampagers do not 'snap'. In almost all cases, the attacks are premeditated. The attackers systematically procure the necessary weapons, make lists of their targets and plot their plan of attack.

School rampagers aren't, as one would expect, loners. In most cases, they have a tight network of friends with whom they discuss specifics about their planned attacks. In some cases, people knew in detail what was going to happen, while others knew in vague terms that 'something spectacular' was happening on a particular date. Those who knew in advance sometimes encouraged the attacker and/or helped him widen the scope of the plan. Rarely, though, did those who knew about the plan warn anyone. In the aftermath, all the friends who knew – and those who came to watch the carnage – always claim that they never believed the attacker would do it.

In almost all cases, the attackers behaved strangely and hinted at what they were going to do in front of adults. But these adults didn't pay attention to the warning signs and remained oblivious to the shooter's growing desperation.

In most cases, the attackers would practically broadcast their intentions to whoever would listen. Before the

Columbine attack, the local sheriff had been given copies of one attacker's website. The printout, obtained by a concerned parent, described the rampager's pipe bombs and was loaded with threats against everyone: 'You all better fucking hide in your houses because im comin for EVERYONE soon, and I WILL be armed to the fucking teeth and I WILL shoot to kill and I WILL FUCKING KILL EVERYTHING.' The sheriff, who probably thought the threats were the ramblings of a bored teenager, didn't take them seriously and never looked into it.

Contrary to what one would expect, only a few of the shooters have been diagnosed with a mental illness or have had histories of drug or alcohol abuse. That is, until after the attack. Then their defending lawyers dredge out some syndrome like Intermittent Explosive Disorder or Bipolar Disorder and go for an insanity defense.

But more than half of the shooters had a history of depression. Some were on antidepressants like Prozac before the attacks; about three-quarters either talked about suicide or tried to kill themselves before the attack. Six did kill themselves during their attacks. In a jailhouse interview, Luke Woodham, the wannabe Satanist shooter from Pearl High, told the Secret Service researchers, 'I didn't really see my life going on any further. I thought it was all over with . . . I couldn't find a reason not to do it.'

The main motivation for most shooters is revenge. Some shooters mentioned in their journals a polymorphous sense of hatred against everyone and everything as the main factor for their actions. In his journal, Kip Kinkel, an Oregon student who killed his parents and two classmates, wrote: 'Hate drives me . . . I am so full of rage . . . Everyone is against me . . . As soon as my hope is gone, people die.'

The most common problem encountered in school by the shooters was bullying and scapegoatism. Many thought that launching an attack was the only way to stop the abuse. Two-thirds of the attackers described feeling persecuted, bullied and threatened by their peers. Loukaitis wrote in his journal: 'Some day people are going to regret teasing me.'

More than three-quarters of the attackers were known to hold a grievance, real or imagined, against their target and/or others. In most cases, this was the first violent act against the target. Some shooters were acting out over having their heart broken, while others acted out in response to something as simple as an expulsion, a suspension, or a failing grade.

Most school rampagers were not bullies. On the contrary, their problems stemmed from being the ones who were continually bullied. Furthermore, rampagers were rarely involved in fights and were not victims of domestic violence. Some, but not many, harmed animals. Six in ten showed interest in violence in movies, music and video games. About half kept detailed diaries of their growing rage. Some dabbled in the occult and were interested in Satanism. Very few, apart from Klebold and Harris, showed interest in extremist philosophies like Nazism.

In more than three-quarters of the incidents, the attackers had difficulty coping with a major change in their lives. A romantic breakup or a humiliating failure could be the trigger for an attack. 'I actually had somebody I loved and somebody that loved me for the first time in my life, the only time in my life,' Woodham said in a jailhouse interview. 'And then she just, all of a sudden one day she broke up with me and I was devastated, I was going to kill myself.'

Many of the killers made lists of targets and some were specific about the order in which they would perpetrate the killings. In about half of the cases, people who were not included in the original hit list were shot. Also, once the shooting started, about half of the rampagers were gunning for maximum body count.

For most attackers, the easiest part of their plan was getting weapons. These young killers were able to get their guns at home or from friends. They were also able to buy them at stores and gun shows. Some stole the weapons from a neighbor or relative. Ironically some received them as gifts from parents. More than half had a history of gun use, with many of them taking trips to a gun range with their fathers. Curiously, only a few had a 'fascination' with weapons.

Most school rampages were very brief. Almost two-thirds of the attacks were over before police arrived. The attacker was usually stopped by students or staff members or had run out of bullets. Sometimes the attacks ended with the killer taking his own life. In general, SWAT teams were unnecessary and perhaps even – as seen in the aftermath of Columbine – detrimental. In only three cases studied by the Secret Service did police have to discharge their weapons.

BRAIN CHEMISTRY

'Why did God just want me to be in complete misery? I need to find more weapons. My parents are trying to take away some of my guns! My guns are the only things that haven't stabbed me in the back. My eyes hurt. They hurt so bad. They feel like they are trying to crawl out of my head. Why aren't I normal? Help me. No one will.' – Kip Kinkel

Adult rampage killers tend to be better educated than typical murderers, which concurs with the fact that many teen rampagers are honor students or, at least, do well in school. Adult rampage killers tend to be driven by some sort of mental illness, which would indicate that teen rampagers would also be mentally unbalanced. At the time of their attacks, several teen rampagers were being treated for depression or antisocial behavior. Could their violent behavior be directly linked to the toxic chemical cocktails that were being prescribed for them?

Columbine killer Eric Harris was being treated by a psychiatrist with the drug Luvox. Like Prozac, Zoloft and Paxil, Luvox is a selective serotonin reuptake inhibitor, which means that it tries to control depression by changing the serotonin levels in the brain. Luvox is typically prescribed for obsessive-compulsive disorder, although many doctors prescribe it for depression. Kip Kinkel was on Prozac when he killed his parents and two students in Springfield, Oregon. Not surprisingly, Lewis A Opler MD, author of *Prozac and Other Psychiatric Drugs*, writes: 'The following side effects are listed for Prozac: apathy; hallucinations; hostility; irrational ideas; paranoid reactions; antisocial behavior; hysteria; and suicidal thoughts.'

After Andrew Golden and Mitchell Johnson pulled a fire alarm at their school in Jonesboro, Arkansas, and shot at exiting students, Dr Alan Lipman, of Georgetown University, remarked that at least one of the boys had been treated for violent behavior. Because of the age of the suspects, the identity of the boy getting treated was never made public. Was the youngster treated with Prozac, Zoloft or Luvox? Or with a dangerous combination of the three? Though serotonin reuptake inhibition is touted by some experts as a potential cure for violence, it is seen by others in the psychiatric community as a causative factor in violent behavior.

Recent child development studies have uncovered an increase in childhood psychopathy. Many children are grow- ing up with no sense of morality or respect for others. These youths have failed to develop affectionate bonds that allow them to empathize with others. Instead, they are arrogant, dishonest, narcissistic and remorseless. Furthermore, they learn at an early age to be deceptive, manipulative and uncaring. But this profile of the 'fledging psychopath' is equally suited to the bullies who drive teen rampagers to murder their peers.

Brain studies suggest that psychopaths and children diag- nosed with Antisocial Personality Disorder have, not surpris- ingly, abnormal serotonin levels in the brain. Children with antisocial tendencies tend to be fearless and have a weak behavioral inhibition system. According to Canadian theorist Dr David Lykken, most antisocial behaviors in children come from poor parenting. Lykken believes that antisocial behaviors like aggressiveness and lack of fear of punishment are a result of absent fathers and inadequate mothers who fail to properly socialize their children.

INTERMITTENT EXPLOSIVE DISORDER

'It clicked in my head, I had to kill Manuel.' – Barry Loukaitis

Another clinical term bandied around teen rampagers has been Intermittent Explosive Disorder, which is associated with impulsive aggressive acts that are grossly out of proportion to any precipitating psychosocial stressors and that lead to violent outbursts. Episodes of Intermittent Explosive Disorder have been variously referred to as rage attacks, anger attacks or episodic dyscontrol, but cannot be attributed to other mental disorders like Antisocial Personality Disorder, Borderline Personality Disorder, Conduct Disorder, or Attention-Deficit/Hyperactivity Disorder.

Intermittent Explosive Disorder is characterized by frequent and often unpredictable episodes of extreme anger or physical violence. Between episodes, the individual functions normally and exhibits no evidence of violence or physical threat. The disorder is, at best, rare, with the majority of cases occurring when the individual is between late adolescence and late twenties. Again, the neurotransmitter serotonin is believed to play a role in it.

People with Intermittent Explosive Disorder may have a significant history of unstable interpersonal relationships, dangerous behavior and substance abuse. Some believe that a diagnosis of Intermittent Explosive Disorder, which is still a vaguely-defined entity, is a cop-out by enterprising lawyers seeking a way to spare their clients from the death penalty or life in prison.

As with other troubling aspects of modern living, there are no quick answers to the rise in teen rampaging. As a society we look for its causes and try to ascertain who is to blame. Is it uncaring parents? Elitist social hierarchies? School bullies? Violent video games? Self-indulgent rock stars? Murderous movie fantasies? Many in courtrooms and the media have tried to blame pop culture icons like Marilyn Manson, Pearl Jam, Stephen King, *Natural Born Killers*, *The Basketball Diaries* and the video game 'Doom', but such scapegoatism is merely an attempt to whitewash ourselves of any blame.

Perhaps the answer lies in the prophetic words of Charles Manson: 'You made your children what they are . . . These children that come at you with knives, they are your children. You taught them. I didn't teach them. I just tried to help them stand up . . . You can project it back at me, but I am only what lives inside each and every one of you . . . I am only what you made me. I am a reflection of you.'

ROMANTICIZING DEATH

'I am the epitome of all Evil! I have no mercy for humanity, they tortured me until I snapped and became what I am today.' – Luke Woodham

A recent study by the United States Department of Education concluded that vigilance is the best way to avoid the next rampage. But police-state tactics do not always work. Dr Peter Stringham, the adolescent violence prevention counselor at the Department of Pediatrics and Adolescent Medicine in East Boston, believes that the key to reducing teen rampages is to ensure that all children are made to feel valuable: 'We have, as a society, to make each individual feel that they have worth.'

At the root of all school rampages, according to Dr Stringham, there is a teenager who's been rejected, socially and institutionally, for not being special. 'Problems do occur when we transmit the message to young people that they only have a place in the universe if they are smart, if they are good athletes, if they look a certain way or have a certain sexuality. Young people who do not conform to that ideal will be more likely to experience problems.'

Coupled with this rejection is the romantic notion of death – the Kurt Cobain syndrome – and not understanding that the consequences of their violent actions are permanent. Cobain was both tragic and heroic, and teenagers romanticize this duality without understanding the finality of death.

'Violence is often a problem for people who have some kind of emptiness,' said Dr Stringham. 'Teenagers do not have strong egos, so they fill that space with something. There are healthy things to fill it with like academic achievement, sport or altruism. There are extremely negative things to fill it with like cults, inappropriate sex, inappropriate behavior like sex or drugs.

'The thing that sets America aside from the rest of the world,' he adds, morosely, 'is that any moron can get a gun.'

2. THE HIT LIST

'When I snap, I want the firepower to kill people. – Kip Kinkel

In the late 1990s, school rampages reached epidemic proportions. Yet the following timeline shows that since 1974 gun violence in schools has been on the rise. Most attacks occurred in the United States and were perpetrated by teen and pre-teen boys. However, since Columbine, school rampages have taken a more international aspect with attacks in Canada, The Netherlands, Germany and Bosnia.

30 DECEMBER 1974 – OLEAN, NEW YORK
ANTHONY BARBARO, 18
During Christmas recess, Barbaro, an honor student, broke into his high school and set several fires. He then holed up in a room on the third floor with his rifle and shot at people responding to the fire alarm, killing three – a custodian and two bystanders – and wounding nine others. Hours later, a SWAT team found him asleep with his headphones on playing 'Jesus Christ Superstar'. At his home, police found several handmade bombs and a diary detailing how he had been planning the attack for five months. Barbaro hung himself while awaiting trial. In a suicide note found in his cell, he scribbled: 'I guess I just wanted to kill the person I hate most – myself. I just didn't have the courage. I wanted to die, but I couldn't do it, so I had to get someone to do it for me. It didn't work out.'

22 FEBRUARY 1978 – EVERETT HIGH, LANSING, MICHIGAN
ROGER NEEDHAM, 15
A smart but troubled loner, Needham was constantly picked on by classmates. That is, until he brought a German-made Luger to school and shot two students. One died. Then he

surrendered to a social studies teacher and said, 'I'm tired of being pushed around. Now I'm even.' After serving four years in a juvenile facility, he was released. Needham went on to get his PhD in mathematics and taught at the City College of New York. He has never been arrested again.

15 OCTOBER 1978 – LANETT, ALABAMA
ROBIN ROBINSON, 13
After an argument with a student, Robinson was paddled by the school principal. Pissed off, he went home, returned to school with a gun and shot the principal when the man threatened to paddle him again.

29 JANUARY 1979 – CLEVELAND ELEMENTARY SCHOOL, SAN DIEGO, CALIFORNIA
BRENDA SPENCER, 16
Using a rifle her father had given her for Christmas, Spencer shot at children entering the Cleveland Elementary School across the street from her home. She killed two adults, and wounded eight children and a policeman.

21 JANUARY 1985 – GODDARD JUNIOR HIGH, WICHITA, KANSAS
JAMES ALAN KEARBEY, 14
Although he intended to shoot at the athletes that had been picking on him for years, Kearbey shot and killed the school principal, and wounded two teachers and a student. Kearbey spent seven years in a state youth center before being released on his 21st birthday.

4 DECEMBER 1986 – LEWISTON, MONTANA
KRISTOFER HANS, 14
Failing French, Hans threatened to kill his teacher, but instead shot and killed her substitute, and injured the school's vice principal and two students.

2 MARCH 1987 – DEKALB, MISSOURI
NATHAN FERRIS, 12

An overweight honor student, Ferris vowed to bring a gun to school to stop his classmates from humiliating him. When he did pull out a .45-caliber pistol during history class, classmate Timothy Perrin laughed at him and said it was a toy. Ferris shot him dead, then turned the gun on himself. Ferris had warned his friends not to attend school that day, but, like always, they didn't listen to him.

26 SEPTEMBER 1988 – OAKLAND ELEMENTARY SCHOOL, GREENWOOD, SOUTH CAROLINA
JAMIE WILSON, 19

Jamie Wilson killed two third-graders and wounded seven other students and two teachers when he started firing shots in the school's cafeteria and in a classroom. Wilson's relatives said they made two attempts to have him involuntarily committed during the couple of years before the killings. The rampager pleaded guilty but mentally ill. The court, however, sentenced him to death for his killing spree.

16 DECEMBER 1988 – VIRGINIA BEACH, VIRGINIA
NICHOLAS ELLIOTT, 16

Loaded with a semi-automatic pistol, 200 rounds of ammunition and three firebombs, Elliott went to school and killed a teacher, wounded another and fired on a student who had called him a racist name. In court, the teen rampager pleaded guilty to murder and thirteen other charges and received life plus 114 years in prison.

5 OCTOBER 1989 – ORANGE COUNTY, CALIFORNIA
CORDELL 'CORY' ROBB, 15

After telling other students he wanted to get his stepfather to school so he could kill him, Robb – armed with a shotgun and semi-automatic pistol – took his drama class hostage and shot a student who taunted him.

1 MAY 1992 – LINDHURST HIGH, OLIVEHURST, CALIFORNIA
ERIC HOUSTON, 20

Angry over the perceived treatment he had received in high school, Eric Houston wrote: 'My HATEtrid tord humanity forced me to do what I did . . . I know parenting had nothing to do with what happens today. It seems my sanity has slipped away and evil taken its place . . . And if I die today please bury me somewhere beautiful.' Then he returned to Lindhurst High with a 12-gauge shotgun and a sawn off .22 rifle and killed Robert Brens, a teacher who flunked him in history class, and three students. He also wounded thirteen other pupils. He took seventy students hostage for eight and a half hours before surrendering to the authorities.

11 SEPTEMBER 1992 – PALO DURO HIGH SCHOOL, AMARILLO, TEXAS
RANDY EARL MATTHEWS, 17

During a morning pep rally, Matthews pulled out a gun and shot six students. A seventh student was trampled by the escaping mob. All the injured recovered. Matthews was charged with attempted murder, aggravated assault and unlawfully carrying a weapon on school grounds. He was sentenced to eight years in prison.

14 DECEMBER 1992 – SIMON'S ROCK COLLEGE, GREAT BARRINGTON, MASSACHUSETTS
WAYNE LO, 18

A sophomore at the exclusive Simon's Rock College, Wayne Lo had told a school official that he had 'the power to bring the college to its knees'. On the day of the rampage a school administrator found that Lo, who repeatedly made racist and homophobic remarks and joked about killing people, had received in the mail a package from an ammo company. After meeting with him, he allowed the youngster to keep the package. Then Lo went to a Pittsfield gun shop and bought a Chinese-made SKS semi-automatic rifle. When Lo returned to his dorm, a student anonymously phoned another school administrator and told him that Lo had a weapon and wanted to hurt somebody. Again, no one did anything about it. That night, acting on 'a command from God', Lo rampaged through the school's small campus killing a professor and a student and wounding four others.

18 JANUARY 1993 – EAST CARTER HIGH SCHOOL, GRAYSON, KENTUCKY
GARY SCOTT PENNINGTON, 17

Upset over a bad grade on his report card, Pennington, armed with a .38-caliber revolver, shot and killed his English teacher and a custodian, and held his seventh-period English class hostage. Over the next hour he released the students, letting them go in groups of two and three. Then he surrendered to police without further bloodshed. Pennington had previously told a friend that his goal was to kill two people so he could be eligible for the death penalty.

24 MAY 1993 – UPPER PERKIOMEN HIGH SCHOOL, PENNSBURG, PENNSYLVANIA
JASON MICHAEL SMITH, 15

Tired of being bullied, Smith broke into his mother's boyfriend's locked gun cabinet and stole a .9mm Ruger. He took the weapon to school and, during Biology class, fired twice at point-blank range at sixteen-year-old Michael Swann's face. Swann, according to classmates, had been bullying the youngster since the seventh grade. After the attack, Smith calmly walked out of the school and waited for the police to arrive and arrest him.

12 APRIL 1994 – BUTTE, MONTANA
JASON OSMANSON, 10

After a playground dispute over a ball, little Jason Osmanson shot and killed one of his classmates. When asked why he did it, the youngster answered, 'Nobody loves me, anyway.' After the shooting, school personnel learned that his divorced parents both had Aids and the other kids had been teasing him about it.

26 MAY 1994 – RYLE HIGH SCHOOL, UNION, KENTUCKY
CLAY SHROUT, 17

Before going to school Clay Shrout shot and killed his parents and his two sisters. When he arrived at Trigonometry class, Clay pulled out his gun and announced that he was taking them hostage. When a student asked him why, Clay replied, 'I have had a really bad day, I've just killed my family.' After about thirty minutes, he released his hostages. In court, he was found mentally ill but guilty and sentenced to life in prison without parole for 25 years.

23 JANUARY 1995 – SACRED HEART SCHOOL, REDLANDS, CALIFORNIA
JOHN SIROLA, 14

Angry that he had to wear a school uniform to his Catholic school, John shot the principal in the face and shoulder with a sawn-off shotgun stolen from a family friend. Fleeing the scene, he tripped and accidentally shot and killed himself.

12 OCTOBER 1995 – BLACKVILLE-HILDA HIGH SCHOOL, BLACKVILLE, SOUTH CAROLINA
TOBY SINCINO, 16

While on suspension for making an obscene gesture, Toby, who was regularly picked on by other students, returned to the school with a gun, killed a teacher and wounded another. He then killed himself.

15 NOVEMBER 1995 – RICHLAND SCHOOL, GILES COUNTY, TENNESSEE
JAMIE ROUSE, 17

Dressed in black, Jamie headed for school packing a .22-calibre Remington Viper handgun and shot two teachers in the head, killing one of them. Then he aimed at the school's football coach, but a female student walked into his line of fire and was killed instead. Rouse told five friends what he was planning to do. Not one of them chose to warn any adults.

2 FEBRUARY 1996 – FRONTIER JUNIOR HIGH SCHOOL, MOSES LAKE, WASHINGTON
BARRY LOUKAITIS, 14

Another honor student with an axe to grind. Loukaitis showed up at Frontier Junior High School with two pistols, 78 rounds of ammunition, and a high-powered rifle under his black duster. He fired four shots in Algebra class killing two students and a teacher and wounding a third student.

27 JANUARY 1997 – CONNISTON MIDDLE SCHOOL, WEST PALM BEACH, FLORIDA
TRONNEAL MANGUM, 14

After stealing a watch from Johnpierre Kamel, a handicapped fourteen-year-old classmate, school bully Tronneal Mangum fired three times and killed the youngster. Tronneal was tried as an adult, convicted of murder and received a life sentence. In prison, Mangum has attended auto repair classes. Ironically, though he now knows how to fix cars, he will never get the chance to drive one.

19 FEBRUARY 1997 – BETHEL HIGH SCHOOL, BETHEL, ALASKA
EVAN RAMSEY, 16

Tired of being called 'retarded' and 'spaz' by the other kids, Evan brought a shotgun to school and killed a fellow student and the school principal. He also injured two other students. Prior to the killings, Evan discussed his planned revenge with two classmates.

1 OCTOBER 1997 – PEARL HIGH SCHOOL, PEARL, MISSISSIPPI
LUKE WOODHAM, 16

After his girlfriend broke up with him, baby-faced Luke stabbed his mother to death, then went to school with a hunting rifle. There he shot and killed his former girlfriend and another girl and wounded seven others.

1 DECEMBER 1997 – HEATH HIGH SCHOOL, PADUCAH, KENTUCKY
MICHAEL CARNEAL, 14

Wannabe Satanist Michael Carneal brought a pistol, two rifles, two shotguns, and 700 rounds of ammunition to school and, just before the start of classes, opened fire on a small prayer group. Three girls died and five others were wounded. Earlier he threatened to 'shoot up' the school, but no one had taken him seriously.

15 DECEMBER 1997 – STAMPS HIGH SCHOOL, STAMPS, ARKANSAS
JOSEPH 'COLT' TODD, 14

Hiding in the woods next to the school parking lot, Todd launched a sniper attack on fellow students. Using a .22-caliber rifle he wounded Leticia Finley, fifteen, and Grover Henderson, seventeen. In custody Todd said, 'I was tired of being picked on.'

24 MARCH 1998 – WESTSIDE MIDDLE SCHOOL, JONESBORO, ARKANSAS
ANDREW GOLDEN, 11, AND MITCHELL JOHNSON, 13

Dressed in camouflage and loaded down with weapons, Golden and Johnson gunned down fifteen people after pulling a school fire alarm and ambushing the exiting students. Four girls and a female teacher were killed.

24 APRIL 1998 – J. W. PAKER MIDDLE SCHOOL, EDINBORO, PENNSYLVANIA
ANDREW 'SATAN' WURST, 14

After telling his fellow students he planned to 'make the dance memorable', class rebel Andrew Wurst shot and killed a popular science teacher and wounded two students at the end of their eighth-grade graduation dance. The rampage happened in a banquet hall near the school as the last song – 'My Heart Will Go On' from the movie *Titanic* – was playing.

19 MAY 1998 – LINCOLN COUNTY HIGH SCHOOL, FAYETTEVILLE, TENNESSEE
JACOB DAVIS, 18

Three days before graduation, honor student Jacob Davis used a rifle to shoot and kill Robert 'Nick' Cresonto, his ex-girlfriend's new boyfriend. After the shooting, Davis reportedly put the gun on the ground, sat down next to it and put his head in his hands. He was sentenced to 51 years in prison.

21 MAY 1998 – THURSTON HIGH SCHOOL, SPRINGFIELD, OREGON
KIPLAND KINKEL, 15

Having just been expelled from school for carrying a gun to class, Kipland killed both his parents, spent the night next to their bodies, then returned to Thurston High with a semi-automatic rifle. He started shooting in the school cafeteria, killing two students and wounding 22 others. At the time, Kip had been prescribed Ritalin and Prozac, two powerful antidepressants. Not surprisingly, he told the arresting officers after the rampage: 'I had no choice.'

16 APRIL 1999 – NOTUS JUNIOR–SENIOR HIGH SCHOOL, NOTUS, IDAHO
SHAWN COOPER, 16

Another youngster on Ritalin, Shawn boarded the school bus with a shotgun wrapped in a blanket and a death list in his pocket. When he got to school, he fired twice, barely missing students and school staff.

20 APRIL 1999 – COLUMBINE HIGH, LITTLETON, COLORADO
ERIC HARRIS, 17, AND DYLAN KLEBOLD, 18

In the bloodiest chapter in high school rampages in the US, Harris and Klebold, armed to the teeth with guns and homemade bombs, killed twelve students, one teacher and themselves in their morning attack on Columbine High. According to their journals and a website, they had planned the carnage for over a year. Like Kip Kinkel and Shawn

Cooper, Harris was being treated for depression and had been prescribed Prozac.

28 APRIL 1999 – W R MYERS HIGH SCHOOL, TABER, ALBERTA, CANADA
UNIDENTIFIED BOY, 14

Marking the first post-Columbine attack, an unidentified fourteen-year-old boy, who had dropped out to begin home schooling, returned to his high school at lunchtime with a .22 caliber rifle. He fired four shots, killing Jason Lang and injuring his best friend, Shane Christmas, both seventeen. The shooter, who has a congenital heart condition, spent the rest of the year in a coma and was charged with murder.

20 MAY 1999 – HERITAGE HIGH SCHOOL, CONYERS, GEORGIA
THOMAS SOLOMON, 15

Upset about being dumped by his girlfriend, Solomon brought a gun to school and wounded six students. After shooting at his classmates, he put the gun in his mouth to shoot himself, but was talked out of it by an assistant principal. Like others, Thomas repeatedly talked about bringing a gun to school. He too was taking the antidepressant Ritalin.

19 NOVEMBER 1999 – DEMING MIDDLE SCHOOL, DEMING, NEW MEXICO
VICTOR CORDOVA, JR., 12

Dressed in camouflage, twelve-year-old Victor Cordova shot and killed thirteen-year-old Aracely Tena after lunch in a school courtyard. Cordova also pointed his .22-caliber gun at two other students, the school's principal and the assistant principal before surrendering to police officers. A classmate said that the day before the rampage, Cordova showed him several bullets and boasted that he would open fire at school. 'Watch, I'm going to make history blasting this school,' he told his friend. Under state law, the youngster cannot be tried as an adult and will probably be released after serving at least two years in juvenile prison.

5 DECEMBER 1999 – FORT GIBSON MIDDLE SCHOOL, FORT GIBSON, OKLAHOMA
SETH TRICKEY, 13

Though an A-student and popular with his classmates, Seth pulled a gun from his backpack while standing in front of the school and fired fifteen rounds into a crowd of about seventy students, wounding several. When asked why he did it, he replied, 'I don't know.' He was convicted on seven assault charges and will remain in jail until he's nineteen.

7 DECEMBER 1999 – DE LEIJGRAAF HIGH SCHOOL, VEGHEL, NETHERLANDS
UNIDENTIFIED BOY, 17

A feud between two Turkish families led a seventeen-year-old student, who cannot be named under Dutch law, to open fire at a school in Holland. The shooter, whose father was waiting for him in the family Mercedes outside, fired his gun at least ten times in a school hall and in a computer class. Three students and a 46-year-old female teacher were wounded. The shooter's father then drove him to the police station where he surrendered. One of the wounded students, a nineteen-year-old, was romantically involved with the shooter's fifteen-year-old sister. One can assume the shooter was unhappy about their relationship.

20 FEBRUARY 2000 – BUELL ELEMENTARY SCHOOL, MOUNT MORRIS TOWNSHIP, MICHIGAN
UNIDENTIFIED BOY, 6

A six-year-old boy, called 'Johnny Elementary School' by the media, shot to death Kayla Roland, a fellow first-grader, after they argued in the playground. Apparently the shooter, who lived in a crack house, told little Kayla: 'I don't like you!' To which, she answered: 'So?' Then the six-year-old took out a .32-caliber handgun and shot her. The girl died thirty minutes later. The attacker was not prosecuted because of his age. In searching for someone to blame, the boy's nineteen-year-old uncle was arrested for possessing the gun used by the youngster. The uncle was sentenced to two to fifteen years in prison.

20 APRIL 2000 – CAIRINE WILSON HIGH SCHOOL, OTTAWA, ONTARIO, CANADA
UNIDENTIFIED BOY, 15

Five minutes before the students and faculty of Columbine started a one-year memorial service in their gym, a fifteen-year-old male student stabbed five of his classmates with a kitchen knife outside his school's library. No names were made public, and all victims survived.

26 MAY 2000 – LAKE WORTH COMMUNITY MIDDLE SCHOOL, FORT LAUDERDALE, FLORIDA
NATHANIEL 'NATE' BRAZILL, 13

On the last day of school, Nate and a fellow seventh-grader were sent home by a school counselor for starting a water balloon fight. Nate told his friend that he was going to get a gun, return to school and shoot the counselor. 'You wouldn't do that, would you, Nate?' the girl asked him. 'Watch, I'm gonna be all over the news, ' Nate answered. Nate did as he said, but instead of killing the counselor, he killed one of his favorite teachers. Two days before the shooting, Nate joked to his friends about having a 'hit list', but no one took him seriously. He also showed them the gun, which he had stolen from a relative's house. The youngster was tried for second-degree murder as an adult and sentenced to 28 years in prison.

24 OCTOBER 2000 – PIONEER ELEMENTARY SCHOOL, GLENDALE, ARIZONA
SEAN WAYNE BOTKIN, 14

Wearing a mask and camouflage and armed with a 9mm handgun, Botkin took thirty children and their teacher hostage in a portable building at Pioneer Elementary School. After negotiating the gradual release of the hostages, Sean demanded that the helicopters hovering overhead leave. When they did, he surrendered to authorities.

5 MARCH 2001 – SANTANA HIGH SCHOOL, SANTEE, CALIFORNIA
CHARLES ANDREW 'ANDY' WILLIAMS, 15

Andy Williams used to say that he wanted to 'pull a Columbine' but no one took him seriously. He finally made good on his word after the school disciplined him for tardiness. He brought a gun to school and started firing randomly in the hallway, killing two and wounding thirteen others. Like many rampagers, he complained about being picked on because of his scrawny physique.

7 MARCH 2001 – BISHOP NEUMANN HIGH SCHOOL, WILLIAMSPORT, PENNSYLVANIA
ELIZABETH BUSH, 14

Two days after the Santana High rampage, Elizabeth Bush, an eighth-grader who was ostracized and ridiculed by her classmates, shot a popular cheerleader in the school's cafeteria. The cheerleader, thirteen-year-old Kim Marchese, was wounded on the shoulder. Apparently Marchese and her friends relentlessly mocked Elizabeth with 'name-calling and slurs and innuendoes'. Before attending the Catholic school, Bush – who believed she was able to talk to God – had attended a public school in the Jersey Shore Area where classmates would call her a lesbian. The teenager was sentenced to an indeterminate term at a treatment facility for juveniles where she may be held until her 21st birthday.

22 MARCH 2001 – GRANITE HILLS HIGH SCHOOL, EL CAJON, CALIFORNIA
JASON HOFFMAN, 18

Irate at the school vice principal, senior Jason Hoffman pranced outside the administration building with a .22-caliber semiautomatic handgun and a 12-gauge shotgun in his hands. He fired ten shots from his shotgun, wounding six students and two teachers. An El Cajon police officer who was in the administration building at the time exchanged fire with Jason, wounding him in the face and buttocks. After pleading guilty,

Jason hanged himself in his jail cell with his bed sheets while he awaited sentencing.

15 JANUARY 2002 – MARTIN LUTHER KING JR. HIGH SCHOOL, MANHATTAN, NEW YORK
VINCENT RODRIGUEZ, 18

In one of the few school shootings in Manhattan, eighteen-year-old Rodriguez seriously wounded Andrel Napper and Andre Wilkens with a .380-caliber automatic pistol in a fourth-floor school hallway. The high school, like many in Manhattan, uses metal detectors in its entrance, but many students enter through unmonitored side doors. Apparently, the two youngsters were shot because they had been teasing Rodriguez's girlfriend.

19 FEBRUARY 2002 – FREISING, GERMANY
UNIDENTIFIED FORMER STUDENT, 22

A former student in an Economics school in Freising killed his ex-boss and a foreman at a home furnishing company in Munich where he had just been fired. He then took a cab and traveled twelve miles to his old school. Although he was looking for a particular teacher, the rampager shot another teacher in the face and shot and killed the school headmaster. He ended the rampage by setting off several pipe bombs and blowing himself up. The teacher who was shot in the face survived the attack.

26 APRIL 2002 – JOHANN GUTENBERG HIGH SCHOOL, ERFURT, GERMANY
ROBERT STEINHAEUSER, 19

The deadliest school shooting to date. After being expelled from school, Robert Steinhaeuser returned to walk the halls of the Gutenberg Gymnasium wearing a mask and a ninja outfit, and hunted down his former teachers. Using a 9mm Glock handgun and a pump action shotgun, Steinhauser killed thirteen teachers, two students and a female police officer with pin-point precision. The siege ended when his art and history teacher tore off his mask and pushed him into a classroom. There, the teenager put a bullet to his head as police commandos closed in on his location.

29 APRIL 2002 – ST APOSTOLA PETRA I PAVLA SCHOOL, VLASENICA HIGH SCHOOL, VLASENICA, BOSNIA
DRAGOSLAV PETKOVIC, 17
Three days after the massacre in Erfurt, Dragoslav Petkovic shot and killed his history teacher outside the school. Then he shot his math teacher in her classroom before committing suicide.

3. I DON'T LIKE MONDAYS

Name: Brenda Spencer
Born: 3 April 1962
Age at time of rampage: 16
Date of attack: 29 January 1979
Number of victims: 2
Victim profile: the school's principal and head custodian
Arsenal: .22-caliber rifle given to her for Christmas
Media keywords: Boomtown Rats
Early warning signs: dug an escape tunnel in the backyard
Probable cause: didn't like Mondays
School: Cleveland Elementary School
Location: San Diego, California
Status: serving 25 to life at the California Institution for
   Women in Corona

*'I had asked for a radio and he bought me a gun. I felt like he
wanted me to kill myself.'* – Brenda Spencer

SNIPER ATTACK

On 29 January 1979, sixteen-year-old Brenda Spencer, the
original school rampager, perched herself on her bedroom
window across the street from San Diego's Cleveland Elementary School and fired forty shots at students and teachers
entering the building. Spencer, using a .22-caliber rifle with a
telescopic sight that her father had just given her for
Christmas, killed two men, the school principal and the
head custodian, and wounded eight pupils and a police
officer.

The twenty-minute-long sniper attack began at 8.30 in the
morning, when the school bell signaled the start of classes and
children were pouring in from the playground. Witnesses said
at first it sounded like firecrackers, but the sight of sprawling
bodies made it painfully clear that it was an armed assault.

The first person mortally wounded was Burton Wragg, the 53-year-old school principal. He was struck twice in the chest as he ran out to help wounded children. Then Michael Suchar, the 56-year-old head custodian, was also struck in the chest when he went to the principal's aid. One youngster described how Suchar, agonizing on the floor, kept asking about his shoes. 'But he had his shoes on,' the girl said. Principal Wragg, a family man with three children, died while undergoing surgery. Suchar, the custodian, was pronounced dead on arrival at a local hospital.

The wounded children ranged in ages from seven to ten years old. Two underwent abdominal surgery and were reported in critical but stable condition. Three of the wounded youngsters were discharged from the hospital after being treated. One pupil, seven-year-old Audrey Sites, never let go of her coat and lunch bag as the doctors treated her gunshot wound.

Eight-year-old Mary Clark didn't tell anyone a bullet had passed through her abdomen until hours later when she was evacuated from the school. 'She didn't tell anyone she was shot,' a police officer said. 'She just went back to her class. She was afraid to talk to anybody.' The first officer at the scene, rookie patrolman Robert Robb, was struck in the neck by a bullet that lodged itself under his shoulder blade. Veteran police officer Theodore Kasinak commandeered a nearby garbage truck to block the sniper's line of fire and to pull the wounded to safety.

'There couldn't have been a worse time for it,' said Darryl Barnes, the assistant principal. 'The bell had just rung, the kids were streaming in and suddenly there were these shots.' Those inside the school remained trapped for three hours. Some students ran into closets and bathrooms to take cover. Others hid in the school auditorium or in their classrooms.

When the shooting stopped, Brenda, who had attended Cleveland Elementary, barricaded herself inside her home. For the next six and a half hours she held over one hundred police officers at bay, including San Diego's elite SWAT team, until she surrendered.

As the sniper attack developed into a stand-off, police cordoned off a sixteen-block area of La Mesa, a suburban, middle-class neighborhood in the northeast section of San Diego. Hoping to resolve the situation, veteran police negotiator Paul Olson established phone contact with Brenda. Authorities also brought in her father, three friends from Patrick Henry High School and two school counselors who knew her. Her father, it was reported, 'was in no condition to talk'.

On the phone, Spencer was juvenile and belligerent. On one occasion she told Olson she had reloaded her weapon and was going to start shooting. She also said she was drunk and taking barbiturates. To her friends she said that she was 'really wasted' and that she enjoyed the chaos she was causing.

Contradicting her implied state of mind, the then San Diego Police Chief William Kolander said after her arrest: 'She's very coherent. She knows who's she talking to.' Toxicology tests performed on her revealed no traces of illegal drugs in her blood. Arresting officers did find empty liquor bottles strewn around the house.

Brenda also chatted with enterprising reporters who telephoned her for quotes. She told one reporter she enjoyed aiming at 'the red and blue jackets' and that it had been 'a lot of fun seeing children shot'. When asked by a *San Diego Evening Tribune* reporter why she did it, she blurted out the often quoted: 'I just don't like Mondays. This livens up the day.' She then abruptly ended the interview saying: 'I have to go now. I shot a pig (police officer), I think, and I want to shoot some more.'

A little after 3 p.m., Brenda grew bored with the mayhem and calmly walked out of the house, laying down her rifle and pellet gun on the driveway. She went back and, a few minutes later, re-emerged from the house with her cache of several hundred rounds of ammunition and surrendered. A swarm of heavily armed SWAT officers took her into custody and drove her out of the scene in a waiting patrol car.

Of the 319 students attending Cleveland Elementary on the day of the shootings, only 69 were absent the next day. Two years later, next to the flagpole, a brass monument was erected in honor of the two dead men. The school closed in 1983 due to a sharp drop in enrollment. It's been used for a variety of purposes since.

The brass monument was erected on the very spot where Monika Selvig, then eight, was shot. After the shooting, little Monika was praised for being brave and cheerful throughout the ordeal. Now all grown up and freshly out of drug rehab, Selvig knows why things went wrong for her after the attack: 'I just didn't deal with it, and I never got any crisis help or counseling or therapy until I was in my late teens,' she said. 'By then I was really screwed up.'

TOO SMALL TO BE SCARY

From all accounts, Brenda was a walking contradiction. While some people described her as loving and reserved, others said she was cruel and boastful. Though she said she loved animals, she also enjoyed torturing them. But, at barely five-foot-two and 89 pounds, she was not the image of a gun-toting maniac.

The *San Diego Union* said that Brenda was 'too small to be scary'. One neighbor remembered her as a doe-eyed, freckled-faced, red-headed girl, sitting alone by the window with her arm around her dog. 'She was a tiny, lonely little youngster,' the neighbor recalled, 'a wisp of a girl.' Others remembered her playing in the front yard of her home with her cat or drawing cartoon animals for the neighborhood children.

But underneath the benign surface, according to friends, was a troubled tomboy who lived in a fantasy world of violence, drugs, death and killing policemen. Though there were subtle and not so subtle signs of her rage, no one imagined the fateful events that lay ahead.

A neighbor, whom the *San Diego Union* called her boyfriend, said that they would sit around all the time talking about 'wasting' people and 'going hunting'. When his mother asked him what that meant, the youngster said: 'Oh, you know, going out and killing a cat, or killing a cop.' They would also make elaborate fantasy plans of how to 'kill pigs'.

In one sadistic fantasy, she would approach a cop car and ask the officer if he knew any widows. When he said no, she would reach for his weapon and blow him away while saying, 'Now you do.'

The weekend before the shooting, she told her neighbor/boyfriend – who had recently moved away – she was planning something big. 'I'll call you Monday night if it doesn't come off,' she said. 'If it does, you'll know about it, because it'll be all over TV.' That night, she showed another friend a row of .22-caliber bullets lined up on her night-table.

Dawn White, one of her best friends, said: 'She was a good shot. I went into the desert with her last year to go target shooting and she killed a lot of lizards and squirrels. She almost never missed.' Another friend said she was 'crazy about guns. She liked to kill. She used to say she's gonna make her living being a sniper.'

One classmate from Patrick Henry High, where she was a junior, told the *Los Angeles Times*, 'she was always talking about guns, bragging about the guns her father had.' Another said: 'I don't think she had any friends. But it wasn't like she was real sad or anything. You'd see her smiling and laughing sometimes.' Other classmates described her as quiet and weird.

At school she had a reputation of being a 'stoner'. A neighbor said she bragged about smoking 'tons of pot' and doing PCP. Others believed her tales of drug exploits were merely attempts 'to impress the younger kids'. One friend said Brenda enjoyed 'saying things that just were not true in order to get attention'.

Schoolmates acknowledged that she was very artistic and had won a color television set as first prize in a Humane Society photo contest. However, her school photography teacher, Neil Heinberg, said that she was a completely average student: 'The only thing that set her off from the other students was her bright red hair.'

Relatives talked about her fondness for animals. On the one hand, her grandmother described how Brenda's pet cages were 'staked high' in the family home. Several weeks before the rampage, she talked to her grandmother about pursuing a career as a veterinarian. On the other hand, a friend recalled how, 'Just for the hell of it, she pumped her pellet gun three times and shot her neighbor's cat.' Sometimes, she would torture stray dogs and cats and set their tails on fire using lighter fluid.

Brenda mostly got in trouble for things petty criminals are made from: truancy, drugs and shoplifting. Her classmates said she boasted of being a good shoplifter. A year before the shootings she was caught shoplifting ammunition at a nearby drugstore. But her most serious scrape with the law came the summer before the rampage when, together with a friend, she was arrested for shooting out the windows of Cleveland Elementary.

LIFE IN A VACUUM
'Brenda has to accept the responsibility, but to some extent she's a victim,' said Trudy Hobel, the wife of her maternal grandfather, implying that her step-granddaughter's anger did not grow out of a vacuum. 'She didn't seem like a bomb,' she added, 'but then, sometimes bombs are silent too.'

As a child, Brenda, the youngest of three, was a 'spindly tomboy, no bigger than a bar of soap'. Her father, Wally, was the audio-visual supervisor at San Diego State University. Her mother, Dot, was the bookkeeper for the Andy Williams San Diego Golf Tournament. By all accounts they were a typical middle-class family with no evident dysfunction. Brenda was a happy, loving and active little girl. From a young age she was involved in baseball, soccer, bowling and golf. She was an especially good golfer and was ranked high in the San Diego Jr. Golf Association.

But everything in her life took a turn for the worse when her parents divorced in 1972. She stopped playing golf. She started spending more time by herself. Unfortunately for Brenda, her father was awarded custody of the children. Wally was incommunicative and clearly was unable to connect with her in any way.

Ruth Hobel, her grandmother, said that her daughter Dot 'was a wonderful mother and that the reason the judge awarded the children to the father was because the two other children – teenagers at the time – chose to go with the father and Brenda was also sent along because the judge didn't want to break up the family'.

Almost overnight, everything in Brenda's life changed. From peppy and cheerful, she became sullen and strange. After the divorce, Brenda grew more distant from her father. Wally, on the other hand, had no idea of how to maintain any type of family structure for Brenda. He rarely disciplined her or set any type of boundaries or restrictions.

Sensing that his daughter was drifting away, Wally tried to reconnect with her by buying her the one thing she wanted for Christmas: a .22-caliber rifle with a telescopic sight. 'I'm tired of hearing people at work saying what kind of father would give a kid a gun,' a family friend told the *San Diego Union*. 'I know it wasn't a blatant, I-don't-care-sort-of-thing. It was out of love.'

But her father never had a clue of what was going through little Brenda's mind. Police said the pint-sized sniper had been actively planning the attack for over a week. She allegedly had a 'fortress' in her garage stocked with weapons and ammunition. She had also dug a tunnel in the backyard where she planned to hide or escape. The day of the shootings she said, 'My dad will flip out when he finds out about this.' He did, of course, as did everyone else who knew her.

Just as Brenda thoroughly abused her fifteen minutes of fame, Bob Geldof, the singer of the Irish new wave band The Boomtown Rats, read about the shooting incident and wrote a song based on her 'I don't like Mondays' statement. The song procured the band their one and only bonafide hit. Unfortunately, it also made Brenda worldwide pop-culture legend.

THE CALIFORNIA INSTITUTION FOR WOMEN

Spencer was charged with two counts of first-degree murder, nine counts of attempted murder, eight counts of assault with a deadly weapon and one count of assault with a deadly weapon on a policeman. In her first arraignment, the freckle-faced killer pleaded not guilty by reason of insanity. After two court-appointed psychiatric examinations, Michael McGlinn, her lawyer, alleged she suffered from a rare form of epilepsy called 'temporal lobe epilepsy' that had led her to lose her mind on the day of the shootings.

Due to media saturation coverage in San Diego, the trial was moved to Santa Ana in neighboring Orange County. On 1 October 1979, the day before the trial was to start, Brenda changed her plea to guilty to two counts of first-degree murder and eight assault charges. In court, the bespectacled Spencer murmured the word 'guilty' as each charge was read. 'I shot from my house,' she told the court. 'I killed two people and wounded nine.'

In exchange for her plea, prosecutors dropped the attempted murder charges on each of the non-fatal shootings as well as the 'special circumstances' factor of the two first-degree murder charges. The 'special circumstances' factor stemmed from committing more than one murder and for 'laying in wait' for her victims. It would have meant life in prison without parole.

McGlinn filed a motion to keep Brenda in a Youth Authority Detention Facility while serving the first portion of her term, because, 'She is too young, too physically frail to go to a women's prison.'

But when Spencer was sentenced to 25 years to life in prison she was sent to the California Institution for Women in Corona. Since then, other than minor disciplinary problems, little has been seen or heard from the now forty-something prisoner. In two parole hearings in 1993 and 2001, Spencer sabotaged her chances of freedom by painting two very divergent – and unrealistic – pictures of herself and the motivations behind her Monday morning killings. In both cases, the members of the board unanimously denied her parole.

On 21 January 1993, Brenda – who had turned 30 – had her first parole hearing. Although she did not appear in person, she presented a written statement to the three-member Board of Prison Terms panel claiming that she planned to file a legal challenge to her conviction on the murder and assault charges, contending that authorities conspired against her.

In the written statement, Spencer claimed that at the time of her schoolyard sniper attack, she was under the influence of alcohol and the hallucinogenic drug PCP. She also claimed that police, prosecutors and her defense attorney conspired to fabricate laboratory test results showing that, at the time, she had no drugs in her system.

Spencer, searching for sympathy from the members of the board, wrote: 'I live with the unbearable pain every day of knowing that I was responsible for the death of two people and caused many others physical and emotional pain and suffering, but I'm not a murderer.'

MIND-ALTERING DRUGS

According to the statement that was read by Richard Jallins, an El Cajon lawyer who represented her at the hearing, the morning of the attack Brenda was shooting at hallucinated commando-type paramilitary troops advancing towards her home. She also suggested that the victims may not have been hit by bullets from her rifle, claiming that they might have been shot by police and that police officers lied about not firing any shots during the stand-off.

For two years after her arrest, Brenda alleged that she was given mind-altering drugs and, at the time, had not realized that she had pleaded guilty to two first-degree murder charges. 'People who saw me say I was a zombie,' Spencer said in her statement. 'I said what they told me to say, I did what they told me to do.'

Spencer claimed that she had been active in a prison group of about fifty women who claim that they were given mind-altering drugs while awaiting their trials. The group, she said, was planning to file a federal civil rights suit and was seeking help from state legislators and members of Congress. She also noted that, while in custody, she graduated from high school and had taken several college courses on electronics.

Charles Patrick, a Municipal Court judge who was formerly the prosecutor who handled her case, and Michael McGlinn, Spencer's former attorney, vehemently denied that there was any tampering of evidence preceding her 1979 conviction. 'It's just absolute nonsense,' Patrick said. 'There was never any indication that any test results were in any way falsified.'

McGlinn, who wrote a letter on Spencer's behalf that was read at the parole hearing, said Spencer got the best defense he could give her. 'It obviously was a tragic case, but we couldn't do any better than we did. She got our fullest attention.'

Not surprisingly, her statement elicited little sympathy from the members of the parole board. The chairman of the board, James Nielsen, a former state senator, said that Brenda's acknowledgement of responsibility for the killings was 'woven in a web of denial, excuse and blame-claiming'. Deputy District Attorney Dave Berry urged the rest of the board members not to grant her parole, citing her lack of remorse and the fact that she had been planning the rampage days before it occurred.

MIDDLE AGE

A middle-aged Brenda Spencer showed up in person to her second parole hearing on 1 April 2001. In her new request for parole, Spencer, who wore her long hair in a thick braid, said that she felt responsible for the many school shootings that have followed her 1979 sniper attack. 'I know saying I'm sorry doesn't make it all right,' she said, adding, 'With every school shooting, I feel I'm partially responsible. What if they got their idea from what I did?'

In the new hearing, Spencer was represented by University of Southern California Professor Denise Meyer and students from the school's Post Conviction Justice Project. 'What could have caused our children to behave this way?' the attorney asked, rhetorically referring to Spencer and all the other school rampagers. 'She told us why – a terrifyingly abusive home life.'

Spencer, in a surprising statement, claimed for the first time that her violent outburst that fateful Monday morning grew out of an abusive home life in which her father beat her and sexually molested her for years. 'I've never talked about it before,' she said at the hearing. 'I had to share my dad's bed 'til I was fourteen years old.'

Brenda told the board that her father gave her the rifle she used in her sniper attack as a subtle hint to commit suicide. 'I had asked for a radio and he bought me a gun,' she said. 'I felt like he wanted me to kill myself.' She also said she shot at the school in the hope that police would kill her – an act now known as 'suicide by cop'. 'I had failed in every other suicide attempt. I thought if I shot at the cops, they would shoot me.'

Her father, Wally, has never spoken publicly about the shootings. He lives with his new wife – Brenda's seventeen-year-old cellmate when she was being held at Juvenile Hall – in the same house across the street from the former Cleveland Elementary School, which is now the San Diego Hebrew Day School.

BEING MISERABLE

The hearing disclosed that Spencer had been under treatment for epilepsy and depression. 'I don't get depressed like I did,' she said, acknowledging that she is now taking antidepressants. 'I'm not scared all the time.'

The parole board unanimously denied her second chance for parole, saying they doubted the truthfulness of some of her remarks, especially the sexual abuse allegations. Brett Granlund, the board's chairman, questioned the fact that she had never mentioned being sexually or physically abused to her numerous counselors and psychiatrist. Brenda answered that she had, but they had ignored her. 'I'm just going to tell you,' he said to Brenda, 'you are either involved in a situation with counselors and psychiatrists who are covering up, or you are making this up' – which is what the parole board believed she was doing.

San Diego County Deputy District Attorney Richard Sachs, who prosecuted Spencer 22 years before, said her crime remains 'unthinkable'. Sachs added that Spencer 'probably was and still is a miserable person through and through. But

her way of dealing with the misery was to spread it around.'
To make his point he remarked that a recent breakup with a
fellow female prisoner led Spencer to carve the words
'courage' and 'pride' onto her chest. She claimed it was just a
simple, handmade prison tattoo.

Brenda Spencer's next parole hearing will be in 2005.

4. JEREMY SPOKE IN CLASS TODAY

Name: Barry Loukaitis
Born: February 1981
Age at time of rampage: 14
Date of attack: 2 February 1996
Number of victims: 3
Victim profile: two students and a teacher
Arsenal: two guns and a high-powered .30/30 lever-action
   hunting rifle
Dress code: black cowboy hat, black pants, black shirt, black
   boots, black duster
Media keywords: The Pearl Jam Defense, 'Jeremy', *Natural
   Born Killers*, *A Fistful of Dollars*, Clint Eastwood, Stephen
   King, *Rage*
Early warning signs: Mom's suicidal fantasies, three
   generations of family depression, shopping for a black
   duster
Probable cause: anger at another student for calling him a
   'fag'
School: Frontier Junior High School
Location: Moses Lake, Washington
Outcome: convicted of two first-degree murder charges, one
   second-degree murder charge, one attempted murder
   charge, one second-degree assault charge, and fifteen
   kidnapping charges
Status: serving two life sentences without possibility of parole
   plus 205 years in Clallam Bay Correction Center near Port
   Angeles

'It's my first murder
I'm at the point of no return
I look at his body on the floor
Killing a bastard that deserves to die.' – Barry Loukaitis

GROUNDHOG DAY

School gun violence is nothing new, but recently its form and visibility have morphed into something much more disturbing. School shootings in the 70s, 80s and early 90s were isolated cases of mostly one-on-one attacks. Between 1992 and 1994, there were 97 acts of school violence involving weapons in which 99 students and teachers were killed. But in 1996, when fourteen-year-old Barry Loukaitis showed up to his Algebra class looking like an evil Clint Eastwood, everything changed.

Loukaitis's rampage at Frontier Junior High in Moses Lake, Washington, was the first in a series of school assaults in rural communities during the late 90s that were chillingly similar and fearfully effective. All perpetrators were excessively well-armed, white, middle-class youngsters and their meticulously crafted plans of attack yielded increasingly higher body counts. Their rosy cheeks, freckled faces and seemingly 'boy next door' looks made the perpetrators objects of worldwide media attention, changing forever the concept of school shootings.

On 2 February – Groundhog Day – Barry Loukaitis, a ninth-grade honor student with an above-average IQ of 116, told his dad that he was going to walk to school. Instead, he spent the morning in preparation, putting on black pants, a black shirt, black cowboy boots and a black cowboy hat. On his hips, he strapped two holsters with loaded pistols. Across his chest, draped bandolier-style, two ammunition belts holding 78 rounds. On top of it all, a black duster. The duster had the pockets ripped open, enabling the youngster to shoot his father's high-powered .30-30 lever-action hunting rifle without taking his hands out of his pockets.

A .30-30 lever-action hunting rifle is an extremely powerful weapon – think of it as the weapon used by Robert DeNiro in *Deer Hunter*. Its cartridge is the size of a man's pinky. When it leaves the muzzle it is travelling at a speed of 2,200 feet per second with an impact equivalent to the force of a 1,800-pound object being moved one foot. It can drop a deer from 500 feet. Needless to say, when used at close range, it proves devastating.

When Barry arrived at the door of Room 15 – his classroom – he stood for a minute and gathered his thoughts. Then he burst in, took four steps, and fired three shots in quick succession. The first hit fourteen-year-old Manuel Vela, the object of his ire. The bullet exploded through his chest, killing him instantly. The second shot hit Arnie Fritz, also fourteen, who was sitting behind Manuel. The bullet passed through his arm, his right lung, his heart, his left lung and exited his lower back. Though the wounds were mortal, the youngster did not die immediately. Instead, he stumbled to the back of the classroom where he fell on the floor and started choking on his own blood.

The third bullet hit thirteen-year-old Natalie Hintz as she got up from her seat directly behind Arnie. The bullet impacted her on the stomach, blowing out her liver and diaphragm, then ripped through her right elbow, nearly severing her arm. In extreme pain, she asked the youngster why he had shot her.

Loukaitis then turned and fired the fourth and final bullet at 49-year-old Leona Caires, the Algebra teacher. The bullet hit her on the back as she wrote a binomials equation on the blackboard. Leona, a mother of four, crumpled to the floor with her magic marker in one hand and an eraser in the other and died instantly.

After the four shots, Loukaitis turned and pointed the rifle at the rest of the class and retreated into a corner. 'This sure beats Algebra, doesn't it?' he said, quoting a line from *Rage*, a Stephen King novel about a school shooting. Several classmates who were cowering under their desks pleaded to 'get help for Arnie,' who was gurgling on the floor, but still breathing. 'Just let him lie there and die,' Loukaitis told them. Later, the students remarked that Loukaitis was chillingly calm and organized throughout the attack. Many thought his actions seemed 'rehearsed'.

Jon Lane, the school's gym teacher, heard the shots and ran to the classroom where he found himself at gun point. He dived behind Mrs Caires's desk. Barry asked him to come out, but he said he was too afraid. Down the hall, Stephen Caires, the assistant principal and Leona's husband, heard the shots and went to investigate. He opened the class door and saw Lane crouching behind his wife's desk, four spent cartridges on the floor, and his wife's lifeless body.

In a stupor, he called 911. Meanwhile, Barry told Lane, 'If you don't get up, I'm going to start shooting more students.' Lane stood up and asked Barry to put down the weapon. The quick-thinking teacher then started engaging Barry, trying to defuse the situation.

'Natalie was crying out in pain,' Lane said in an interview with the *Seattle Times*. 'I asked if I could take her out. He said yes. I took her out the door and went back. There was a diabetic in distress, and I asked Barry if it was OK to take that student out, and he said OK. Then I heard Arnold breathing, making sounds that were so difficult, and Barry agreed to let us take him out of the room. Two other students helped me drag Arnold out the door, then I went back in.'

Loukaitis, remarking, 'I imagine there's going to be snipers and cops,' told the remaining students to 'chill' and move to the back of the class. He covered the rifle's muzzle with a plastic bag and told Lane, 'I'm going to put this gun in your mouth and you're the hostage.'

Lane, who was a champion wrestler, asserted with a nod, took a step forward and charged the teenager. He knocked the rifle out of his hands, pinned him against the wall and told the students to get the hell out of there. Police, who had just taken positions around the classroom, rushed in and took the boy into custody.

Defiant, Loukaitis told arresting officers, 'I know my rights.' When they asked him why he did it, he said it was because Vela had called him a fag. He didn't have any reason for killing the others, other than remarking that 'reflex took over' and 'it was kinda of crazy'. Then he fell asleep – a monster, in the local jail, sleeping like a child.

THE BLAME GAME

Experts called Barry's rampage 'a wake-up call' for the nation. Since then, there have been many more wake-up calls, but, it seems, we're still asleep at the wheel. Since that snowy February afternoon, pundits and politicians have been searching for an answer as to why Loukaitis and the other teen rampagers that followed were able to unscrupulously take away so many young lives without batting an eyelash.

Where did the system go wrong? Is it the violent pop culture overload? The easy availability of weapons? The powerful antidepressants? The instant media attention? The world feeding off rage? The disintegration of the family? The death of God? Or just poor parenting?

There is no easy answer to explain Barry's willingness to kill. 'What's behind it,' said Dr Ronald Stephens, executive director of the National School Safety Center, 'seems to be a combination of issues that range from the availability of weapons to the culture our kids immerse themselves in to the fact that many youngsters simply have no sense of the finality of death.'

In retrospect, when it came to Barry, there were many signs of the upcoming carnage. His classmates described Loukaitis as a shy and serious loner with few friends. 'His outsized feet, his gangly build, his studiousness, and his cowboy clothing' made him the perfect candidate for bullying.

Ronald Stephens said, 'As we look at the profile of perpetrators, the majority were first victims. When spurned, rejected, or bullied, some adolescents resort to violence. They want to resolve their problems quickly and with a measure of finality that is oftentimes rather scary.' Loukaitis was no exception.

According to fellow students, Loukaitis and Vela had a year-long running feud. Vela, a popular athlete, liked to push Barry around and slap his books out of his hand. 'I guess he finally got sick of it,' said classmate Walter Darden. Other classmates said that Barry had threatened to kill Mrs Caires after she incorrectly marked wrong an answer on a math quiz. Ironically, on his last report card, Caires wrote that Barry was 'a pleasure to have in class'.

For over a year, Loukaitis told friends that 'it would be fun to go on a shooting spree,' and 'it'd be cool to kill people'. He would quote from *Natural Born Killers*, his favorite movie: 'Murder is pure. People make it unpure.' He wrote poems about death and murder. He complained about being teased, about being called 'dork', 'fag' and 'gaylord'. He obsessively read gun magazines. He had 28 books by Stephen King in his bedroom.

Even his English teacher, who'd been reading his poems about 'killing with the cold ruthlessness of a machine' and 'killing a bastard that deserves to die', thought he was simply going through a phase. 'His behavior did not appear obviously different from that of other early adolescents,' wrote a psychiatrist who examined Loukaitis, 'until he walked into his junior high school classroom and shot four people.'

The plan for the assault started to germinate around December 1995, when he started asking his friends about how to go about getting ammunition. Sometime later, he showed a friend a sawn-off shotgun. He retooled a gun-belt to fit more ammunition. He had his mother drive him to seven stores to find the perfect duster to fit his pre-rampage fantasy. Barry and his mother, JoAnn, found the black duster at a local store called Skeen's Western Wear and bought it for $240.

Two weeks before the rampage he asked several friends what they would think if he killed Manuel. They didn't take him seriously, saying that he was just 'being Barry', the morose little nerd obsessed with killing. Julia Moore, a psychologist who treated Barry after the killings, believes Barry snapped about a week before the attack. 'It clicked in my head,' he told Moore. 'I had to kill Manuel.' Two days before the shootings, Loukaitis told a classmate he was 'going to kill something that was annoying him'. The teenager thought Barry was talking about killing an animal and didn't tell anyone about it.

Every detail of the rampage was carefully plotted. He orchestrated each aspect of the attack around a hand-picked pop cultural reference. From the Oliver Stone movie *Natural Born Killers*, which Barry had rented seven times, he got the idea for the black cowboy outfit. From *Rage*, a Stephen King novel found on his night table, he took the idea of holding his Algebra class hostage. From the Clint Eastwood film *A*

Fistful of Dollars, which was found in his video cassette player, he fashioned his outlaw attitude.

King, using the pseudonym Richard Bachman, wrote *Rage* when he was barely past his teens. Back when he wrote it, he said in a subsequent Court TV interview, he felt 'rejection, of being an outsider, what it was like to be teased relentlessly, and to entertain visions, fantasies of revenge on the people who'd done it to you – the system that had done it to you.' King said that the novel, which is about a student who takes his Algebra class hostage and shoots two teachers, was 'a troubling book' and, in retrospect, regrets having written it.

THE PEARL JAM DEFENSE

The trial, which was held more than a year after the shootings, was moved from Moses Lake – a small farming community of 13,000 – to Seattle because the appointed judge could not guarantee that an impartial jury could be found in Grant County. After several delays, the proceeding started 24 August 1997. Grant County Prosecutor John Knoddell charged Loukaitis as an adult with three counts of aggravated first-degree murder, one count of attempted murder, one count of second-degree assault, and sixteen counts of kidnapping. Mike Frost, his lead attorney, said his client pleaded innocent by reason of insanity.

Knodell told jurors that Loukaitis despised his father, envied popular kids in his school, 'and in a number of ways was angry at the girls he thought were rude to him'. Frost blamed his crimes on 'mood swings' caused by a previously undiagnosed bipolar personality disorder, and by the severe emotional neglect he experienced from his parents. The public prosecutor implied that Loukaitis, who had never undergone psychiatric counseling until after the shootings, was faking mental disease, noting the boy had requested information about Bipolar Disorder before seeing any doctors.

Mike Frost painted a picture of Barry as the product of an explosive home life. He grew up in a chaotic and disruptive household under the sway of his father's violent temper and his mother's suicidal depression. His father kept a large number of guns around the house and taught Barry how to shoot at a very young age. Of the three weapons he brought to Algebra class, two – the high-powered rifle and the .25-caliber semi-automatic pistol – came from an unlocked gun cabinet in the living room; the third, the .22-caliber handgun, came from the trunk of his mother's car.

Two months before the attack, JoAnn Phillips, his mother, filed for divorce. A few days later, she told Barry that on Valentine's Day she planned to kidnap her estranged husband and his new girlfriend, tie them up, force them to hear all the suffering they caused her, then commit suicide in front of them. Barry – parroting the advice Stephen King gives his readers in the preface to *Rage* – told her to channel her energies into writing: 'Mom, don't kill yourself. I don't want you to die. Just write about it. Write it into a play.'

Countering the defense's portrayal of Loukaitis as a mentally deranged victim, Knodell said the shooter was using his alleged mental state as a way to avoid having to take responsibility for the killings. 'He is a very, very angry, angry young man who coldly and methodically avenged himself upon the world.' The careful, premeditated steps he took to prepare for the carnage spoke louder about his state of mind than anything the defense team could claim. 'Just as a judge wears a robe in court to project respect, the defendant wore a black coat to inspire fear,' Knodell said. 'He was to project an image that would inspire fear and terror in his victims.'

Hintz was the first witness to testify. During the shootings, she said, 'time seemed to slow down to a crawl – as if everything was happening in slow motion.' The crippled youngster recounted how Loukaitis entered the class, guns ablaze: 'The only way I can describe it is pure terror and confusion . . . As I recall it, the door swung open, and I slowly looked up, and I saw somebody in a long trench coat and a cowboy hat, and in the air I saw a long, big rifle, and my first instinct was "Was this really happening, was it real?" '

In defense of his client, Frost claimed that Loukaitis was mentally deranged when he entered the classroom of Frontier Junior High School and opened fire. 'If you just dislike someone . . . you don't need to dress up like Clint Eastwood in a costume of this kind unless it is part of a delusional system,' Frost said.

'Certainly there may be some merit out there that the insanity defense is overused,' he said in explanation of his insanity defense. 'But this case has merit. This is really a clear case of insanity. My client clearly suffers from a mental illness – Bipolar Disorder – and there is a long history of the disorder in his family.'

Part of the delusion, according to Frost, was his obsession with the rock video 'Jeremy', by the Seattle grunge band Pearl Jam. In the video, Eddie Vedder sings about a lonely kid, Jeremy, who shows up to class one day and commits suicide. The song was based on a news story about Jeremy Wade Delle, a teenager from Richardson, Texas. One day, during second period, the teacher asked the sixteen-year-old to get an admittance slip from the office because he had missed the previous class. When he returned, he pulled out a gun and shot himself in front of thirty classmates.

In what was called 'the Pearl Jam Defense', the jury watched the 'Jeremy' video to discern if the band was to blame for Barry's mayhem. The *Seattle Times* described the jury as pensive while they studied the 1992 clip that turned Pearl Jam from a local bar band to a blockbuster grunge act with heavy MTV rotation. The video shows manic close-ups of Eddie Vedder singing 'Jeremy spoke in class today' intercut with shots of a boy who comes to school shirtless and leaves his classmates splattered with blood. Barry, who was very much like the kid in the video, memorized the words to the song and, according to his mother, became 'fidgety and uncomfortable' when he watched the video.

Not laying the blame squarely on Vedder and the boys, Barry's mother also conceded that her family had a history of depressive illness, which stretched back for four generations. Terry Loukaitis, Barry's father, said he too was burdened with three generations' worth of depressives in his family.

Barry's lawyer contended that the family's move to Moses Lake and the change to a new school were difficult and traumatic for the youngster. Those, coupled with the knowledge of his mother's suicidal fantasies and his troubled home and school life, were most likely the triggering factors for the carnage. 'It would be enough to make anybody snap.'

John Petrich, a psychiatrist for the defense, said that Barry experienced delusional, godlike feelings before his deadly rage. 'He felt like God and would laugh to himself . . . He felt he was superior to other kids.' Then, those feelings of superiority were replaced by 'hate, disdain and a sense of not measuring up . . . He was under the influence of his psychosis and it was distorting his thinking.'

Petrich, who was brought in to bolster the claim that the youngster was insane at the time of the killing, said that Loukaitis experienced 'identity diffusion', a psychological symptom characterized by feelings of not fitting into the world and having no sense of reality. He attributed Loukaitis's feeling of not belonging to his relationship with his parents, specifically to his mother's influence. 'He was deprived of the opportunity to identify with his father . . . His mother dominated him . . . His identity was so much linked to his mother's.'

After nearly four weeks of testimony and four days of deliberations, the jury found Loukaitis guilty of aggravated first-degree murder in the deaths of Manuel Vela and Arnold Fritz; guilty of second-degree murder in the death of teacher Leona Caires; and guilty of first-degree assault against Natalie Hintz. He was also convicted of assaulting Jon Lane, a teacher who managed to disarm him, and of kidnapping fifteen students. Two weeks later, on 25 September, the sullen teenager was handed two consecutive life terms plus 205 years, meaning that he will never again see the light of day outside the confines of prison.

Some of the victims' relatives wept. Others hugged. 'Either verdict would have been a tragedy,' said Alice Fritz, mother of victim Arnie Fritz. 'There's no happy ending here.' Through written letters read aloud by their mother, Arnie's three sisters said they forgave Barry. 'If I let myself hate you, I wouldn't be the kind of person my brother would want me to be,' Nyla

Fritz wrote. Natalie Hintz said she also forgave Barry and considered a life sentence just. 'You have condemned my classmates and I to a life sentence.'

Speaking on behalf of his client, Frost said Loukaitis felt 'great remorse about what happened', adding that 'he still doesn't know why it happened'.

AFTERSHOCKS

Six months after the shootings a local fourteen-year-old boy who had told friends he wanted 'to go out in a blaze' broke into a house, fired three shots from a hunting rifle and held a man hostage while invoking the name of Loukaitis. The youngster eventually surrendered to police without bloodshed. Six months later, Aaron Harmon, a ninth-grade student at nearby Chief Moses Junior High School, shot and killed his mother and his sister with a hunting rifle, then killed himself. Police said Harmon was distressed over the death of his cousin, Arnie Fritz.

Since the rampage, meetings have been held, civil suits filed, public-health counselors dispatched, and the citizens of Moses Lake have tried to reach 'closure'. As for the 6,000-student Moses Lake School District, it formed a task force, then a focus group, then a committee, then another, and finally they tightened its dress code, installed surveillance cameras, posted guards at two schools, and set up a hotline. And for closure, they turned Frontier Junior High into a middle school.

The Fritz, Hintz and Vela families each filed separate lawsuits against the Loukaitis family and the Moses Lake School District, alleging that officials were lax with school security and failed to monitor Loukaitis's troubling behavior. Terry and JoAnn Loukaitis eventually divorced. Their property repeatedly became a target for vandals. The family coffee shop was closed and they both filed for bankruptcy.

A few of the young survivors from Frontier Junior High worry that their schools, with their metal detectors and high-tech gadgetry, will fail to prevent the next rampage from happening. Bullying and harassment among students were checked sharply right after the tragedy, but within a year things crept back to normal. 'I think it's gone back pretty close to the way it was before the shooting,' said Jennie Luiten, one of the surviving classmates. Barry's name surfaces from time to time in classroom discussions, but students are not sitting in the classroom worrying about who'll be the next one to go postal.

During renovations, the school tore down a wall in Room 15 where surviving students painted a rainbow in memory of Arnie, Manuel and Leona. Relatives and survivors were upset, but a year later, a stone memorial for the three who died and the sixteen who survived was placed outside. 'I want us to be remembered,' said Emily Stuber, another survivor. 'Not that we were part of what happened, but that we overcame it and moved on.'

'The first year after it happened it was really hard,' said Jennie Luiten. 'We felt like nobody would talk to us about it.' According to Larry Smith, the principal of Moses Lake High, the high school most shooting survivors went to after Frontier Junior High, the school was unaware of any of the kids still having problems. 'That's because nobody bothers to find out,' Jennie explained. 'They wait for a problem to happen, then they pay attention.' Since the shootings, she said, she had been having suicidal fantasies: 'I feel the guilt of being alive.'

Though Moses Lake raised thousands of dollars to help pay for Natalie Hintz's seven surgeries and her physical rehabilitation, many people in town avoid her when they see her on the street or in a store. 'By not facing me, they're not facing the problem,' she said. After extensive reconstructive surgery to save her arm, Natalie can barely hold a pencil or tie her shoes with it. 'Some feeling in her hand is coming back,' Natalie's father said. But she will never have full use of it again.

'We were careful not to put her in PE, where other girls would have to look at her (scars),' her father said. 'And then, of course, she's worried about the different scars on her body. (In finding) a husband, she will have to find someone who is a very understanding man who won't be worried about the scars. So that bothered her.'

GRADUATION

In the spring of 2001, Natalie, who turned seventeen, together with her twin sister Breanna and the other survivors of her ninth-grade class, graduated from Moses Lake High. The bubbly and charismatic youngster has struggled to recover physically, but she now seems to have won all her battles and is well on her way to leading a healthy and productive life.

'I hope that I never get over it,' Natalie said in a pre-graduation interview with the *Wenatchee World*. 'I don't know how to explain that except that this is something that will be carried with me for the rest of my life and has shaped who I am today.' If she hadn't been shot, Natalie wouldn't be involved in Students Against Violence Everywhere, a group devoted to helping kids solve problems peacefully.

Whenever another school shooting happens, she knows first-hand what students there are going through. 'My first reaction was the deepest kind of pain,' she says. 'You understand so fully what they're going through.'

Among those still trying to deal with the after-effects of the violence is her friend Alice Fritz, the mother of Arnie. If it weren't for Loukaitis, her son would have graduated with Natalie. As a tribute to him, Alice – who left Moses Lake and moved a hundred miles away to Spokane – came to Natalie's graduation ceremony. Moses Lake High, remembering the lives that were lost not so long ago, awarded an honorary degree to Alice on behalf of her son. 'This is the year he would have graduated,' she said. 'I think it's important for the people who loved Arnie that I'm there.'

Over the past four years, Alice has maintained a friendship with Shea Haynes, Arnie's best friend. 'He really loved my son and my son really loved him,' she said about the boys. 'They were kindred spirits.' Shea also left Moses Lake after the shooting. One day, he called Arnie's mom and asked her if she wanted to hang out and talk. 'I was so thrilled,' she recalled. Since then, their friendship has filled a void for both.

Sometimes, they talk about Arnie.

5. SATAN'S HITMAN

Name: Luke Woodham
Born: 5 March 1981
Age at time of rampage: 16
Date of attack: 1 October 1997
Number of victims: 3 dead, 5 wounded
Victim profile: female students, his mother
Arsenal: Marlin .30/30 lever-action hunting rifle
Accomplices: Grant Boyette, Justin Sledge, Lucas Thompson, Donald Brooks II, Delbert Allen Shaw and Wesley Brownell
Media keywords: Friedrich Nietzsche, Hitler, satanism, The Kroth, *Falling Down*
Early warning signs: enjoyed setting his dog on fire. Joined a demonic cult
Probable cause: angry at being dumped by his girlfriend
School: Pearl High School
Location: Pearl, Mississippi
Outcome: guilty on all counts
Status: found Christ in prison

'I am the hatred in every man's heart! I am the epitome of all Evil! I have no mercy for humanity for they created me, they tortured me until I snapped and became what I am today . . . Hate what humanity has made you! Hate what you have become! Most of all, hate the accursed god of Christianity. Hate him for making humanity. Hate him for making you! Hate him for flinging you into a monstrous life you did not ask for nor deserve! Fill your heart, mind, and soul with hatred; until it's all you know. Until your conscience becomes a fiery tomb of hatred for the goodness in your soul. Hate everyone and everything. Hate where you were and are. Hate until you can't any more. Then learn, read poetry books, philosophy books, history books, science books, autobiographies and biographies. Become a sponge for knowledge . . . Make your own rules. Live by your

own laws. For now, truly, you should be at peace and your own true self. Live your life in a bold, new way. For you, dear friend, are a superman.' – Luke Woodham, April 1997

MISSISSIPPI DEATH TRIP

On 1 October 1997 – not a week after Barry Loukaitis was sentenced to life in prison – another teen rampager struck at a high school in the backwoods of Mississippi. This time it was in Pearl, a small, Baptist farming community of 22,000 in the heart of the Bible belt.

Luke Woodham, a chubby and bespectacled sixteen-year-old, woke up at five in the morning with demonic voices in his head. Guided by the evil voices, Woodham killed his mother, then went to his high school where he pulled out a hunting rifle, killed two students and wounded seven others. Adding an unexpectedly lurid twist to this southern gothic revenge-of-the-nerds tale, rumors that Luke was the chosen assassin in a Satanic cult led to the arrest on conspiracy charges of six other teenagers.

The morning carnage began when Mary Ann Woodham bumped into her son in the hallway of their home. Luke, who had fought with her the night before, attacked his mother with a butcher knife and a baseball bat. The mother, trying to stay alive, retreated into her bedroom where her six-foot-one, 267-pound son overpowered her and stabbed her to death. Police found the fifty-year-old divorcee dead on her bed with a pillow case covering her head, numerous stab wounds in her chest and slashing cuts on her hands and arms. Obviously, the woman struggled with her son before succumbing to the knife wounds in her chest.

For the next three hours, the teenager cleaned the blood off the walls and the floor, then threw the bloody towels and his jeans in the washing machine and took a shower. Before leaving for school, Grant Boyette, his satanic mentor, called him on the phone. Next, his classmate Lucas Thompson called. Both wanted to know if he did it, to which he answered: 'Yes.'

A little before eight, Luke picked up his brother's .30/30 hunting rifle, ammunition, and several notebooks, threw them in the trunk of his mother's white Chevy Corsica, and set out for Pearl High. There, he took the weapon out of the trunk and hid it under his big, blue trench coat. He also grabbed the notebooks and headed for an area of the school known as the commons. The commons is a huge lobby created between two structures that is used for eating during lunch. It is also a popular gathering spot for students, especially in the morning, when they arrive at school.

As Luke walked into the commons he was approached by his friend Justin Sledge. Luke whispered something into his ear and handed Sledge his notebooks. Justin turned and walked away, grabbing another kid by the arm and telling him not to look back, no matter what happened next.

Moments later, gunfire erupted. Woodham first shot his ex-girlfriend, sixteen-year-old Christina Menefee, and her best friend, seventeen-year-old Lydia Dew. Christina, whom he had dated for three weeks a year before, was hit at close range on the neck, exploding her jugular artery and killing her instantly. Lydia, hearing gunfire, turned to run and was hit on the back. She, too, collapsed on the floor and bled to death.

'I just did it,' he told police detectives in a videotaped confession. 'I went up to Christina and I shot her, then I shot Lydia, then I just shot into the crowd. I don't know why I killed Lydia.' Witnesses said he methodically moved through the commons blasting 'anybody he could find'. In the ensuing pandemonium, students and teachers ran screaming, looking for cover. 'I wasn't aiming at anyone,' he said after his arrest. 'It was like I was there, and I wasn't there.'

One student, Jerry Safeway, saw Woodham firing and dove on top of his girlfriend to protect her. He then felt the stinging of a bullet in his leg. Woodham stood over him and apologized. 'I didn't realize it was you. I thought you were Kyle,' Luke told him, referring to the mayor's son, Kyle Foster. In custody Luke said wanted to kill Foster, the son of a local celebrity, for shock value.

Another student, Connie Safely, saw what happened next: 'He walked over there and he cussed at Alan and said, "You turned your back on me for the last time" and opened fire.'

According to investigators Alan Westbrook, the targeted student, was one of the main instigators of the constant bullying endured by Woodham.

Joel Myrick, the school's assistant principal, said: 'I knew immediately it was gunfire that I heard. After the first few shots, the other kids realized it, too, and they all ran out. Luke was standing in the middle of the commons and I thought, these kids . . . these kids are going to die today.'

Realizing he had to stop the chaos, Myrick ran to his car in the parking lot to grab a .45-caliber automatic pistol he had hidden in the trunk. He loaded the weapon and went back searching for Woodham. Luke also ran out to the parking lot. He jumped into his mother's Corsica and tried to drive away, but was blocked by the terrified students pouring out of the commons. Myrick, who unwittingly became a hero for the anti-gun control forces in the US, spotted Luke in the Corsica as he spun out on the grass and crashed into a tree.

Myrick, gun in hand, cautiously approached the car. At gunpoint he told Woodham to drop his weapons and get out. Then he forced the teenager to the ground, searched him, and pinned him with his foot on his neck until the police arrived. 'I kept asking him, why, why, why?' Myrick later recalled. 'Mr Myrick, the world has wronged me,' Woodham answered, 'and I just can't take it any more.' Then, bizarrely, Woodham, who worked at a Domino's Pizza, said: 'Oh, Mr Myrick, I'm the one that gave you the discount on the pizza the other night.'

REVENGE OF THE NERDS

'I am not insane,' Woodham wrote as an explanation for the shootings in one of the notebooks he handed Justin Sledge. 'I am angry. This world shat on me for the final time. I am not spoiled or lazy, for murder is not weak and slow-witted, murder is gutsy and daring . . . I killed because people like me are mistreated every day . . . I am malicious because I am miserable.'

Acting like his publicist, Sledge made copies of a particular page from the notebooks earmarked by Luke and handed it to reporters. The text, which was called by the press 'his manifesto', included a passage from Friedrich Nietzsche's 1887 book *The Gay Science*, in which the Prussian philosopher wrote about the death of God and the rise of the madman: 'I have come too early . . . My time is not yet.' The alleged manifesto ended with the ominous coda, 'Grant, see you in the holding cell!' An obvious reference to his firend Grant Boyette.

Sledge – dressed in a black trench coat, a black shirt and black glasses – told reporters that his friend Luke killed because 'He was simply pushed to a pivotal point in his life in which the world has spit on him for the last time, and he was fixing to spit back.' Speaking perhaps for himself, Sledge added that his rampaging friend 'did it because society as a whole put down the thinkers and the true geniuses of the world,' and his friend 'was tired of society dealing the thinkers, the learners, a bad hand, and watching Johnny football player get the glory.'

Classmates remarked that Luke was fed up with the bullying and the cruel school social hierarchy in which people like him were always getting a raw deal. 'A lot of people would put signs on his back calling him names,' said Stephanie Wiggins, one of the students wounded during the shooting spree. 'They said, like, "You fat thing," mean things . . . They called him dork. I would think that he looked like it bothered him.'

When police took Woodham into custody, an officer asked him why he fired on his fellow students. Woodham answered that he was tired of being called a 'fat motherfucker'. Another officer remarked that after being arrested Woodham appeared euphoric, as if he had just won a prize fight. High on adrenaline, the teen assassin eagerly gave a twenty-minute videotaped confession filled with bravado and swagger: 'I wanted attention, someone to notice me. I guess the world's going to remember me now.'

Spotting a cut on his hand, Detective Roy Dampier asked him how he got it, to which, he replied, 'Killing my mom.' Until then, police had no idea of what had happened before the school shooting. 'He appeared to be very proud of what he'd done when I asked him,' the detective said.

The next day, school officials found a sheet of scorched paper taped next to the school's entrance, with a skull and crossbones, an Iron Cross, and the words: 'Luke is God. From your friends at Pearl High School.'

THE KROTH

'My investigation has led us to believe that there is satanic activity occurring in this county,' announced Rankin County District Attorney John Kitchens. 'I'll just say the devil exists in Pearl just as well as he does in Kentucky, Oregon and anywhere else,' added Tim Surratt, the first police officer to reach the school after the shooting.

'You can see signs of it. You can see stickers on cars. Most of our officials don't know what the stickers mean,' said Aleene Robinson, who runs the Resource Center Network, a domestic and sexual abuse shelter in Pearl. 'I feel like, that our people, our teachers, our principals and our superintendent fell asleep at the wheel.'

At first, city and school officials underplayed the existence of a satanic cult among their children. 'There's all kinds of rumors flying around,' said a school official. 'There are some things in this that could be considered satanic, but to jump out there to say it is satanic, that they are devil-worshippers, is jumping to conclusions.'

'No!' said Mayor Jimmy Foster, holding to the belief that their town was not ruled by the Lord of Darkness. 'It's outsiders who say that. Let me put it to you this way: When you're talking about a true satanic, devil-worshiping cult, no, we don't have that.' Not in Pearl, a peaceful-looking town with 41 churches and no bars – a place that is as God-fearing as God-fearing can get: the heart of the American heartland. 'I was on the Pearl police department for nineteen years, worked the midnight shift six years. If there was an occult out there, I'd know about it.'

But, within a week of the killings, Pearl Police Chief Bill Slade arrested on conspiracy charges six teenagers who were all part of The Kroth, a wannabe demonic cult that worshipped Satan for money, power and influence. The arrested satanists were the previously mentioned Grant Boyette, Justin Sledge and Lucas Thompson, as well as Donald Brooks II, Delbert Allan Shaw and Wesley Brownell. All cultists were sixteen years old, except Brooks, who was seventeen, and Boyette, who was eighteen. All attended Pearl High except Boyette, who had graduated the year before and was attending Hinds Community College in nearby Raymond.

Brooks and Boyette were also charged with plotting to murder Brooks's father, a local firefighter. Brooks, under the instigation of Boyette, planned to poison his dad who had discovered that they had surreptitiously used his credit card to buy computer equipment. In court, Donald Brooks Sr. stood by his potentially patricidal son refusing to believe the youngster wanted to harm him.

The kids of the satanic group were mainly awkward bookworms who modeled themselves after Michael Douglas's vengeful nerd character in the film *Falling Down*. Though they considered themselves intellectually superior to their peers, in reality they were societal misfits who complained of being 'always beaten, always hated' by the more popular and athletic students. Several of them were A-students, some belonged to the Junior Classical League, a Latin study group. They all were obsessively involved in role-playing games, which in time became satanic rituals.

Boyette, whom the others called 'father', was by all accounts the leader of The Kroth. 'There was a mastermind to this particular group and Mr Boyette was it,' testified police investigator Greg Eklund. 'He was the one that called the shots.' Through Boyette, the geekish gang of youngsters discovered esoteric literature and the bombastic writings of Nietzsche. They also discovered Satan, and in a twisted sense, a way toward boosting their fledging egos.

Woodham and the others said their charismatic leader was able to cast spells that would conjure up to six different demons and was in direct contact with the Dark Lord himself. Boyette told Luke that he had to be as faithful as he was to Satan because the Horned One had specifically singled him out to do 'great things'.

In court, Boyette was characterized as someone living two completely separate lives – a community college student and Baptist church member by day, a Hitler-loving, Nietzsche-quoting, demonic cult leader by night. Billy Baker, Boyette's former Sunday school teacher, described the teen as 'courteous, engaging and sober ... He was to me more of a follower, not a person who would be a leader.' But his friends told a different story of a obsessively manipulative youngster who lived by the motto 'We cannot move forward until all of our enemies are gone,' and adamantly prayed to Satan.

TRUE BEAUTY

Luke Woodham was born 5 March 1981 in Rankin County. The second of two children, he always resented his older brother, whom he called 'Mr Popular'. From the time Luke entered the Brandon Academy Kindergarten to when he finished Junior High, he recalled being constantly bullied and alienated by his classmates.

His parents' divorce, coupled with his lack of friends, his weight and the overbearing nature of his mother, molded his memories of childhood into a series of unhappy disappointments, the worst being when his mother and his brother were the only ones to show up for one of his birthday parties.

In his early teens Luke found solace in learning how to play the guitar and listening to rap and rock bands like Aerosmith and Marilyn Manson. 'Writing and playing the guitar helped me deal with my depression ... I stopped hating the world ... It gave me a way to channel everything.' At school he excelled in art and was considered a voracious reader. He faithfully kept a journal that unwittingly became a document tracking his spiraling self-esteem and mounting hatred toward everyone and everything.

The true terror of Woodham's psyche comes through clearest in his writing. In one journal entry he fantasized about being his English teacher, Valerine Neal: 'If I could spend a day as Mrs Neal, I would be very, very nice to Luke Woodham and pass him for the year. Then I would knock the crud out of the "omniscient dork" for putting junk on my computer. Then I would go crazy and kill all of the other teachers. Then I would slowly and very painfully torture all of the principals to death. Then I would withdraw all of my money in the bank and give it to Luke Woodham. Then I would get all of the other teachers and principals' bank account numbers, withdraw all of the money and give it to Luke Woodham. Then I would do acid. Then I would get a gun and blow my brains out all over the dog-gone room and leave my house to Luke Woodham.'

During the summer before the rampage, Luke wrote about making his first kill. The target, his beloved dog, Sparkle. The horrifying scene, described in detail, shows that he was a ticking time bomb ready to implode: 'I will never forget the howl she made, it sounded almost human. We laughed and hit her hard ... I took the night stick and hit her in the shoulder, spine and neck ... I'll never forget the sound of her bones breaking ... The foolish dog opened her mouth & we sprayed [lighter] fluid down her throat, her whole neck caught on fire, inside & out. Finally, the fire went out and she was making a gurgling noise. I silenced the noise with the club again. I hit her so hard the crusted burnt scar on her shoulder fell off ... Then we put her in the burned bag and chucked her in a nearby pond. We watched the bag sink. It was true beauty.'

LOVE LOST

Bob Menefee, the father of one of the girls killed, said his daughter Christina was targeted for showing some interest for her geeky schoolmate. Though Luke and his daughter went out for three weeks, Woodham became completely obsessed with the bubbly teen. He ecstatically referred to the time when he met Christina as 'the most changing year of my life'.

But then, the hammer fell. Christina soon grew bored with Luke and broke off the relationship. He was devastated and threatened to kill himself, but she talked him out of it. 'No one truly loved me. I only loved one thing in my whole life and that was Christina Menefee. But she was torn away from me ... I didn't eat. I didn't sleep. I didn't want to live. It destroyed me,' he wrote in his journal. Putting his broken heart beyond good and evil he wrote that he started hating God because Christina 'claimed to be a Christian'. He also started spending more time with his Hitler-loving friend, Grant Boyette.

By January 1997, Woodham found himself completely under Boyette's spell. 'No one else took care of him,' Boyette told the *Jackson Clarion-Ledger*. 'When he cried, I held him. When he was in trouble, I helped him when no one else did.' Sick of hearing his chubby sidekick bemoan little Christy, Boyette said he should kill her so he wouldn't have to see her again. 'At the time I really didn't care and he said that Satan wanted me . . . He said I didn't know what to think and Grant said he knew I had been hurt by Christina, and he said there was a way to get revenge of her. He said Satan was the way. He said anytime Satan needs something you put your thumbs on this pentagram and put it on your forehead and you ask Satan for whatever you want . . . Satan would give me anything . . . money, power, sex, women, revenge.'

Luke became a true believer after he and Boyette cast a spell from the satanic book the *Necronomicon* on a teenager they both knew. The next day, incredibly, the kid was run over by a car and killed. 'One second I was some kind of heartbroken idiot and the next second I had power over many things,' he said. 'My mind didn't know how to take it.'

Flushed with success over their first satanic outing, the two teens, together with their other nerdy wannabe-satanist friends, started planning how to send demons to terrify their enemies. 'We started a satanic group and through the hate I had in my heart, I used it to try and get vengeance on people.'

For over ten months, the young satanist clique held secret meetings in Woodham's room under a map he had on the wall with the slogan 'One Nation Under My Gun'. There, they ordered a 'bunch of pizzas' and enthusiastically plotted an elaborate assault on the school that involved setting off napalm bombs and cutting telephone lines before killing a selected group of teachers, parents and students and fleeing to Louisiana, Mexico and, ultimately, Cuba.

Once Luke was chosen – by Satan, no less – as the group's assassin, the plan of attack refocused on killing Christina and Mary Woodham, Luke's mom. In the weeks preceding the assault, the group met several times to convince Woodham 'that murder was a viable means of accomplishing the purposes and goals of their shared belief system'.

'He was going to kill his mother because he was going to use the car and was going to take his brother's gun and kill the girlfriend and kill some other people. He said he was tired of everything,' Lucas Thompson recalled discussing with his friends. The day before the attack Luke had said, 'I figure I'll be in a shootout with the cops and die.' Thompson, chillingly, kept quiet and told no one about the brooding carnage.

100,000 DEMONS
Woodham was charged separately for the hacking murder of his mother and the assault on Pearl High. Both trial dates were set for early June 1998. Because of pre-trial publicity, both trials were moved from Pearl to the nearby towns of Philadelphia, Mississippi and Hattiesburg. In both cases Woodham pleaded not guilty by reason of insanity.

The first trial held in Philadelphia, began on 1 June and lasted five days. Woodham was charged with the murder of his mother, Mary Ann Woodham. In court Luke came off as a meek and victimized youngster, someone driven to murder by society and/or his evil mentor. As prosecuting attorney John Kitchens showed the bloody baseball bat and kitchen knife Luke used to bludgeon and stab his mother to death, the youngster wept.

He kept weeping as he watched himself on video saying why he killed his mother. 'She never loved me. She always told me I wouldn't amount to anything.' In the tape, he told the arresting officers that the weekend before the killings, '[he] stopped caring for some reason'. He also said his mother constantly berated him and often spent nights away from home. 'I didn't want to kill my mother. I do love my mother. I just wanted her to understand,' said the misunderstood teen. 'It's real hard to live with the things I've done.'

Luke claimed he was under the spell of '100,000 demons' conjured by Grant Boyette the morning he plunged a butcher's knife into mommy dearest. 'I remember I woke up that morning and I'd seen demons that I always saw when Grant told me to do something. They said I was nothing and I would never be anything if I didn't get to that school and kill those people.'

The demons, apparently, had been appearing at night in Luke's bedroom, all summer long. In court he described each type of infernal creature as 'red-cloaked with red glowing eyes,' 'tall, slumped over,' 'spikes on head,' or the fetching ones with 'no hair'. These demons would come 'eight times' every night and 'say exactly what Grant had told me . . . Satan would want me to command some demons to attack somebody.'

Between sobs, he recalled getting the knife, the aluminum bat and the pillow and walking to his mother's room. All along, he could hear Boyette's voice telling him what to do. 'I just closed my eyes and fought with myself because I didn't want to do any of it. When I opened my eyes, my mother was lying in her bed.' When asked if he could remember the actual killing, he said: 'I don't know, sir. I don't know and it's eating me up every day.' The fact that he covered her face with a pillow during the attack indicates a certain awareness of the horror he was perpetrating.

Though the three psychologists who examined Woodham disagreed over his sanity, they all agreed he had narcissistic traits, which included lack of empathy and hypersensitivity to insult, and erratic coping skills. 'Luke's head is apparently filled with craziness about his world . . . and himself,' wrote defense psychologist Dr Michael Jepsen. 'It's my opinion that as a result of the vulnerability of this very psychologically disturbed young man, Grant was able to exploit him,' the good doctor said, adding that Woodham suffered from 'psychotic processing', meaning he had perception and judgment problems and had a borderline personality disorder.

Dr Reb McMichael, who examined Woodham for the prosecution, agreed that the killer had a personality disorder, but did not seem to suffer from any form of psychosis that would have deemed him insane at the time he committed matricide. 'He is not so wrong that I would consider him to have a major mental disorder.'

Woodham's attorney, Leslie Roussell, said the conflicting portraits of his client had made it difficult to view him as the troubled teen that he is. 'When this story first broke, all the news reports portrayed Luke as somebody who's been picked on, abused psychologically by his parents. Now you're reading that he's a hitman for Satan. That's the way the public sees him – he's no longer the poor, mistreated kid and that first version is much more accurate. You could talk to anybody who went to school there; he's been picked on since kindergarten. He's overweight, wears glasses. For lack of a better word, he fits the nerd syndrome.'

District Attorney John Kitchens said the defense lawyers were using the insanity plea as a 'smokescreen' to divert from the fact that the youngster was perfectly conscious when he brutally killed his mother. The jury believed the DA's side of the story, rejecting the insanity plea and finding him guilty of first-degree murder. On 5 June Luke was sentenced to life in prison. 'I'm going to heaven now,' said the handcuffed and shackled teenager as he was led out of the courtroom.

Three days later, Luke was back on the docket, this time in Hattiesburg, a hundred miles away from where he spilled his schoolmates' blood. Facing a new jury, Woodham was charged with two counts of murder for the shooting deaths of Christina Menefee and Lydia Dew, and seven counts of assault. Again, the vengeful nerd rambled on about seeing demons who, under the spell of Grant Boyette's voice, forced him to do evil.

Against the advice of his counsel, Luke took the stand and said that Grant, through demonic voices in his head, told him to kill: 'He told me I had to get the gun and the car and go to school and get my revenge on Christy and cause a reign of terror.' Boyette, he continued, said he would be 'spineless and gutless' if he failed to follow Satan's commands.

Ominously, he warned that the day following his testimony, the same demons that talked to him would be descending on the court to do evil. Though Rankin County Circuit Judge Samac Richardson and the others were watchful for any unexpected demonic activity, nothing out of the ordinary was reported that day.

END GAME

On 13 June Luke was found guilty once again. This time the jury took five hours to pass guilty verdicts for the two murder charges and seven attempted murder charges. 'I am sorry for the people I killed and the people I hurt,' Woodham told the courtroom. He was handed two life sentences plus seven twenty-year sentences. 'The reason you don't see any more tears is I have been forgiven by God,' he said. 'If they could have given the death penalty in this case, I deserve it.'

Nita Lilly, Christy's grandmother, called him a genetic waste. 'I don't hate you but I'm terribly disappointed,' she told him, adding that she considered him responsible for all the other school shootings that followed his spree. 'You initiated a chain of events across these United States that's wreaked havoc on our children.'

'I'm so sorry. I'm so sorry,' Luke repeated as he was led out of court. 'It wasn't me. I didn't want to do it.' Though Woodham accepted his sentence, he still blamed his friend Grant Boyette for the murders, saying that his influence led to the deadly events. Enjoying his last moments in the media spotlight, he waved at the reporters and said: 'God bless you all.'

As for his six fellow satanists, shortly after they were charged with conspiracy, the prosecution dropped all charges because, according to Mr Kitchens, it would be 'tough' to convict them in Mississippi. Boyette and Sledge were then indicted on the more serious accessory to murder charges, but by December 1998 the indictment against Sledge was withdrawn because of lack of evidence.

On 12 February 2000 Grant Boyette was sentenced by Judge Samac Richardson to six months at a boot camp-style program and five years of supervised probation for his role as the satanic mastermind behind the killings. Boyette pleaded guilty to the lesser charge of conspiracy to prevent a public officer from discharging his official duties in exchange for prosecutors dropping the more serious charge of accessory to murder. As he headed to the Regimented Inmate Discipline program, the alleged self-professed satanist claimed he was innocent in spite of the guilty plea. 'He should have been completely exonerated,' remarked his attorney, Ed Rainer.

Luke Woodham is rumored to have found Christ in his cellblock. The brooding youngster has allegedly traded the *Necronomicon* for the Bible and has become a born-again Christian. He is now rejoicing to the Word of the Lord at the Mississippi State Prison lock-down maximum-security camp in Parchman, Mississippi.

6. THE EXTERMINATING ANGEL

Name: Michael Carneal
Born: 1 June 1983
Age at time of rampage: 14
Date of attack: 1 December 1997
Number of victims: 3 dead, 5 wounded
Victim profile: Students at a prayer circle
Arsenal: a Ruger .22-caliber semi-automatic handgun with
    three spare clips, two .22-caliber rifles and two sawn-off
    shotguns
Media keywords: *The Basketball Diaries*, atheism, Internet
    porn sites, violent video games, 'Mortal Kombat', 'Doom',
    'Quake'
Early warning signs: stole weapons from father and neighbor,
    told friends something big was going to happen
Probable cause: emotionally immature, peers called him
    'faggot', mental illness
School: Heath High School
Location: West Paducah, Kentucky

*'Like many teenagers, he was hypersensitive to his classmates'
statements about him. He felt inadequate, unworthy, unloved,
unrespected and unaccepted by his peer group. At fourteen
years of age, Michael's peer group was critical to his self-esteem.
Michael felt as if he were a massive failure, doomed to be
different and recognized as a nobody. Michael believed he would
be able to return to school the next day and nobody would make
fun of him again.'* – defense attorney Chuck Granner

THE PRAYER CIRCLE
Two months after Luke Woodham shot two students in Pearl
High, a seemingly identical attack occurred in West Paducah,
Kentucky. On 1 December 1997 Michael Carneal, a fourteen-
year-old high school freshman, descended on a morning

prayer circle at Heath High and fired eight times on his schoolmates, killing three students and wounding five others.

Before leaving for school, Michael assembled his mini arsenal: a .22-caliber Ruger semi-automatic handgun, three spare clips, two .22-caliber rifles, two antique shotguns, 600 rounds of .22-caliber cartridges, four boxes of 12-gauge shotgun shells and several sets of earplugs. He put the handgun, the earplugs and the ammunition in his backpack and wrapped the rifles and shotguns with packing tape and a quilt. He placed the bundle in the trunk of his sister Kelly's car. When his sister asked him what the package was, he told her he was bringing props for a skit he was going to do in English class.

After arriving at school, Michael headed to the middle of the main lobby where the Goth kids would hang out. The Goths were a bunch of social misfits who wore black trench coats, were purposefully antisocial and said they were atheist. Just the type of people Michael liked.

Next to the Goth spot, the Agape Club, a Christian student group, would always hold a morning prayer circle. In previous occasions Carneal and the Goths would heckle, jeer and say obnoxious things to their praying schoolmates. This time, Carneal stood next to a trophy cabinet, waited for the 35 students to finish praying, then calmly inserted a pair of orange earplugs, pulled the .22 Ruger semi-automatic from his backpack, clicked an ammunition clip into place, assumed a two-handed shooter's stance and started blasting. 'As soon as they said amen, he opened up on them,' Bill Bond, the school principal, said. 'Only the first three shots could have been aimed. After that, it was just as fast as he could pull the trigger.'

He slowly fired three shots, then five more in quick succession making an arc around his body. He stopped firing when he saw Nicole Hadley, his friend, on the floor covered in blood. Just a few feet away, his sister Kelly could barely recognize him. She had never seen him 'look so big' as he stood with his arms outstretched and a gun in his hands. For a withdrawn fourteen-year-old who cowered from confrontation and was always scared, it was a dream come true. Finally, he was the one calling the shots.

PLEASE KILL ME

Ben Strong, a pastor's son and the leader of the prayer circle, putting his own life at risk, confronted the teen and talked him into dropping the weapon. 'I was scared once I realized it was real,' he said. 'I seen some people fall, and I seen blood. And I just ran over there. And, you know, I just started talking to him. I was just telling him to be calm, drop the gun, whatever. And he just kind of slouched down and dropped the gun.' Carneal told him, 'I can't believe I'd do this,' then added, 'please kill me.'

Carneal and Strong were good friends from playing together in the school marching band. Before the Thanksgiving break, Michael had told Ben not to come to the prayer circle that Monday, that it was going to be a 'day of reckoning'. Strong thought about it throughout Thanksgiving weekend, but decided it was a joke. 'When we got done praying, I kind of thought everything was going to be OK,' he said. 'And I just heard a pop and I spun around. And I . . . was like, "Mike, what are you doing?" And then he just let a bunch of them go.'

The three students killed were Kayce Steger, Jessica James and Nicole Hadley who were fifteen, seventeen and fourteen respectively. Michael knew Kayce and Jessica casually from the school band, but he was really good friends with Nicole. He talked to her almost daily. Classmates said he had a crush on her. The five injured students were: Craig Keene, fifteen, Hollan Holm, seventeen, Kelley Hard, sixteen, and Shelley Schaberg, fourteen. The most seriously wounded, fifteen-year-old Misty Jenkins, was paralyzed from the waist down for life.

Bill Bond, the school principal, was in his office talking to a parent on the telephone when he heard the gunfire. He rushed out in time to see Ben talking to the youngster and getting him to drop the gun. 'He didn't run. He just stood and talked to him,' Principal Bond said about Ben. 'He's the one who told him to stop, stop. He's the one who had the courage.'

Bond led the rampager to his office where the youngster said he was sorry. 'He acted just like he had been caught with some minor offense.' Bond left him under the custody of his Homeroom teacher, Tobe Dulworth. Mike babbled to his teacher about the weapons he used and somehow believed that he would be coming back to school the next day. Then, he said, 'It was like a dream. And I woke up.'

THE DAY AFTER

The day after the shooting, Sheriff Frank Augustus said Carneal may have had accomplices. He acknowledged the theory was based on a 'gut feeling' and had no evidence to back it up. He explained that the fact that Michael brought four more weapons to school and left them on the floor next to his Goth friends suggested that someone was supposed to join him. 'He did bring five guns,' the sheriff told reporters. 'Is he the only one who was supposed to be there? Are there more people involved in this, who maybe chickened out or used him as a patsy?'

'I've got a fourteen-year-old male who walks into school and commences firing on a group of students,' the sheriff said. 'I don't believe this boy planned this out by himself. I believe there is somebody else in the background that we need to talk to. I think it's other students. I may be totally out of whack, but I just believe there's others involved.' Though he told many of his friends that 'something big' was going to happen beforehand, police were never able to determine if any of these friends actually helped him plan the attack.

Going into total denial mode, the school board decided to hold classes the day after the attack. By not doing so, they claimed, they would be handing a victory to Carneal and those of his ilk. 'This is a terrible tragedy but I still believe in Heath High School,' Principal Bond said. 'I still believe in public education. And we can't let one mixed-up person destroy our society. If someone believes in anarchy and we let that anarchy control us, then he is in control of us. And I don't believe in letting someone control me, so we will go about our business.'

Almost 90 per cent of the high school's student body of six hundred showed up to school that day. Many students, in tears, walked in groups, clinging to each other for support and laying flower wreaths where the three girls were killed. Ben Strong again led the morning prayer group; this time, though, it was attended by nearly two hundred students. 'We had just a time of silence for everyone to reflect and pray,' he said. 'I told them God's the only thing we can turn to in a moment like this.' Outside, a group of students unfolded a large handwritten banner that said, 'We Forgive You, Mike'.

Carneal's parents, through their minister, Reverend Paul Donner, said they were stunned and couldn't explain what might have motivated their son to kill so indiscriminately. 'They really feel very deeply for the whole community and the other families,' said Donner, who baptized the boy as an infant at St Paul's Lutheran Church. 'Absolutely, they have no idea.'

Even the then-President Clinton spoke out in support of the families and students of Paducah. 'Like all Americans, I was shocked and heartbroken by the terrible news,' Clinton said. 'I believe I speak for every American in sending our thoughts and prayers to the parents of Kayce Steger, Jessica James, Nicole Hadley and the wounded children and the entire community of West Paducah. We still don't know . . . why a fourteen-year-old boy would take a pistol and open fire on his classmates. We may never know, but we must redouble our efforts to protect all our children from violence.'

PEER RIDICULE

Heath High principal Bill Bond said Carneal, a freshman who had only attended high school for 71 days, was a 'very intelligent young man' who had 'some minor problems' but was never suspended from school nor was he considered a troublemaker. His disciplinary record involved downloading Playboy photos from the Internet on the school library computers and flecking paint off a wall. The principal said he was your basic B-student who liked to clown around and sought the attention of his peers.

The son of a prominent attorney, Michael was described as small, quiet, sensitive and emotionally immature. Some said he was a 'jokester and a prankster', and a 'fidgety fun-loving guy' who was constantly yearning for acceptance and recognition. Noting that he was bullied just as much as other kids in his class, friends said he was not a loner or a social outcast. At school he liked to hang out with the Goth kids and enjoyed antagonizing the 'born-again Christians' and the 'preps'. But he had an extensive set of friends, including both Goths and Christians. In general, though, he was a marginal participant in several social groups, but was not fully accepted in any of them.

In retrospect, his outward appearance clearly masked an inner turmoil bordering on mental illness that was fraught with fear and steeped in violence. In his mind, he had sunk into a private hell of peer ridicule, social ineptness and feelings of rejection. He had suicidal urges. He was in a fragile stage of development and thought that his lack of social life at school was a sign of his hopeless failure.

Psychiatrists agree that kids like Carneal 'fly under the radar screen' as they proficiently mask the mounting trouble clogging their brains. Generally, they'll cruise along until they start reacting illogically to perceived wrongs. As these frustrations accumulate, their anger explodes into rage and total annihilation becomes the only way out.

Forensic psychiatrist Dianne Schetky, one of the counselors who evaluated him after the shooting spree, said that Michael, for years, had felt marginalized and persecuted by classmates and teachers. Since his preschool days, he said he didn't have any friends. His memories from elementary and middle school always involved some humiliating incident of peer torture and abuse. Students putting frog parts on his shoulder during dissection class, someone tossing his prize class project on the roof, classmates hitting him for no reason, older kids saying he had 'Michael germs' and stealing his lunch. In eighth grade, a student newsletter ran a column called 'Rumor Has It' that said he liked another boy. Since then, it seemed he was called 'gay' and 'faggot' several times a day.

Three months before the shootings, Michael's life started to seriously unravel. In what others saw as a 'deranged' state, he threw his bicycle and a lawn chair into a bonfire during a school band party. Emotionally, he felt that Nicole Hadley, his friend and one of the youngsters he killed, was not returning his affections. He was also hurt that Amanda Jones, who said she was his girlfriend, stopped talking to him and called him 'the biggest loser in the ninth grade'.

'Most adolescents turn to peers, athletics, extracurricular activities or academics to help them negotiate the passage of adolescence,' said Dr Schetky. But Michael did not excel in anything and never developed a safety net to keep from crashing. As he entered the vicious world of the high school 'pecking orders' he went into an unguided free fall. He was constantly baited for being five-foot-two and puny. His only extracurricular activity was the school band, and even there he was ostracized by the older kids.

SIBLING RIVALRY

Though Michael desperately wanted to fit in with his peers, he never achieved the social acceptance of his older sister. Kelly Carneal, unlike her brother, was popular, pretty, a straight-A student, class valedictorian and a National Merit Scholar. She was also a contributor to the school newspaper, played in the marching band and sang in the school choir. How could he, a nobody, an underdeveloped geek with an IQ of 120 and low self-esteem, compete for praise and attention with such a high-achieving sister?

'He said he'd been trying hard to live up to her, but that he kept getting into trouble,' said Dr Schetky. 'Everybody talked about how I was not like my sister,' Michael told the doctor, 'so I figured if I was the exact opposite, people would pay attention to me.'

Perhaps in reaction to his sister's perfect behavior, Michael decided he wanted to be friends with the Goth kids. To impress the leader of the Goths, a ghouly senior who wore a trench coat and painted his nails black, Michael stole a fax machine from his father and gave it to him. He also stole a

$100-dollar bill from his father's wallet and gave it to a couple of the older Goth kids. To show off, he would print pornography from the Internet and sell it or it give away. Nevertheless, all this didn't give him the social status he coveted from his gloomy groovies.

Paducah, a deeply religious farming community of 25,000, is very much like Luke Woodham's hometown of Pearl. Considered part of the Bible belt, it doesn't take kindly to charges of devil-worshiping and atheism. Although the media relentlessly focused on Carneal's 'self-professed atheism', most reports suggest that the youngster was a 'practicing Christian' who had attended church as recently as a month prior to the attack.

'We studied God's word together,' said Reverend Paul Donner, who both confirmed and baptized him. 'Seven months ago, on the first Sunday in May, Michael knelt here at the altar and confessed his faith in Jesus Christ as his Savior . . . Michael is a Christian. What he did was a devastating act. It was not the act of an atheist. It was an act of a sinful Christian.'

Several alarmist sources said that Michael, like other high school rampagers, was 'hunting for Christians'. But counselors and investigators agree that he chose to shoot at the praying students because they made convenient targets. In fact, many of the kids in the prayer circle were his friends from the school marching band. Though he claimed to have perpetrated the attack because he was tired of being teased, none of the students shot had teased him.

MENTAL ILLNESS

Before the killings, no one recognized the depth of Michael's mental illness: his psychological despair, the delusions he suffered, or his desperate need for acceptance and attention. After the attack, according to Dr Kathleen O'Connor, Michael developed the full-blown psychotic symptoms of a paranoid schizophrenic and now lives under heavy anti-psychotic medication. After the Columbine shootings, he went into a deep psychosis and tried to commit suicide because he blamed himself for the assault. Dr O'Connor believes it is now clear that Carneal committed his killing spree once mental illness took over the functioning of his brain and it became impossible for him to cope with society.

In two independent psychiatric evaluations, Michael – in his pre-rampage days – was described as exhibiting the classic disorganized symptoms of a budding paranoiac. Dr Dewey Cornell of the University of Virginia said he suffered from dysthymia (depression) and 'traits of schizotypal personality disorder.'

At home when he showered, he would cover the bathroom air vents with towels because 'people might be looking'. When he'd finish, he would wrap himself in several towels and make a quick dash for his bedroom to avoid being seen naked by the 'spies'. He would sleep out on the family room couch because he feared being attacked by the people lurking under the floor. A month before the slayings, his mother found a stash of kitchen knives under his mattress that he said were there for protection: 'If someone came in, maybe I could stop them.'

All this, inexplicably, never concerned his immediate family.

SELF-EXPRESSION

An examination of Mike's school essays and short stories by Principal Bond revealed that the youngster felt small and weak, and was constantly teased and picked on. In one story, 'Halloween Surprise', a character is attacked by a gang of students called the Preps. The main character, Mike, exacts revenge by opening fire on the preps with a sawn-off shotgun and killing five of them. The story concludes with Mike detonating an atomic bomb.

'The first one he crucified on a metal cross that had been heated up to a glowing red temperature. The second one he tied their hair to a huge bungee cord that just happened to be too long and made them jump off a bridge.

'The third one he heated up a drill bit and drilled it into one of his eyes and then put a pin hole in their wrists and Chinese water tortured them while they bleed to death very slowly. . . .'

Tobe Dulworth, his English teacher, gave him a passing grade for the story. A suit filed by the parents of the dead girls alleged that Dulworth should have reported the story and its violent content to the school principal or another McCracken School District administrator.

Joan Bertin, the executive director of the New York City-based National Coalition Against Censorship, said that disciplining students for such written expression is completely misguided and detrimental. One cannot assume that any expression of violence by a youngster in an art class or a creative writing class would lead to the next rampage. The impulse of turning teachers into criminal profilers on the lookout for 'thought crimes' is in fact highly suspect. A teacher should be teaching, not assessing the violent tendencies of every pupil. Such vigilance would undoubtedly aggravate any real psychological problem that could lead a youngster towards an explosive act of random violence.

Such feel-good, knee-jerk reactions from administrators happen most often when school districts overreact to media-fueled hysteria over school violence. In 1998, after a series of school shootings, the Cabrillo, California, school district suspended a fourteen-year-old student for turning in two violent essays for an English class. The two essays, 'Goin' Postal' and 'The Riot', could be seen as 'disturbing', said Ann Brick, an attorney for the American Civil Liberties Union, but they were still protected by the First Amendment Right of Freedom of Speech.

'The person uttering or writing the words has to intend that the recipient will think it's a threat,' said a suit filed by the ACLU against the school board. 'It has to be unequivocal. It has to be unconditional so that the person who is supposedly threatened is convinced that he or she is in danger.' Otherwise, its suppression is unconstitutional.

SOMETHING BIG'S GOING TO HAPPEN

According to his friends, for weeks the fourteen-year-old 'goof ball' warned them that he was planning 'something big'. They all thought it was some kind of stunt or prank. His friend

Alan Coleman came early to school on the morning of the attack specifically to see what Michael was going to do. 'I was expecting a practical joke of some sort . . . Perhaps fireworks, water balloons, something of that nature.'

About a month before the shooting, Carneal started collecting an arsenal of weapons. First he stole his father's .38 revolver from a locked box in his parents' bedroom. That night he held his father's unloaded .38 to his head because he was depressed and 'didn't think it was worth it to keep on living'. A few days later he brought the gun to school to show his friends and try to sell it. An older kid told him that if he didn't sell it to him he would call the police, and took the weapon. Incidentally, the kid kept the gun and never paid Carneal.

Several days before the attack, Carneal snuck into his friend Toby Nace's dad's garage. There, he stole the .22 Ruger he used in the school attack, and several boxes of ammunition. The Wednesday before Thanksgiving, he brought the .22 to school to impress his friends. The boys, instead of being impressed, made fun of him, saying it was, like himself, too small. After school, he took the gun to a friend's house and used it for target practice on a ball in the backyard.

On Thanksgiving Day, before having dinner with his parents, sister and two sets of grandparents, he rode his bike to Toby's house and snuck into the garage once again. This time he went through a window which he had left open when he stole the .22-caliber pistol. He opened the locked gun cabinet and took a .30/30 rifle, four .22 rifles and ammunition. He put everything in a duffel bag he had previously left in the woods and hid the loot in a crate in his bedroom closet.

The day after Thanksgiving, Michael brought the .30/30 rifle and two of the .22 rifles to a friend's house. Michael Alonso, his friend, said Carneal showed him and his brother the rifles. His brother, a senior in Heath High, warned them not to get into any trouble with the weapons. Michael left the three rifles in Alonso's house when his dad came to drive him home. That night, he managed to steal two old shotguns from his father and hid them with the rest of his arms cache.

The morning of the shooting, his friend Toby Nace said that Carneal was not being himself: 'He acted totally different than he usually did. He wasn't laughing or joking or smiling like he usually was. He just had a blank look on his face.' When Toby noticed the earplugs, he told him, 'Hey, it would be funny if you wore those during class while the teacher is giving a speech.' The two kids laughed. Then, as he saw him pull out the gun, he said: 'Hey, that's my dad's gun.'

'I saw him cock it, and he shot once,' Toby said. 'And I turned toward the cafeteria and he shot again. I started running down the hall saying, "Oh, my God, he's got a gun, get out." I just wondered what he was doing with my dad's gun. It surprised me that he had it. I was wondering why he had it and how he got it.' Wendell Nace, Toby's father, cried when he learned that Carneal had used his gun to kill three students. He said the last time he had seen that gun was in June 1997, locked in the gun cabinet in his garage.

There's no evidence suggesting that Toby helped his friend procure any of the weapons or if he helped him find the key to the gun cabinet. Police did find an email from Toby to Michael referring to the 'timing of the event in the hall'. After the shooting, Toby's parents retained a lawyer, just in case.

SENTENCING

On 11 December, Carneal was charged with three counts of murder, five counts of attempted murder and one count of burglary. On 15 January of the next year, Carneal pleaded 'not guilty by reason of diminished capacity' and was ordered to undergo a battery of psychiatric tests. After spending a year with court-appointed psychiatrists, the day before his jury trial was set to begin, the defense agreed to plea bargain.

McCracken County Circuit Court Judge Jeff Hines agreed to accept a plea of 'guilty but mentally ill' on condition that the maximum penalty – life in prison without possibility of parole for 25 years – would be imposed. Judge Hines asked Carneal if he understood his plea. 'Yes, sir,' the boy said. Judge Hines then asked, 'You are fine today, in terms of your mental health?' 'Yes, sir,' Carneal replied.

The plea allowed Carneal to be confined to a mental institution, rather than prison, for as long as he needs it or until his sentence is completed. On 16 December 1998, Michael was formally sentenced to life in prison with no possibility of parole for 25 years. Judge Hines determined that the school rampager was to be sent to the Northern Kentucky Youth Development Center until the age of eighteen, when his mental health would be re-evaluated to determined if he was ready to be placed within the adult prison population.

From all accounts, Michael was 'cooperative and compliant' in the Youth Development Center. As well as being treated for mental illness, he has been working on completing his high school education.

As for his former school, the McCracken County Board of Education – in an attempt to bring a sense of security back to the campus – went overboard with new security measures. The school safety panel ordered supplementary security officers for the school and a chain-link fence enclosing it. Additionally, in the new 'Heathcatraz' all students are required to wear ID tags when they are on school premises. Ironically, as many students have remarked, measures like the fence and the ID tags, which imply that the threat would be coming from outside the school, would not have stopped Michael.

Within a year of the carnage, three memorials commemorating the victims of the tragedy were erected in Heath High. The first is a marker next to the entrance of the school that is inscribed with the names of the three murdered girls and the dates they would have graduated. Impressed in the marker is Ben Strong's statement at their funeral: 'They saw the face of God on December 1 1997.' Inside the school, in the exact spot where the shooting occurred, there's a simple glass case filled with mementos of the girls.

The third memorial is in a grassy area behind the school building. It is a circular garden with a fountain and stone benches symbolizing a prayer circle. There, too, is a marker with an image of an angel and an inscription from John 14:1: 'Let not your heart be troubled: ye believe in God. Believe also in me.'

EVERYONE IS LIABLE

In the beginning, the victims' families placed the blame where it belonged – on Michael's trigger finger. Joe James, whose daughter Jessica was killed, said, 'He has blamed everyone but himself . . . Other kids are teased just the same way, but they don't take a gun and use it. That's not a solution.'

Unsatisfied with Michael being solely responsible for the killings, the families of the three victims sued 45 people – from the killer himself to his friends, neighbors, parents and twenty educators – alleging that the defendants knew or should have known that Carneal was plotting the shootings, and that they failed to interpret the numerous 'warning signals' he had put out.

'Our schools have become killing fields,' stated the filed document. 'The shootings described in this lawsuit are the direct result of the failure of the family, the educational system, the social organization and structure, and those who lead it.' The suit also alleged that some kids knew that Michael had previously taken weapons to school but failed to report him and that teachers who read or knew about Michael's violent writings, should also have reported him.

Because Michael was revealed to be an avid gamer, an Internet porn junkie and an action movie fan, on 12 April the families also filed suit against 25 media companies. The $130 million federal suit against Internet pornography sites, movie production and distribution companies and the makers of ten computer games alleged that the companies were negligent for not warning consumers that the content they made available could incite copycat violence.

According to documents filed with this second suit, Michael, through the workings of some industrial entertainment conspiracy, had his violent role-playing fantasies turned into nightmarish Technicolor realities that led to the deaths of their three daughters. 'We're not saying the devil or Sony made him do it,' said Michael Breen, a Bowling Green attorney representing the parents, 'but these corporations use focus groups to determine what plot twists influence audiences in some way, and they make their movies based on [those] reactions.'

The companies sued, among others, were: Time Warner, Polygram Film Entertainment Distribution Inc., Palm Pictures, Island Pictures and New Line Cinema, all of which were involved in *The Basketball Diaries*; Atari, Nintendo of America, Sega of America, Sony Computer Entertainment, id software, Interplay Productions, Meow Media, and Network Authentication Systems.

'We believe the Heath shooter was influenced by the movies he watched, the computers games he played and the Internet sites he visited,' said Sabrina Steger, Kayce's mother. 'The lawsuit is intended to hold accountable certain media corporations which recklessly incited fourteen-year-old Michael Carneal to murder these three precious girls,' added Mr Breen.

THE BASKETBALL DIARIES

Toby Nace said that a year before the shooting he watched *The Basketball Diaries* with Michael. After the movie Michael told him that 'it would be neat to go in the school and shoot people that you don't like . . . and take over the school.' Based on the Jim Carroll novel, the 1995 film – starring a young Leonardo DiCaprio – featured a drug-induced dream sequence in which the DiCaprio character takes a gun to school and starts firing at random.

Two hours after the shooting, under questioning by investigators, Michael made a vague reference to the movie. Investigators asked him if he had ever seen anything like what he did before, to which he answered, 'Yes, I have seen this done in *Basketball Diaries*.' Though the movie connection was widely reported by the media, Carneal himself is said to be angered by pundits trying to blame a movie for what he did.

Part of the suit contended that Michael became proficient at shooting from playing video games. Sabrina Steger, the mother of one of the deceased girls, appeared before a congressional committee on the effects of video games on youth violence, and said that Carneal learned to shoot from playing first-person shooter games. Though he had hardly ever fired a real gun, it's hard to believe that Michael's eight hits on eight shots fired were because he had played a lot of 'Doom' or 'Quake'. And as anyone who has fired a gun will say, there's virtually no similarity between using a joystick and squeezing a trigger.

The multimillion-dollar nature of both suits led many to believe the victim's families were less interested in justice and more in cashing in on their losses. As a consequence of the civil suits, the families experienced a backlash from the community who had embraced them at their moment of loss. Some even started sending them hate mail.

On 31 March 2000, McCracken County Chief Regional Circuit Judge Will Shadoan dismissed the families' lawsuit against Michael's family, friends and neighbors. The judge said that friends who had been in contact with him prior to the shooting may have had 'a moral or Christian duty to do something, but there was no legal duty'. As for Wendell Nace, the owner of the pistol used by Michael, he was 'not negligent in leaving the .22 pistol outside a locked cabinet'.

The judge also ruled that the board members, administrators, and teachers named as defendants in the suit were all protected from liability by sovereign immunity under Kentucky law. In a written order, Shadoan said it is the job of educators to 'see that all children receive the best education possible. We cannot expect those teachers and administrators to be psychiatrists, lawyers, psychologists, or physicians. They are to educate our children, nothing more and nothing less.'

The only person the judge found liable for the deaths of the three girls was the shooter himself, Michael Carneal. The judge set damages to be paid by Carneal at the symbolic amount of $42 million. The money, in this writer's opinion, will never be collected.

A week later, on 6 April, US District Judge Edward Johnstone dismissed the families' $130 million lawsuit against the media conglomerates. According to Johnstone the companies were not liable since Michael's acts could not be foreseeable by the makers of the video games, the movies, and the Internet porn site. The judge based his opinion on a similar case from the late 80s in which the 6th US Circuit Court of

Appeals held the makers of 'Dungeons & Dragons', a popular role-playing game, not liable for a McCracken County teenager's suicide.' 'This was a tragic situation, but tragedies such as this simply defy rational explanation and the courts should not pretend otherwise,' Johnstone wrote in his opinion.

POST MORTEM

On 2 June 2001 – the day after his eighteenth birthday – Michael entered Kentucky's adult prison population. A 102-pounder at the time he was arrested, Carneal is now over six feet tall and weighs more than 250 pounds. Beth McGuire, who heads the prison's mental-health unit, said he was sent to a medium-security Kentucky State Reformatory near La Grange, where he will be kept 'somewhat segregated' until officials can assess the reaction of other inmates to his presence.

The day before, Michael's parents watched as he was awarded a high school diploma in a private, informal ceremony at the Northern Kentucky Youth Development Center. In his new prison, Michael will be a patient in the reformatory's mental health hospital.

Ultimately, the goal of the treatment in the hospital is to stabilize Michael so he can be moved into the general inmate population. Court documents indicate Carneal has responded well to treatment but has occasional relapses that leave him depressed and suicidal.

7. THE PINT-SIZED RAMBOS

Names: Andrew Golden and Mitchell Johnson
Born: June 1986 & 11 August 1984
Age at time of rampage: 11 and 13
Date of attack: 24 March 1998
Number of victims: 5 dead, 10 wounded
Victim profile: female classmates and one teacher
Arsenal: Golden – .30-caliber carbine, .38 special two-shot, Ruger .44 Magnum, Ruger Security Six .357-caliber revolver, FIE .380 handgun, a Star .380-caliber semi-automatic, pocketknife, two speed loader clips for the Ruger and over 300 shells of various calibers
Johnson – .30-06 caliber Remington model 742, Smith/Wesson .38-caliber pistol, Double Deuce Buddie two-shot derringer, Charter Arms .38 special pistol, two pocketknives and over 150 shells of various calibers
Dress code: camouflage
Media keywords: NRA, action shooting, Southern hunting culture, rap music, TuPac Shakur, Bone Thugs-N-Harmony, Choirboy, Wannabe Gangsta
Probable cause: have gun will travel. Johnson was dumped by his girlfriend; Golden was tired of taking crap from teachers
School: Westside Middle School
Location: Jonesboro, Arkansas
Sentence: both found delinquent for 5 murders and 10 assault charges
Status: in juvenile detention until they turn 21
Outcome: Mitchell wishes he could go to the school prom. Both are unhappy with the food in jail.

'There is a very special relationship between a man and his gun, an atavistic relation with its deep roots in prehistory, when the primitive man's personal weapon, so often his only effective defense and food provider, was nearly as precious to him as his

own limbs.' – Franklin Orth, executive vice president of the National Rifle Association

'That was my deer rifle, and it was set deadly accurate . . . At 200 yards, if that crosshair was on it, you pull that trigger . . .' – Doug Golden, bragging about the accuracy of the rifle used by Mitchell Johnson

'I hope your boy gets raped in jail and killed.' – an anonymous caller to Doug Golden

CAMOUFLAGE

On 24 March 1998, Mitchell Johnson, thirteen, and Andrew Golden, eleven, perpetrated one of the most heinous attacks on school grounds in US history. Nothing imaginable could prepare the nation for their calculated carnage. Nothing, that is, until Columbine . . .

The morning of the sniper attack started with Mitch, a garrulous and well-mannered youngster, telling his mother a funny story about how an elderly lady pulled his ear while he was singing with a Christian group at a Jonesboro nursing home. The yarn went on for too long, and by the time he was done, the school bus had already passed by. Mitch told his mom that he would catch a ride to school with his stepfather, Terry Woodard. Unbeknown to her, Woodard had already left.

When his mother, Gretchen, saw the family's 1991 Dodge Caravan van drive away, she didn't think twice about it. But it was Mitch behind the wheel. He had previously filled the vehicle with food, camouflage netting, ammunition, hunting knives and survival gear for after the school attack, when Drew and him would hide in the woods until it was 'cool' for them to come back.

Mitch picked up Drew and they drove to Drew's house where his father had a steel vault full of weapons. Though younger than Mitch, Drew was a gun-obsessed troublemaker who grew up with weapons and shooting and played gun sports. Drew's parents – both, ironically, postal workers – were already gone. Alone in the house, the two youngsters tried to open the gun vault with a hammer and a blowtorch.

Though the steel vault proved impenetrable, they found three unsecured handguns throughout the house; a .38-caliber Derringer, a .38-caliber snub-nose and a .357 Magnum.

The youngsters donned on their camouflage outfits and set out to their next stop, Drew's grandparents' house. The two boys, who could hardly reach over the steering wheel, noticed that the van was low on gas. They had to stop in three different gas stations before they were allowed to fill up the tank. Incredibly, none of the three gas station attendants reported the sight of two little kids driving around unsupervised in their parents' minivan.

Doug Golden, Drew's grandfather, worked for the Arkansas Game and Fish Commission. The boys knew he had an extensive gun collection just waiting to be raided. Using a crowbar they cracked open a basement door and snuck into the house. Once inside, the boys marveled at the living room's wall-length gun-rack with 48 weapons. Though the guns were secured with a steel safety cable, Drew used a bolt-cutter to break them loose. The boys helped themselves to three rifles; one of them, chosen by Mitch, was Doug Golden's favorite 'deadly accurate' .30-06 deerhunting rifle. They also took four unsecured handguns they found stashed under the mattress and about 3,000 rounds of ammunition.

Next, they drove to a cul-de-sac near the back of Westside Middle School in the outskirts of Jonesboro. Parking to the side of the road, they climbed out of the van, hauling their arsenal of ten weapons and over 450 rounds of ammunition. The two baby Rambos headed into the woods to a place they had previously scouted: the perfect spot to hunt their unsuspecting schoolmates. Perched at an elevation, about 100 yards from the school wall, the shooters had a clear view of the playground. The surrounding three feet of sage grass, kudzu vines and an array of sapling oaks, sweet gums and acorn trees provided the perfect cover for a sniper assault.

FIRST BLOOD
Just after the school lunch hour, Drew ran down to the school building and pulled the fire alarm. He quickly returned to his

position, grabbed his grandfather's Universal 30-caliber carbine with a 15-round clip, and waited for the students and teachers to file into the kill zone. The older boy, Mitch, cocked the massive Remington .30-06 hunting rifle with telescopic sight and aimed at his friends below. As 120 students and teachers walked into the ambush, the adolescent executioners started blasting, at first methodically, then faster and faster, orchestrating the slaughter of innocents with the precision of a military ambush attack.

With apparent deliberation, the shooters aimed high at their targets, where bodies are most fragile. In less than four minutes, the boys fired 22 rounds, hitting fifteen people, killing five and wounding ten. Giving a psychosexual tone to the bloodshed, the five dead and nine of the ten wounded were female. The only boy hit was Tristan McGowan, Drew's cousin.

As the gunfire erupted, the local 911 emergency board 'lit up like a Christmas tree'. All county emergency personnel and sheriff deputies headed to the school. The first officers to respond, John Varner, chief criminal investigator for the Craighead County sheriff's office, and Deputy John Moore, arrived at the scene within eight minutes of the first emergency call. A group of construction workers working on the roof of one of the school buildings saw the shooters and pointed the cops in the right direction.

The officers drove to the cul-de-sac and confronted the boys as they crossed the road towards the minivan. They ordered them to drop to the ground. 'The youngest one, he dropped real quick. The older one hesitated,' said Varner. After a second warning, he complied. The deputies handcuffed the boys and searched them. Between them, they had two high-powered rifles, seven guns and an assortment of ammunition. Drew was carrying the Universal 30-caliber carbine with an empty clip. Mitch had the deadly .30-06 caliber Remington with three shells in the clip and one in the chamber. In a clearing in the brush, fifty feet away, police found a third rifle, a Ruger .44 Magnum, next to two piles of spent shells.

Sheriff Varner searched the pockets of Drew's camouflage fatigues, finding 312 shells ranging in caliber from 'rat shots' to the bullets for a .357 Magnum. He also found two 'speed loaders', which allow quick reloading, a pocketknife, a loaded Davis Industry .38 special two-shot, a cocked FIE .380 handgun with five shells in the magazine and one in the chamber, and a Ruger Security Six .357-caliber revolver. Mitch had 142 live shells of various calibers. He also had a Smith & Wesson .38-caliber pistol with two spent shells and four live shells, a Double Deuce Buddie two-shot derringer, a loaded Charter Arms .38-special pistol with five rounds and a Star .380-caliber semi-automatic.

THE KILL ZONE

'The fire alarm went off at our school and we all came outside and all of a sudden there was shooting,' said eleven-year-old Amber Vanoven. 'I saw my best friend, Natalie Brooks, get killed – shot twice in the head. She started running over there on the concrete screaming and stuff, blood coming out of her head, and yelling, "This is real, this is real." You know? "Run," she said, "run." '

The first one hit was Stephanie Johnson. The twelve-year-old girl took a piercing round to her chest, exploding her heart and killing her instantly. At first, authorities were unable to determine who the shooter was. But further analysis of four bullet fragments found in her body and the angle of the bullet's trajectory indicated that Mitch was the one who killed her.

Next, thirteen-year-old Brittney Lambie was hit as she stood there hand-in-hand with her best friend, Whitney Pucket. When Brittney collapsed, her friend recalled telling her, 'Get up, Brittney,' but the youngster couldn't. 'When I looked down, there was blood on her legs,' Whitney said. 'I really didn't hear the shooting at first. When I did, I thought it was fireworks, a joke. Then when Brittney fell, I realized it was real.' Two more girls, Brittney Varner, eleven, and Whitney Irving, twelve, were hit next. Brittney collapsed as the round pierced through her back and blew out a 3-inch hole in her chest. The same bullet continued its lethal trajectory, wounding Whitney in the abdomen.

Using the .30-caliber semi-automatic carbine, Drew – the more experienced marksman – killed eleven-year-old Natalie Brooks, twelve-year-old Paige Herring and Brittney Varner. He also wounded Whitney Irving and Lynette Thetford, a 42-year-old sixth-grade world history teacher. Mitch, using the .30-06 hunting rifle, killed Stephanie Johnson, Brittney Lambie and 32-year-old English teacher Shannon Wright. He wounded Candace Porter, eleven, and Ashlee Betts, twelve. Police reports were unclear as to who was responsible for injuring Christina Amer, twelve, Jenna Brooks, twelve, Tristan McGowan, thirteen, and Jennifer Jacobs, twelve.

Mitchell Wright, the husband of the murdered teacher, said three of the five shots Mitchell fired hit his wife, suggesting that he was gunning for her. 'It's very easy to let go quickly and hate him,' Wright said. 'I'll admit it, I've often thought of getting my hands around his neck and strangling him. I don't want to lie. But I promised my son that we will see his mother in heaven some day. If I'm going to be a Christian, I can't do that. At the same token, I am struggling with it.'

Sixth grader Amber Vanoven said that Mitchell was in fact aiming at her friend Emma Pittman, who had seen Drew pull the fire alarm. But their teacher, Mrs Wright, bravely stepped in to shield little Emma. 'I think Mrs Wright saw that bullet coming,' Emma told *TIME* magazine. 'She grabbed me by the shoulders and pushed me out of the way. I feel so sorry for her.' Shannon Wright died in surgery from mortal wounds to her chest and abdomen.

Candace Porter, a girl who had dumped Mitch three weeks before the shooting, was also hit. She collapsed against one of the cinder-block walls of the building. One student told her: 'Don't worry, don't worry, it's all fake!' Feeling the blood on her right side, she responded: 'No it's not! I just got shot!' Luckily, the bullet missed all her vital organs as it went through her abdomen.

ANGER MANAGEMENT

When the smoke cleared, the two fledging psychopaths were charged in the Jonesboro juvenile detention center with five counts of first-degree murder and ten counts of first-degree battery. After a single night in jail the two cold-blooded snipers turned into quivering, lonely little kids. As the new picture of the baby-faced killers emerged, it became increasingly hard to see the youngsters as the calculating maniacs they had just proven themselves to be.

Craighead County Sheriff Dale Haas remarked: 'Keep in mind these are little boys, y'all. One little boy asked me some scriptural thoughts, and the other one is real emotional and was crying. He wants his mama, and he wants to go home.' As the charges were read, Mitch, the older boy, holding his mother's hand, wept and appeared remorseful. He said he was sorry, and wished 'he could take it back'. Drew, the younger one, was much less emotional and even managed to crack a smile.

Relatives of both kids described the killers as normal, nice, pleasant boys who enjoyed sports and were good students. Classmate Melinda Henson said Mitch was 'just an average guy' to whom she and her parents would give rides to church on Sundays. But he was also often seen writing 'Crips Killer' on dirty windowpanes. 'He started doing all these gang signs. I told him he should stop that because he was starting to scare me,' Melinda told the *Jonesboro Sun*.

By all accounts, Mitch was a deeply religious choirboy who had recently 'turned bad'. Candace, the girl who dumped him, said they had gone out for only three days. 'I thought he was nice, and then I found out he was trouble. He was always talking about fighting other people. He'd say he was going to beat them up the next day. He called one of our music teachers a bad name that I can't say.'

Several of Mitch's classmates recalled the boy saying that he was going to shoot Candace. A week before the attack, Mitch told his ex, 'he was planning something big', and that he had 'a lot of killing to do'. The day before, he announced to friends: 'Tomorrow you will find out if you live or die.'

Mitch, however, told Arkansas State Police investigator Rick Dickinson that Drew was the one that had planned the assault. When he asked why, Mitch replied, 'Anger, I guess.'

Later, he said, 'He asked me if I would help him do it, and I said "Yes."' He then told Craighead County Sheriff's Deputy Terry McNatt that they did it because 'Andrew was mad at a teacher. He was tired of their crap.'

Investigators believe that perhaps Mitch was not being completely truthful. One teacher said that Mitch was definitely the one calling the shots. Betty Fuller, the 42-year-old teacher, said that the chubby youngster was sneaky, manipulative and a con-man. She added that Mitch had an explosive temper and could be extremely vengeful. 'After I found out it was Mitchell, I wasn't surprised,' Fuller said. 'Even a little boy at school told me Mitchell was after me.'

Mitch's family painted a different picture of the youngster. They said he was an unsuspecting innocent dragged into mayhem by his conniving friend Andrew. 'We're not going to get up and say this child is not guilty,' his mother, Gretchen Woodard, said. Pulling the Christ card, Woodard described her son as a God-fearing choirboy and a devout Christian: 'I can tell you, I'm forty two years old, and I've not read the Bible cover to cover. Mitchell, when he was in fourth, fifth grade, read the Bible cover to cover.'

Drew, in contrast, had been shooting weapons since he was a tot. His father, a well-liked and respected member of the community, had been training him in 'action shooting', an NRA-sanctioned gun sport involving live weapons to shoot at pop-up targets in a fantasy 'war environment'. According to his grandfather, a licensed gun dealer, Drew has been armed since he was a toddler. 'We started buying him popper guns from day one,' said Doug Golden, who taught his grandson how to shoot. 'He worked his way up to BBs and then rifles and pistols. He could also shoot a bow.'

'Santa gave Drew Golden a shotgun when he was six,' wrote Nadya Labi in a cover story for *TIME* magazine. A poster boy for the NRA, Drew had been shooting and hunting since he could walk. In the rural South, where hunting is a way of life, you become a man once you drop your first deer. The year before the rampage, Drew bagged his first duck. 'He was very proud,' his grandfather said. 'Next season, he was going to try a deer.'

MEDIA FRENZY

Merely hours after fifteen students and teachers were gunned down, a invading horde of reporters from all over the world descended on Jonesboro with rapid-fire sound-bites from pundits, talking heads, expert commentators, corporate think tanks, media watchdog groups, nonprofit organizations, Internet chat room gurus, government agencies and public relations firms.

Theories about the reasons for the carnage ranged from the influence of a gun-obsessed Southern culture, to the glorification of violence on television and in rap music, to a mystical 'line of tragedy' running through Bill Clinton's hometown of Hope and connecting the three Bible Belt teenage rampage flashpoints of Jonesboro, Pearl and West Paducah.

Larry Sabato, professor of political science at the University of Virginia in Charlottesville and the author of *Feeding Frenzy*, remarked that the carpet-bombing coverage of the tragic events reached its saturation point even before the blood was washed off the concrete of Westside Middle School.

In fact, the sound-bite overload became a wall of senseless chatter, with everyone with a mike, a laptop and an agenda loudly blaming their favorite scapegoat which, in the Bible Belt, is the media:

'What else can we expect from kids who are exposed to murders on TV? We've desensitized human life through our callousness and disrespect for one another.' – Arkansas Governor Mike Huckabee

'What we see happening, is that there is so much realistic-type violence portrayed in movies and in other situations that certain kinds of kids can't tell the difference between reality and fantasy. They think that if you shoot somebody, they get up.' – Dr Stephen Garber, a child psychologist

'We are horrified, shocked, and full of heartfelt remorse for the community and the victims. It extends beyond any political tit-for-tat. This is not a gun issue, it's a society issue and it's troubling.' – The National Rifle Association

THE INEXPLICABLE

A shocked President Clinton, who was touring Africa with his wife, said the shooting was 'horrifying', and that he and Hillary were 'deeply shocked and heartbroken' over the tragedy in Arkansas, their home state. 'We don't know now and we may never fully understand what could have driven two youths to deliberately shoot into a crowd of their classmates.'

Attempting to explain the inexplicable, Kevin Dwyer, assistant executive director of the National Association of School Psychologists, laid the blame on the 'availability of guns and the misdiagnosis of depression . . . It makes me cry. People don't take these kids seriously . . . They tell friends they're going to do something. They tell adults wait until you see what's going to happen. They send a lot of signals.'

Rap music became the target of the self-appointed spin gods when police announced that Mitch owned and enjoyed two rap CDs. Debbie Pelley, an English teacher at Westside Middle School, told a Senate Commerce Science and Transportation Committee that the angry lyrics of TuPac Shakur and Bone Thugs-N-Harmony had incited Mitch's pre-rampage mindset: 'Mitchell brought this music to school with him, listened to it on the bus, tried listening to it in classes, sang the lyrics over and over at school.'

In a written statement read in Congress, Tina McIntyre, the mother of shooting victim Stephanie Johnson, also said that Mitch and Drew were driven to murder by rap. 'This is so chilling because this is what they did,' McIntyre remarked in her statement, referring to Mitch's favorite rap song 'We Crept and We Came' by Bone Thugs-N-Harmony. 'That is exactly how I felt when I saw my daughter – like she had been hunted down and slaughtered like an animal.'

> 'On the ground, they lay, when I spray that chrome.' – Bone
> Thugs-N-Harmony

Several Senators, in their election year best, expressed concern that the label warning system on CDs was failing to give parents enough information about the music's messages of sex and death. But even if your taste for music is more Burt Bacharach than TuPac Shakur, it is positively insane to blame East Coast Gangster rap for a shooting rampage perpetrated by a couple of white Bible Belt adolescents.

'MY BOY'S NOT A MONSTER'

> 'Hi, my name is Mitchell. My thoughts and prayers are with those people who were killed or shot and their families. I am really sad inside about everything. My thoughts and prayers are with those kids that I go to school with. I really want people to know the real Mitchell some day.' – Mitchell Johnson, read by his father during an interview in the ABC news program 20/20

As authorities and the press tried to piece together the stories of the two terror tots, charges surfaced that Mitch had molested an infant girl in Spring Valley, Minnesota. The youngster, while spending the summer with his father, appeared twice in court for inappropriately touching the girl, who was two or three years old.

Mitch told his friend Andrew O'Rourke, thirteen, that the situation had been 'misunderstood'. Apparently, he said, he was only trying to help the toddler pull up her pants after she went to the bathroom. Under questioning, he admitted taking his pants off too and putting 'his finger inside of her once'. In court, the girl corroborated the statement, pointing to an anatomically correct doll. 'His actions were inappropriate,' his father said. 'I took him to the authorities.'

After the sexual molestation charge came to light, Scott Johnson, Mitch's father, through his attorney, said his son had also been sexually molested when he was young. Tom Furth, Johnson's attorney, told Barbara Walters that Mitch had been molested by a relative of a day-care worker. 'He told me that he had been sexually abused as a child when he was six and seven years old in Minnesota and that it was repetitive.'

Furth suggested that the anger Mitch might have felt from being abused may have led to the schoolyard shooting. 'You don't do something like what he is accused of doing because you break up with a girlfriend or because you're angry at something that happened at school,' Furth said. 'There are reasons for it.'

FROM CHOIRBOY TO GANGSTER

To paint an accurate picture of Mitchell, one has to go back to his early days in Spring Valley, Minnesota, where he lived until 1994, when his parents finalized their divorce. Mitch was the older of two boys. They had an older half-sister from their mother's previous marriage who lived with them off and on. His mother, Gretchen, worked as a counselor in the federal prison system and his father, Scott, worked at a meat-packing plant. Scott, described in the press as a bulldog, had a volatile temper and constantly punched the walls of their home as he clashed with his wife and children.

By the early 1990s, Gretchen and Scott's marriage was falling apart. Home life was a disaster. 'There was dog crap on the kitchen floor,' a family friend told *TIME* magazine. 'Rotting food was lying on the counter for weeks. The yard was not cleaned or mowed.' The friend said that Mitch 'didn't look like someone I wanted my kid to play with'. In 1993 Scott was arrested for stealing meat from work and was fired. Gretchen filed for divorce and moved the kids into a two-room trailer in nearby Grand Meadow to live with Vermona Schwartz, her mother. Conditions there, according to their father, were no better than home. Scott complained that the 'boys have no space for themselves' and slept 'in the living room, one on the couch, and the other on the floor'.

Gretchen, with her divorce finalized, moved the boys to London, Kentucky, where she had a new job as a correctional counselor for the Federal Correctional Institution in nearby Manchester. Around the same time, she started seeing Terry Woodard, whom she had first met when she worked at the Federal Medical Center in Rochester. Back then Terry was doing time on methamphetamine and gun charges. When Gretchen discovered she was pregnant, she relocated her family once again, this time to Jonesboro, a town of 55,000 residents and 75 churches, 130 miles north-east of the state capital of Little Rock. There she married Woodard and settled in Bono, in the outskirts of Jonesboro, to live as a homemaker.

Mitch was known as a courteous, polite, respectful and well-mannered youngster. By all accounts, he had a good relationship with his mother and stepfather. In school, he was a good student who got mostly As and Bs. He played football, basketball and baseball, performed in the school choir and, on the weekends, sang in a nursing home with a Christian youth group. He enjoyed reading the Bible and attended church every Sunday. He impressed adults with his piety and his love of Christ. 'He made a profession of faith and decided to accept Jesus Christ as his savior,' said Christopher Perry, the youth minister at the Central Baptist Church in Jonesboro.

But there was also a dark side to his 'model child' exterior. Yes, he was the well-behaved, respectful and hard-working boy who made his mother proud. But he was also an abusive, manipulative and threatening youngster who spooked and scared his classmates. People knew him as a choirboy, a football player, a gentleman and a decent student, but they also knew him as a bully, a weirdo, a wannabe-gangster and, eventually, as a merciless killer.

In middle school, Mitch was never considered a trouble-maker, though he had been sent to in-school suspension three times in the two years he'd been there.

The third suspension was three weeks before the shooting, when he refused to take off a Nike cap he was wearing inside the school building. Betty Fuller, his English teacher, de-scribed how, with the help of another teacher, she wrestled the cap from him. School policy prohibits students from wearing hats or caps indoors. For detention, Fuller assigned Mitch to write an essay about what had happened. 'I hate in-school suspension,' he wrote. 'It was the only Nike hat I had left.' Then, in what the teacher took as veiled threat, he wrote about killing squirrels. 'I have a pellet gun and I am not afraid to use it.' Fuller showed the essay to the school principal, Karen Curtner, who called Mitchell's parents in for a meeting.

Within the last month before the attack Mitch was also kicked out of the basketball team for engraving his initials on his shoulder. Then he got caught using his father's debit card to make hundreds of dollars' worth of sex-talk calls. To top it off, Candace, his girlfriend, dumped his chubby ass.

The youngster stopped going to church and started identifying with gangsters. He wore a red bandana in his back pocket and boasted that he had joined the local chapter of the Bloods, the lethal South Central Los Angeles gang of mostly black and Latino thugs. The Bloods are best known for drive-by shootings and the street sale of crack cocaine. Together with their rivals, the Crips, they have entered mass consciousness through Snoop Doggy Dogg videos and the 1993 Rodney King race riots. Incidentally, the 55,000 residents of Jonesboro are mostly white, working-class, churchgoing 'bubbas' – not the type that are 'down' with the South Central LA gangster scene.

A BRAT WITH A GUN

Unlike Mitch, Drew did not pretend to have a good and an evil side. With Drew, it was all evil. Friends and neighbors described him as wicked, demented, immature, 'more than mischievous' and out of control. Grown-ups said he was a spoiled brat who was in need of a spanking. Although only eleven, he was well-tutored by his dad in the fine art of shooting rifles, shotguns and pistols.

For his parents, Drew was their 'miracle baby', the apple of their eye. His mother, Pat, who had two children from a previous marriage, had undergone tubal ligation. When she married Dennis Golden, she surgically reversed the procedure in order to have a baby with her new husband. Friends of the family said that Drew was 'the center of their world'. Always doted on, never disciplined, the youngster could do no wrong. By the time he was four, a neighbor said he would 'curse like a sailor'. But his father and grandfather would laugh and goad him on, saying that it was cute and manly.

Drew would ride his bike and terrorize the neighborhood while his parents were at work. Friends said Drew constantly shot his BB gun at other kids and bragged about killing squirrels. One young neighbor said he kept a cat in a box for over a week and starved it to death.

At school, Drew talked about 'taking over' the place and once stood on a table during the lunch hour and announced: 'You're all going to die.' If a classmate pissed him off, he would say: 'Man, he's making me so mad I should just take my gun and start blasting him in the butt for it.' For a school project, the gun-obsessed child presented a script for a 'Quick Draw McGraw' puppet show that ended in a gun battle. In the first grade, Drew was paddled after shooting sand into a girl's face with a pop-gun.

GUNS & AMMO

One doesn't need to look too far to understand what might have led Drew to shoot at his schoolmates. In the family photo album there is a chilling picture of a six-year-old Drew, dressed in camouflage and holding a shotgun. The picture, used for the cover of the 6 April 1998 *TIME* magazine issue, is a frightening reminder of everything that's wrong with Southern gun culture.

The FBI estimates that there are 250 million firearms in private hands in the US, with 5 million new ones being purchased every year. As a nation, the US averages per year over 2 million violent crimes and 24,000 murders. Seventy per cent of those murders are the result of someone shooting a firearm. In a typical week, more Americans die by gunfire than in all of Western Europe in a year.

Drew's home was registered with the state of Arkansas as the office of the Jonesboro Practical Pistol Shooters Association. The group, whose founder and head was Dennis Golden, was affiliated with the US Pistol Shooters Association. Through the association, Dennis had started teaching Drew combat shooting. The premier gun sport, according to the GunGames Kids website, combat shooting involves handing a youngster a loaded weapon and putting him or her inside a 'shoot-to-kill' fantasy set. As the shooter moves through the environment, he or she scores points by shooting at pop-up targets.

While many would be horrified by the idea of giving a loaded weapon to a tween and setting him or her loose in a lurid combat environment, the USPSA is using its web page actively to recruit children to join its rank and file and hopes to some day turn combat shooting into an Olympic sport. The USPSA web page shows a picture of three smiling Aryan-looking youths with holstered handguns, ammunition clips tucked into their pants, and a caption that reads:

'Julian, Izak and Chase are just your regular pre-teens who love to shoot. As the official members of 'GunGames Kids–America's Youth' team, they will be touring the different major shooting events across the country to promote more youth participation in the different gun sports.'

The website also contains information on 'Camp Shootout', which is described as a 'practical pistol camp for USPSA Junior Members' aged twelve and over. The 'main objective of the Junior summer camp program is to teach young shooters the basic techniques and skills required to successfully compete in USPSA style practical pistol matches.'

After the Jonesboro shooting, many blamed the irresponsible Southern culture for the carnage. Ironically, Doug and Dennis Golden, the two most influential adults in Drew's young life, myopically failed to see the correlatation between their gun-loving lifestyles and the tragedy besetting their 'miracle baby'. Guns were not the issue, they said. The problem was the virulent media, mental illness, unrequited love, bullies, Mitchell, anything except their beloved guns.

LEGALESE

After visiting Mitch in the Craighead County Jail, Gretchen Woodard complained that her son had lost forty pounds. 'Mitch is hungry all the time,' she said. 'He's so thin. There are times he actually licks his plate.' Craighead County Sheriff Dale Haas responded that a dietician prepares a balanced menu for all prisoners and she shouldn't be worried about her son being underfed.

'This is a jail,' Haas said. 'We serve nutritional meals that meet the guidelines. Those are frivolous, ridiculous complaints. We are inspected and we comply with jail regulations. This is not a comfortable environment. But this is not a motel. It's a jail.' Craighead County Jail administrator Rick Duhon said Drew often refused to eat and had also lost weight. 'He doesn't like what's served,' Duhon said. 'But it's not a restaurant.'

On 11 August 1998, the two boys had their final adjudication hearing. A tearful Mitch, who turned fourteen that day, told a Craighead County courtroom that Drew and he never intended to kill anyone. 'I really thought that no one would actually be hurt,' he read from a typed statement. 'I thought we would just shoot over everyone's head. When the shooting started, we were not shooting at anybody or any group in particular.'

Drew did not apologize. His lawyer instead argued that he was unable to understand his actions and was insane at the time of the shootings. After three hours, Craighead County Circuit-Chancery Judge Ralph Wilson Jr. rejected the insanity argument and found the two youngsters 'delinquent' of five counts of capital murder and ten counts of first-degree battery. That night, authorities used a National Guard helicopter to transfer the two schoolyard killers from the Craighead County jail in Jonesboro to the Alexander Youth Services Center in Bryant. Hopefully the food will be better.

Because the killers were under fourteen, the worst punishment that could have been handed to them under Arkansas law was confinement in a state youth facility until age 21. Though there are no suitable facilities in Arkansas to keep them beyond eighteen, Governor Mick Huckabee vowed to build a prison, if necessary, to house them until the very last day of their sentence.

The day before the adjudication hearing, the relatives of two Jonesboro victims filed a wrongful death lawsuit against the two boys, both sets of parents, Drew's grandfather and the manufacturers of the two weapons used in the shooting.

The suit, which was filed on 10 August on behalf of Mitchell Wright, the husband of slain teacher Shannon Wright, and Renee Brooks, the mother of slain student

Natalie Brooks, contended that there was ample evidence that the boys were anti-social, obsessed with weapons, and had a 'propensity to commit acts which could normally be expected to cause injury'. This, the suit argued, should have alerted the parents to be more watchful of their two delinquent sons.

Jonesboro attorney Bobby McDaniel said his clients would seek damages from gun-makers Remington Arms Co. Inc. and Universal Firearms for not equipping their weapons with trigger-locking devices. NRA bulldogs were quick to react to the suit, defending the gun-makers' right not to have to install trigger-locks on their weapons and downplaying the advantages of such devices. 'Locks are not a substitute for safety,' said Tracy Gonzalez, a spokesman for the National Rifle Association in Fairfax, Virginia. 'They give a false sense of security.'

Poinsett County Circuit Judge David Burnett dismissed the charges against the gun manufacturers, saying they were removed from any liability because the two weapons were stored in a locked gun cabinet. He also dismissed the suit against Doug Golden because the kids broke into his house and he could not be held responsible for what they took. Golden, who's suffered a heart attack from the stress following the shooting, was visibly relieved by the decision.

It is unclear what has been the final outcome of the civil suit against the two boys and their parents. But what is clear is that on 11 August 2005, whether he's rehabilitated or not, Mitchell Johnson will be free again. Two years later, so will Drew.

8. JUST KILL ME

Name: Kipland Kinkel
Born: 30 August 1982
Age at time of rampage: 15
Date of attack: 21 May 1998
Number of victims: 4 dead, 22 wounded
Victim profile: two students, his parents
Arsenal: .22 Ruger semi-automatic rifle, .22 Ruger semi-automatic handgun and a .9 Glock semiautomatic pistol. 5 active bombs, 15 inactive explosive devices
Dress code: tan trench coat
Media keywords: Prozac, Internet, *Romeo and Juliet*, media violence, violent video games, Most Likely to Start World War III
Early warning signs: anger-management issues, revenge fantasies, gun collecting, bomb-making, cruelty to animals
Probable cause: shame about being expelled from school, mental illness
School: Thurston High School
Location: Springfield, Oregon

'I have just killed my parents! I don't know what is happening. I love my mom and dad so much. I just got two felonies on my record. My parents can't take that! It would destroy them. The embarrassment would be too much for them. They couldn't live with themselves. I'm so sorry. I am a horrible son. I wish I had been aborted. I destroy everything I touch. I can't eat. I can't sleep. I didn't deserve them. They were wonderful people. It's not their fault or the fault of any person, organization, or television show. My head just doesn't work right.' – Kip Kinkel

WILDERNESS
'There are three things you need in order to shoot and kill effectively and efficiently,' retired military psychologist David

Grossman writes. 'The gun, the skill, and the will.' Kipland Kinkel, a freckle-faced fifteen-year-old from Springfield, Oregon, clearly had these three things in mind the day he killed his parents and the next day when he shot 51 rounds into the crowded cafeteria of Thurston High.

On 21 May 1998, a day after being suspended from school for buying a stolen gun from a schoolmate, Kip returned to Thurston High School and opened fire in the cafeteria, killing two students and wounding 25 others. The attack was brought to a halt by seventeen-year-old Jake Ryker who, despite being shot on the arm and chest, tackled Kip as he tried to reload his weapon. Several other students quickly piled on the spindly freshman until police arrived.

When it was all over, seventeen-year-old Mikael Nickolauson was dead on the scene. Ben Walker, also seventeen, died in the hospital twelve hours later from a head wound. Twenty-five more students were wounded, nineteen of them from the gunfire, the rest from the ensuing stampede away from the gunshots.

The day before the rampage, Kip was arrested for the gun incident and released to his father's custody. By all accounts Kip was horrified by the shame his actions would bring to his parents. He'd long felt belittled that he couldn't live up to his popular and athletic older sister, Kristin Kinkel. He felt that he had no other option, that all hope was lost. From that moment forward, Kip set in motion the lethal chain of events in which he would kill his parents, then get back at his classmates.

Following the school rampage, he told investigators they would find his parents, Bill Kinkel, 59 and Faith Kinkel, 57, dead in separate rooms of their A-frame home in an affluent riverfront neighborhood, which he had booby-trapped with homemade explosive devices.

Investigators searching the Kinkel home found five active bombs throughout the house and fifteen inactive explosive devices in a crawl space under the porch. One bomb was placed in the garage under his mother's cold corpse. In Kip's room, investigators found two bombs, one made out of two soda cans and a second made out of a fire extinguisher. They also found an extensive collection of knives, several books with bomb-making instructions, some chemicals, a sawn-off shotgun, two Howitzer shell casings and a hand grenade.

The morning of the school attack, Kip left the soundtrack to Baz Luhrmann's 1996 film *Romeo and Juliet* playing continuously on the living-room stereo and hundreds of rounds of .22 caliber ammunition strewn all over the floor. On a table he left the above-quoted note saying, 'I have killed my parents . . . I am a horrible son.' Using masking tape he strapped a hunting knife to his leg and an X shape on his chest with one .22 caliber bullet and one .9mm bullet underneath – to kill himself, in case he ran out of bullets.

In his backpack he stuffed a .22-caliber Ruger semi-automatic handgun, a 9mm Glock pistol, several clips of ammunition and about a hundred more loose rounds. He grabbed his high-powered .22mm Ruger semi-automatic rifle and drove his mother's green Ford Explorer to school. Twenty minutes later, he walked into the cafeteria hiding the rifle under a tan trench coat with the intent to kill as many people as he could.

FAMILY LIFE

'God damn these VOICES inside my head. I want to die. I want to be gone. But I have to kill people. I don't know why. I am so sorry! Why did God do this to me. I have never been happy. I wish I was happy. I wish I made my mother proud. I am nothing! I tried so hard to find happiness. But you know me I hate everything. I have no other choice. What have I become? I am so sorry.' – Kip Kinkel

William and Faith Kinkel, by all accounts, were good parents. Theirs was not a chaotic home. They were attentive, caring and loving towards both their children. Bill was retired from teaching Spanish at Thurston High and was teaching night classes at Lane Community College. Faith taught Spanish at nearby Springfield High. His sister, Kristin, a 21-year-old student at the University of Hawaii, had reportedly been placed fourth with a partner in the 1998 college cheerleading national championship.

Unlike the families of the killers in previous chapters, the Kinkels did not have a relationship with guns. They were educated, intelligent parents who cared and were involved in the lives of their children.

Kip seemed to have had the perfect childhood. The parents were not remotely amiss in their parenting duties. Instead they took their two kids hiking and camping, and were involved with their school and their friends. 'This was a trustworthy, middle-class, high family values kind of family,' said their neighbor, Dr Dennis Ellison. 'We watched Kip grow up. This was not a weird kid. This was a trustworthy, boy scout type of kid.'

Kip's second-grade teacher testified at his sentencing hearing that he was an average second grader with no disciplinary problems. He might have lacked maturity and he might have been physically and emotionally underdeveloped for his age, but that was all. She said that Kip was frustrated with his writing and language skills. His parents asked the school to test him for a learning disability to see if he was eligible for special education services.

According to the school counselor, Kip scored above the 90th percentile on the intelligence test, average on the neurological screening test, but remarkably low on the motor/hand skills test and the spelling test. The counselor observed that during the 25-minute spelling test, Kip was very diligent, but had difficulty spelling even his own last name.

By third grade Kip qualified for special education and was given an honor award at the end of the year 'for improvement in reading and working hard to overcome his frustration'. In fourth grade he was diagnosed as dyslexic, which explained his troubles with school work. Though he was in the special education services, he also was placed in a Talented and Gifted program for excelling in science and math. But still, he felt like a failure who couldn't measure up to the achievements of Kristin who was a perfect student and popular with everyone.

ANGER MANAGEMENT

'I sit here all alone. I am always alone. I don't know who I am. I want to be something I can never be. I try so hard every day. But in the end, I hate myself for what I've become.' – Kip Kinkel

Starting with seventh grade, Kip began his downward spiral that would end with murder and mayhem. Kristin transferred in her sophomore year of college from the University of Oregon to Hawaii Pacific where she received a full cheerleading scholarship. With Kristin gone, Kip became much more secretive. He wanted to turn himself into someone that others regarded as 'dangerous'. He hung out with a rougher crowd of kids and got into shoplifting and guns.

At school, Kip and his friends downloaded bomb-making instructions from the Internet. When they were caught, his parents told him how deeply disappointed they were. Then he was caught shoplifting CDs from a Target store, bringing the disappointment level of his parents to an all-time high. Around this time he also started secretly collecting guns. He bought a sawn-off shotgun from another kid in school and kept it hidden in his bedroom. His writings demonstrate a degree of anger and violence that is incongruous with his life as a normal teenager with the occasional behavioral blemish.

Over Christmas break Kip went to a snowboarding clinic in Bend, Oregon, where he was arrested with another boy for throwing rocks at cars from an overpass. The two boys were referred to the Department of Youth Services in Eugene, Oregon. Following the arrest, Kip's mother sent him to him to see Dr Jeffrey Hicks, a psychologist specializing in anger-management counseling. Faith was specially concerned with Kip's 'extreme interest in guns, knives, and explosives' his 'anti-social acting out' and his deteriorating relationship with his father.

Hicks wrote that 'Kip became tearful when discussing his relationship with his father.' The doctor said that Kip thought his mother viewed him as 'a good kid with some bad habits' while his father saw him as 'a bad kid with bad habits'. In fact his mother once said that she thought he had no conscience, while his father believed his son was actually dangerous. Dr Hicks diagnosed Kip with Major Depressive Disorder and concluded that 'Kip had difficulty with learning in school, had difficulty managing anger, some angry acting out and depression.' The doctor prescribed the drug Ritalin to bring the boy and his anger under control.

In his last year in middle school Kip was suspended twice from school for anger-related outbursts. The first time, he was suspended for landing a karate kick on the head of another boy after the youngster shoved him. The day he returned from suspension, he was suspended again for throwing a pencil at another boy.

To control his anger, Dr Hicks recommended changing his prescription from Ritalin to Prozac, an antidepressant that works by altering the levels of serotonin in the brain. However, recent studies have linked Prozac and other serotonin inhibitors to uncontrollable explosions of anger, just like that which led Kip to kill four people.

Soon after he began taking the drug, Kip's mood seemed to improve substantially and he no longer appeared depressed. The doctor noted that Kip was 'sleeping better. No temper outbursts, taking the medication as prescribed without side effects.' Was he in the road to recovery? Or was it the calm before the storm?

WARNING SIGNS

'I am so full of rage that I feel I could snap at any moment. I think about it every day. Blowing the school up or just taking the easy way out, and walk into a pep assembly with guns. In either case, people that are breathing will stop breathing. That is how I will repay all you mother fuckers for all you put me through.' – Kip Kinkel

Suicide rates for the young in the United States have increased over the last four decades and have leveled off near their all-time highs. According to the National Institute of Mental Health, more than 1.5 million Americans under age fifteen are seriously depressed. The American Academy of Child and Adolescent Psychiatry believes the number might be twice as high. The point is, the youth in America is in constant psychological pain.

In a literature class, Kip read a passage to the rest of the class about his plans to 'kill everybody'. School superintendent Jamon Kent said that Kinkel was not referred to counseling after the incident because it's more than commonplace for students to express their anger toward others. 'Teachers considered him an average, everyday kid,' he explained. 'If we detained every student who said I'm going to kill someone, we would have a large number of students detained.' Remember, at least 1.5 million youngsters in the US are seriously depressed. A depressed, insecure child is one thing, but that same child with a gun is a tragedy waiting to happen.

Kip gave a talk in speech class about how to build a bomb, which caused a stir, but a classmate gave a speech about how to join the Church of Satan, which was just as controversial. According to classmate Nissa Lund, fourteen, Kip would brag about torturing animals and once told her he stuffed a handful of lit firecrackers in a cat's mouth. Rachel Dawson, Kip's former girlfriend in middle school, said he boasted about shooting little cats. Clearly a serial killer in the making, Kip also talked about blowing up a cow. On the other hand, friends said when he was not busy with revenge fantasies, bomb-making and killing animals, Kip was a normal, boisterous, high-school freshman who enjoyed rocking out to Nirvana and playing the guitar.

A lot of the warning signs about Kip's impending implosion were ignored largely because he was from a good family who lived in a big beautiful house on the right side of town. People assumed his parents would keep him under control. People assumed that his extreme manifestations of cataclysmic violence were a just a phase; that he would soon get over it. After all, he hung with the other preppy kids. He was a purple belt in karate and played football. He was a joker, a boaster, a good kid, not a budding psychopath or a junior Charlie Manson.

When he told his friend Destry Saul that he wanted to put a bomb under the bleachers at a pep rally and block the doorway so students couldn't get out, Destry thought it was a joke. 'If I ever get really mad, I'd go and hit the cafeteria with my .22,' Kip told Destry. 'I have lots more rounds for my .22 than my 9 and I'll save one for myself.' Destry took it as another boast. Sadly, that's exactly what he did.

One day, he showed friends a pipe bomb stored in his school locker. The *New York Daily News* quoted his classmates Walter Fix and Shawn Davidson saying Kip showed them a hit list of enemies he kept. 'He was always talking about killing people,' Shawn said. 'He liked to get revenge a lot.' Investigators never found the rumored hit list.

Friends said his out-of-control antics seemed typical angst-ridden teenage pranks from a hormonally challenged kid going crazy over girls and school work. 'He had a temper but he's not a villain,' classmate Chrystie Cooper told AP. 'He was the guy that made you smile in the hallways.' In the same interview Cooper, fifteen, called Kip a 'country boy who liked to blow things up.' No wonder he was voted in middle school 'Most Likely to Start World War III.'

ARMED AND DANGEROUS

—

'I feel like everyone is against me, but no one ever makes fun of me, mainly because they think I am a psycho. There is one kid above all others that I want to kill. I want nothing more than to put a hole in his head. The one reason I don't: Hope. That tomorrow will be better. As soon as my hope is gone, people die.'
– Kip Kinkel

Though his parents were not gun freaks, they were painfully aware of his all-consuming gun obsession. 'We weren't allowed to watch *Bugs Bunny* because it was too violent. Violence in our house was a huge no-no,' Kristin Kinkel said in an interview on PBS's *Frontline*.

In an attempt to turn his son's fascination with weapons into a supervised hobby, his father took him to buy him a gun and attached a set of rules to the use of it. 'Bill felt that the boy was obsessed enough with guns that he would have a gun, one way or another,' said Rod Ruhoff, a friend of the father. 'The way Bill could control the situation is if he owned the gun and had control over it.' Little did the father know that Kip had already purchased a shotgun from a kid in school and was already working on his own private armory.

On 27 June 1997 Bill Kinkel took his son to buy a 9mm Glock pistol. The understanding between them was that Kip would do the research on which model gun he wanted and would pay for it with his own money. He could not use the gun without his father present. Bill would store the gun and it would not become Kip's until he turned 21 years old. Furthermore, they would both take a course in marksmanship and safety, and the gun would be kept under lock and key.

But Kip had his own gun-purchasing agenda and bought a second handgun from a friend in school. By the beginning of his freshman year in Thurston High, Kip already had three weapons in his possession: the Glock his father had bought, and two weapons he secretly bought from friends – a sawn-off shotgun and a Ruger .22 target pistol.

That fall, Kip convinced his father to let him buy a rifle. Given Kip's moods and temper, the parents debated over whether to get him a single-loading bolt-action weapon or something with more rapid-fire capability. They settled – in retrospect, tragically – on the faster shooting .22-caliber semi-automatic Ruger rifle, the weapon he ultimately used to fire fifty rounds in the school cafeteria. As with the Glock, the rifle was bought with his own money and under the condition that he would use it only under adult supervision.

'The kid had them by the throat,' said Dr Bill Reisman, who profiles deviant youth behavior for law-enforcement officials. 'They were terrified of his interest in guns, but they went out and bought him guns.'

The father, at his wits' end, even sought the advice of a stranger he met in San Diego airport. After discovering the man was an expert in antisocial behavior and juvenile delinquency, Bill Kinkel poured his heart out about his potentially psychopathic son. Dan Close, an Oregon University professor, recalled meeting Bill six months before the shooting. Bill told him about Kip's obsession with guns. 'I told Bill that raising kids is the toughest thing we'll ever do,' Close said. 'And Bill said, "If we survive." '

A few days before the shooting, Bill told his tennis partner that he was 'pleased with Kip's progress' in controlling his anger. It seemed to Faith and Bill that their son was finally settling down. Perhaps buying the weapons he so much coveted had calmed his anxieties. Even his doctor, whom he had stopped seeing, thought he was well on his way to recovery.

TWENTY FOUR HOURS

All the progress changed on 20 May when Kip was arrested for buying a stolen gun on school property. Kip had arranged the night before to buy the gun from his friend Korey Ewert, who had stolen it from Scott Keeney, the father of a schoolmate. After paying $110 in cash for the loaded Beretta semi-automatic pistol with a 9 round clip, Kip put the weapon in a paper bag and hid it in his locker.

A little later that morning Scott Keeney called the school to report that his gun was missing. He thought that a friend of his son had stolen it and gave the school a list of about a dozen suspects. Though Kip's name was not on the list, by 9.15 a.m., Detective Al Warthen was questioning him about the weapon. Kip admitted to having the Beretta in his locker and both he and Korey were immediately arrested. They were escorted off the school premises in handcuffs and were suspended, pending certain expulsion.

At the police station Kip was fingerprinted, photographed, and charged with possession of a firearm in a public building and the felony charge of receiving a stolen weapon. According to Detective Warthen, Kip was very worried about how his parents were going to react to this new disgrace. By 2.00 p.m. the youngster was released to his father's custody.

According to Kip's confession, all hope was gone and he saw, with cold clarity, what he had to do next. As his father was sitting at the kitchen counter drinking coffee, Kip went for th e .22 rifle from his room, got ammunition from his parents' room, returned downstairs and fired one shot to the back of his father's head. Kip then dragged his father's body into the bathroom and covered it with a sheet.

About an hour after killing his father, his friends Tony McCowan and Nick Hiaason called. Patched together in a conference call he talked about the school incident over the gun and said he would probably end up doing something really stupid to get back at those who got him suspended. As he talked he watched out the window, weapon in hand, waiting for his mom to arrive.

Kinkel told his friends that he was 'mad at himself' for everything. Then he ominously stated: 'It's over . . . everything's over . . . it's done . . . nothing matters now.' During the rest of the conversation, Kip went back and forth between being upset and angry. According to Tony, he also kept asking, 'Where's my mom . . . when is she going to be home?'

His mother arrived around 6.00 p.m. According to his audio-taped police confession, he met her in the garage with his handgun to his side. As she turned to head up the stairs, he told her he loved her, then shot her twice in the back of the head. Faith didn't die instantly so he shot her three times in the face and once more through the heart. Then he dragged her body across the garage floor and covered her with a sheet. With his parents growing cold downstairs, Kip flipped on his favorite TV show, *South Park* and watched the episode in which Kenny falls into a grave and gets squashed by a tombstone.

The next morning, at around 7.30 a.m., Kip headed for school. He parked his mother's Ford Explorer about a block away and walked down a dirt path, past the school's tennis courts and into the back parking lot. At 7.56 a.m. he was caught on a school security camera as he walked through a hallway towards the cafeteria. Right then, he shot Ben Walker in the head and Ryan Atteberry in the face. Walker died twelve hours later in the hospital.

Kip continued on his path of destruction, entering the school cafeteria, where there were nearly 400 students gathered for a farewell ceremony for seniors. There, he whipped out the .22 rifle from under his trench coat and started firing from the hip, deliberately emptying the rest of the fifty-round clip into the crowd of students.

'He was swiveling back and forth, firing at everyone,' said sixteen-year-old Jonathan Crawford. 'He just mowed 'em down,' said Michelle Calhoun. 'It was just sort of happening in slow motion.' The bullets shattered the huge plate-glass windows of the cafeteria as terrified students ran for cover and dived under tables. With all hell breaking loose, suddenly the gunfire stopped and the only sound heard was the clicking of empty shells bouncing on the concrete floor.

Jakob Ryker, whose girlfriend, Jen Alldredge, had been shot in the arm, torso and chin, decided he had seen enough. He rushed Kip as the shooter was reaching in his backpack for another clip. Ryker, a seventeen-year-old champion wrestler, tackled Kip to the ground. As the two struggled, Kip was able to grab the Glock 9mm in his backpack and fired one final round, hitting Ryker in the hand and chest. Then another five boys, including Ryder's younger brother, Josh, piled on the shooter until police arrived. As they waited, Kip pleaded, 'Please, just kill me.'

Springfield Police officer Dan Bishop arrived on the scene a mere eight minutes after the first shot was fired. As Bishop got the students off Kip, one boy punched Kip in the face. By 8.04 a.m., Bishop had already searched and handcuffed Kip and was reading him his Miranda rights. Bishop transferred custody of Kip to the first detective to arrive on the scene. Soon after, Detective Al Warthen arrived and recognized Kip as the kid he had arrested the previous morning for having the stolen gun.

At the Springfield Police Department, the freckle-faced killer was left handcuffed in an interview room while Detective Warthen went to secure his weapon. While he was alone in the room, Kip swung his cuffed hands to the front and pulled out the hunting knife that had been strapped to his leg. In an attempt to commit suicide by cop, Kip – yelling 'Kill me, shoot me' – lunged at Detective Warthen with the knife. The veteran detective quickly stepped back and used pepper spray to subdue the desperate youngster. Then Warthen asked him, 'How's your dad?' After a beat, Kip revealed the true proportion of the horror he had perpetrated.

DEAD SOULS

'I have spent days trying to figure out what I want to say. I have crumpled up dozens of pieces of paper and disregarded even more ideas. I have thought about what I could say that might make people feel just a little bit better. But I have come to the realization that it really doesn't matter what I say. Because there is nothing I can do to take away any of the pain and destruction I have caused. I absolutely loved my parents and had no reason to kill them. I had no reason to dislike, kill or try to kill anyone at Thurston.' – Kip Kinkel

On 16 June, Kip was indicted on 58 felony charges including four counts of aggravated murder. On 24 September 1999, three days before jury selection was set to begin, Kip's lawyers agreed to forgo his planned insanity defense in exchange for pleading guilty to the lesser counts of murder and attempted murder. The lawyers chose to do this in reaction to Lane County Circuit Judge Jack Mattison's announcement that he would be trying the fifteen-year-old as an adult.

Under the plea agreement, Kip said he was guilty to four counts of murder and 26 counts of attempted murder (25 for the students wounded and one for assaulting a police officer). The Oregon mandatory sentencing statute, Measure 11, required a sentence of 25 years for each of the four counts of murder. The prosecutors agreed to recommend that those sentences be served concurrently, so that Kip could serve as little as 25 years for the murders. Both sides also agreed to the mandatory minimum sentence of seven and a half years for each of the attempted murder charges. But the final length of the sentence was left to Judge Mattison to decide.

In a six-day sentencing hearing, Judge Mattison allowed psychiatrists, psychologists, victims and Kip's sister to testify. Dr Orin Bolstad testified for the defense on Kinkel's mental state at the time of the killings. After his arrest, the doctor interviewed Kip for over 32 hours. In court, the doctor described a 'very depressed, alienated child who saw adults as unfair, arbitrary and untrustworthy'. Like other rampage killers, he had low self-esteem, and was manipulative and paranoid. Kip had a series of delusional beliefs ranging from his fear that the Chinese were going to invade America – for which Kip had prepared by storing explosives under his house – and how Disney was planning to take over the world and substitute the Disney dollar for the real one. He also thought the government had planted chips in his head, which indicated that he was watching too much *X-Files*. The doctor also reported the existence of mental illness, depression, alcoholism and institutionalization on both sides of the Kinkel family.

Not unlike Luke Woodham, Kip told Dr Bolstad that voices in his head led him to commit murder. The voices, according to Kip, began in sixth grade. Kip told the doctor that the first time he heard a voice it said, 'You are a stupid piece of shit. You aren't worth anything.' He tried to quiet the voices with music, TV, or by punching his head, but to no avail. He said he never mentioned the voices to anyone because he didn't want people to think he was crazy. The only pre-rampage occasion that these voices were mentioned was in 1998 when he disrupted English class by shouting, 'God damn this voice inside my head!' Then again, such an interruption could be explained as a goofy prank by a bored student to entertain his classmates.

Dr Bolstad said he believed that Kip murdered his parents and opened fired in the school cafeteria because of these voices. Kip said the voices told him to shoot his father. 'I had no choice. The voices said I had no choice.' Later, after killing his mother, the voices told him to 'go to school and kill everybody. Look what you've already done.' During cross-examination, Bolstad stated, 'I think the primary thing that was operating in his feeling and need to kill ... were the voices.'

Dr William Sack, another child psychiatrist who interviewed Kip twice after his arrest, said that Kip was 'a very very sick psychotic individual'. Though reluctant to diagnose a fifteen-year-old whose brain was still developing, Dr Sack theorized that Kip will eventually develop 'into the schizo-affective category or into paranoid schizophrenia'. Like Bolstad, Sack said Kip was probably driven to kill by his auditory hallucinations: 'I feel his crimes and his behavior over those two days are the direct result of a psychotic product that was building over three years that suddenly emerged, taking over his ego.'

NEW DAWN FADES

'I take full responsibility for my actions. These events have pulled me down into a state of deterioration and self-loathing that I didn't know existed. I am very sorry for everything I have done, and for what I have become.' – Kip Kinkel

On 2 November Judge Mattison sentenced Kip to 111 years in prison, without the possibility of parole. Immediately after the sentencing, Kip was transferred to the MacLaren Youth Correctional Facility in Woodburn, Oregon. In MacLaren Kip was sent to the Secure Intensive Treatment Program where he'll finish high school and undergo intensive therapy. He may remain at MacLaren until he turns 25 or until the staff determines that he is ready to join the adult prison population. Kip is the first juvenile to serve a life sentence in the state of Oregon.

Six days after sentencing, Jesse Barton, the chief deputy state public defender, filed a notice to appeal the severity of Kip's sentence. Barton said the primary basis for the appeal was that Judge Mattison misread Oregon's sentencing guidelines and wrongly gave more consideration to the 'protection of society' principle over 'reformation'. In a secondary appeal Barton argued that Kip's sentence amounts to 'cruel and unusual punishment' defined in the Oregon State Constitution as one which 'shocks the moral sense of all reasonable persons'. Arguments for the appeal will begin on 31 July 2002.

The National Alliance for the Mentally Ill and the National Alliance for the Mentally Ill of Oregon have joined the appeal filed by Barton, arguing that Kip's schizophrenia can be treated, and that he can be reformed and eventually should be allowed to return to society when he is no longer considered dangerous.

On the November 2000 national elections Kinkel emerged as a central player in the debate over an Oregon ballot measure that could reduce the sentences of thousands of inmates. 'If Kip Kinkel is resentenced, I will be living in fear every day, along with my family and fellow victims, that if he is released he will hunt us all down,' wrote Jennifer Alldredge, a student wounded by Kinkel, in the state's official voter guide. The Republican candidate for attorney general in Oregon featured Kinkel in his TV ads, accusing the incumbent of supporting the earlier guidelines, which theoretically could free Kinkel by the time he turns 21.

State Representative Jo Ann Bowman, a leading repeal supporter, argued that opponents were using Kinkel as a scare tactic. 'There's no way that anyone could kill four people and wound 25 without spending an extremely long time in prison,' the Portland Democrat said.

The Republican candidate argued that tougher sentences for juveniles would prevent future school shootings. However, it's hard to imagine that harsher laws would have deterred Kip Kinkel. By most accounts, he intended to die when he set out to shoot his schoolmates. It's doubtful that he was thinking about the length of his sentence when he was in the school cafeteria, squeezing the trigger.

9. HIGH SCHOOL ARMAGEDDON

Names: Eric Harris & Dylan Klebold
Born: 9 April 1981 & 11 September 1981
Ages at time of rampage: 18 and 17
Date of attack: 20 April 1999
Number of victims: 15 dead (including themselves), 23 wounded
Victim profile: fellow students, one teacher
Arsenal: two sawn-off shotguns, 9mm Hi-Point carbine rifle, TEC-DC-9 semi-automatic pistol and a total of 95 explosives devices (48 small bombs, 27 pipe bombs, eight 1.5-gallon propane containers and three 25-pound propane bombs)
Media keywords: Trenchcoat Mafia, 'Doom', Goth rock, Marilyn Manson, *Natural Born Killers*, German indusrial rock, Rammstein, KMFDM, *The Basketball Diaries*, Adolf Hitler, Shakespeare, Luvox
Dress code: camouflage, ski-masks, black trench coats
Warning signs: everything
Probable cause: wanted to be famous, hated everyone, have bombs will travel, Hitler's 110th birthday
School: Columbine High School
Location: Littleton, Colorado
Outcome: both dead by self-inflicted gunshot wounds the day of the rampage. Changed gun laws in Colorado, made everyone aware of ticking teenage time-bombs, added 'pull a Columbine' to the national lexicon

'After I mow down a whole area full of you snotty-ass rich motherfucker high-strung God-like-attitude-having worthless pieces of shit whores, I don't care if I live or die.' – Eric Harris

BLACK TRENCH COATS

On 20 April 1999 two students dressed in black trench coats, fatigues and ski-masks opened fire on Columbine High School, located in the comfortable suburb of Littleton, on the outskirts of Denver, Colorado, leaving twelve students and a teacher dead, and 23 wounded. Then, in a final act of defiance, Eric Harris, eighteen, and Dylan Klebold, seventeen, ended their own lives, firing two final rounds to their heads.

Like other recent cases of schoolyard massacres, the youthful gunmen were white, from affluent families, with internet connections, obsessed with violence and had easy access to high-powered weapons.

Armed with 95 explosives devices, two sawn-off shotguns, a 9mm Hi-Point carbine rifle and TEC-DC-9 semi-automatic pistol, the two chuckling killers set out on a carefully planned 'suicide mission'. The mayhem started a little after 11.17 a.m., when two 25-pound propane bombs they had previously placed in the cafeteria failed to detonate. Not discouraged by their shoddy, homemade detonators, the two killers walked into their school, laughing and hollering, and began shooting at their fellow schoolmates with complete abandon.

For the next sixteen minutes the rampagers moved through different areas of the school, starting in the cafeteria and ending in the upstairs library, where the two maniacs inflicted most of the damage. Four and a half hours later the school resembled a burned-out war zone and the two rampagers were found dead in the library from self-inflicted gunshot wounds. Since then, the horrifying words 'pulling a Columbine' have been forever etched into the lexicon of the deranged.

Police said the trenchcoat killers left numerous homemade bombs with timers in and around the school, including the two original 25-pound propane and shrapnel bombs in the cafeteria. More explosive devices were found in their cars and homes. Days after the rampage, a third large incendiary device rigged with a barbecue propane tank was found in the school kitchen. Thankfully, like most of the other explosive devices they manufactured, the timer didn't work.

KILLINGS TOOK SIXTEEN MINUTES

*'About 26.5 hours from now the judgement will begin. Difficult
but not impossible, necessary, nerve-racking and fun. What fun
is life without a little death? It's interesting, when I'm in my
human form, knowing I'm going to die. Everything has a touch
of triviality to it.'* – Dylan Klebold

The morning of the rampage, both teenagers had written
to-do lists that included a little 'chill' time as they prepared
for the assault. Klebold ended his list saying, 'When fir (sic)
bombs go off, attack. Have fun!' Harris ended his with the
more ominous: ' HAHAHA.' Remarkably, the youngsters also
found time to go bowling before setting out to perpetrate the
worst high school carnage in US history.

According to the timeline reconstructed in the 11,000-page
Columbine Report, Harris and Klebold first entered the school
at 11.10 a.m. with the two 25-pound propane bombs hidden
in two duffel bags. The idea was for the bombs to detonate at
precisely 11.17, when at least half of the student body would
be in the cafeteria. They hoped the explosions would inflict
'maximum damage', killing between 250 and 500 schoolmates. When the bombs failed to detonate, they kicked in
plan B. After slipping on their ski masks, they marched
towards the school with their trench coats flapping and guns
ablaze.

Seven minutes after firing the first shot, Harris exchanged
fire with a school resource officer and entered the school
building. Around the same time, the first Columbine police
officer arrived at the scene. Four minutes after that, the killers
reached the library, where the worst carnage happened. In
their first seven minutes in the library, the rampagers
managed to kill ten students and wound fifteen.

The first sixteen minutes of the rampage were the deadliest.
After the library massacre, no one else was wounded or killed,
except for the two rampagers. For half an hour the two
predators pranced between the library and the cafeteria,
admiring their handiwork and detonating more bombs. At

around 12.05 p.m. the two youngsters ended their lives with self-inflicted gunshots to the head. Three and a half hours later SWAT officers reached the library and declared the killers dead. The following timeline is based on the one released by the Sheriff's Department on the Columbine Report

11.10   Both boys arrive at the school parking lot separately. Eric parks his 1986 Honda Civic in a space facing an entrance to the cafeteria. Dylan parks his 1982 black BMW in front of the other entrance.

11.14   Eric bumps into his friend, eighteen-year-old Brooks Brown. He tells him: 'Brooks, I like you. Now get out of here. Go home.' Later Brown told Mark Eddy of the *Denver Post*, 'I didn't think twice about it and went off to smoke my cigarette. Then I heard gunshots so I took off and started running.'

11.15   The killer duo walks into the cafeteria carrying two large duffel bags with two bombs inside. They place the duffel bags on the floor next to a pillar in the center of the cafeteria and walk back out.

11.17   The two bombs are set to detonate at 11.17. Fortunately, they fail to explode. The terrible duo wait in their respective cars. From there, they plan to take out the surviving students as they escape from the explosions.

11.18   Previously the boys set up two backpacks with pipe bombs, aerosol cans and a small propane tank in a field three miles from Columbine High. The timer of this bomb actually works and the diversionary explosion goes off as planned. Someone calls the Jefferson County 911 Dispatch Center and reports it.

11.19   This is when all hell breaks loose. Harris and Klebold toss a pipe bomb on to the school roof and march towards the school. They open fire on a group of five students having lunch on the grass outside, killing one, Rachel Scott, and injuring another. Student Don Arnold hears the first explosion and thinks it's a prank until he sees bodies falling: 'One boy was running and suddenly his ankle just puffed up in blood. A girl was running and her head popped open.' Lindsay Hamilton, fifteen, heard one of the boys scream: 'It's a good day to die!'

Three kids step out of the cafeteria for a smoke and are met with a hail of gunfire. All three – Daniel Rohrbough, Sean Graves, and Lance Kirklin – collapse. Klebold walks up to them and shoots at Daniel Rohrbough and Lance Kirklin at close range. Rohrbough dies instantly, Kirklin somehow survives.

11.22   The sheriff's office receives the first 911 call from Columbine High.

11.24   Harris joins Klebold on top of the stairs, next to an entrance leading to the cafeteria. They toss more bombs onto the school roof. Harris shoots student Anne Marie Hochhalter repeatedly as she stumbles down the stairs. 'These guys opened fire on everything that looked human,' said sixteen-year-old John Cook. One of the gunmen shouts: 'This is awesome!'

11.26   School resource officer Neil Gardner fires at Harris. The boy takes cover inside the school. Leaning out of a broken window, Harris fires ten rounds back at Gardner before his Hi-Point carbine rifle jams. Deputy Paul Smoker, who first responded to the diversionary explosion three miles away, arrives at the scene. He fires three rounds at Harris. Before the morning gunfight is over, police fire up to 144 rounds. According to *Soldier of Fortune*, the two terminators manage to squeeze out over 186 rounds.

11.27   Gardner calls for backup. He hears shots inside the school building. The two gun-toting freaks are in the hallway leading to the cafeteria firing at everyone and anything. Students run in all directions in sheer terror.

11.28   About 400 students in the cafeteria hear the gunfire outside. 'Somebody said it was gunshots and that somebody had been shot', said sixteen-year-old Patrick Simington. 'Then somebody else hollered for us to get under the tables.' When the trench coat killers explode a bomb in the cafeteria, students stampede to the kitchen area and out of the cafeteria through whatever doors they can find.

Teacher Dave Sanders is shot twice in the upstairs hallway leading to the library. Sanders, 47, is able to crawl to the science area where his colleague, Richard Long, helps him to classroom SCI-3. 'The door opened and Mr. Sanders runs in and starts coughing up blood,' said sixteen-year-old Marjorie Lincoln. 'He just poured blood and all the guys took off their T-shirts to fill up the hole.'

Harris and Klebold reach the upstairs and pace up and down the library hallway, randomly shooting and throwing pipe bombs at no one in particular. By now smoke is spreading through the building and the fire alarm is blaring. There are kids everywhere, hiding in classes, locked inside bathrooms, or lying on the hallway with their face blown off. 'It was like a war,' said seventeen-year-old Brian Anderson, who suffered minor bullet wounds to his chest. 'They weren't out to scare people. They were out to kill people.'

11.29 The boys enter the library. Teacher Patti Nielson, who is on the phone to 911, ducks under her desk and somehow manages to crawl into an adjoining room and hide in a cupboard. Over the receiver the dispatcher hears a voice saying, 'Get up! This is Columbine's ground zero.' In the next seven minutes, the terrible twosome fire fifty rounds and detonate several bombs. Of the 53 students in the library, ten are killed and fifteen wounded.

'They were going around asking people why they should let them live,' said fifteen-year-old Evan Todd. 'Once when they shot a black kid one of them said, "Oh my God, look at this black kid's brain! Awesome, man!"' On Columbine's day of reckoning, the jocks were called to the mat. 'All jocks stand up!

We're going to kill every one of you,' Aaron Cohn recalled hearing.

'They were saying, "Who's next? Who's ready to die?"' said Crystal Woodman. 'And every time they'd shoot someone they'd holler like it was exciting.' A girl who would not give her name said: 'He put a gun to my head and asked if we all wanted to die and said that he was going to kill us if we were colored and if we had a hat and if we played sports. I started screaming and crying and telling him not to shoot me so he shot the girl in front of me in the head.'

Nick Foss, eighteen, said: 'I'd never seen anything like it in my life. I've never seen so many dead people ... Kids were trying to crawl out through the ventilator shafts. They were looking for a place to hide and a way to safety.'

11.37	They leave the library and walk through the science area, shooting into empty rooms.
11.39	Police report a possible suspect on the roof. The man is later identified as a worker of a heating and air conditioning company fixing a leak above the girls' locker room.
11.44	The teen rampagers go to the cafeteria to try to explode the two 25-pound propane bombs. They fire several rounds at the propane tanks, but the bombs refuse to detonate. One witness hiding in the cafeteria hears one of the boys say, 'Today the world's going to come to an end. Today's the day we die.'
11.46	Klebold manages to start a fire in the cafeteria that activates the fire sprinkler system.
11.47	Denver's KMGH-TV Channel 7 broadcasts the first news report of the attack.
11.55	The first SWAT team is ready to enter the building.
12.00	The boys return to the library upstairs. All other local television channels begin uninterrupted live coverage of the events.
12.02	The SWAT team uses a fire truck to provide cover as they approach the school. The kids hiding with the

gravely wounded teacher Dave Sanders hold a sign out the window saying: '1 BLEEDING TO DEATH'.

12.04   Students escape out of a side door of the cafeteria. A television news helicopter begins broadcasting aerial images of the school.

12.05   Feeling they've done their job, the killer couple commits suicide. Harris uses a 12-gauge shotgun. Klebold uses the TEC-DC 9.

12.06   The first SWAT team enters the building.

12.15   A trapped student tells a 911 dispatcher that the two killers have committed suicide.

12.17   A boy is detained near Columbine High with an unloaded .22 Caliber rifle and a knife. According to the youngster, he heard about the shooting and thought he could help the police.

12.41   A second SWAT team arrives at the scene.

12.50   SWAT team snipers take position on nearby rooftops with clear views of the library windows and the cafeteria.

13.02   Police identify the shooters as Eric Harris and Dylan Klebold.

13.09   The second SWAT team enters the teachers' lounge. It's chaos inside: the fire alarm is blaring, the strobe lights are flashing and three inches of water is coming from under the cafeteria door.

13.15   Police arrive at the family homes of Harris and Klebold.

13.18   One SWAT team evacuates thirty students and faculty members from classrooms on the upper level.

13.22   A third SWAT team arrives at the scene.

13.32   The second SWAT team enters the cafeteria area. They evacuate students and staff from the teachers' lounge, kitchen area and storage areas. SWAT team members are warned by radio that the school might be booby-trapped.

13.44   Three boys dressed in black show up in a field north of Columbine. They are quickly detained. The kids say they're the Splatter Punks and are just checking out the scene.

14.11   The SWAT teams receive pictures of Harris and Klebold.

14.33   President Clinton mentions the shooting at a scheduled news conference about the economy: 'We all know there has been a terrible shooting at a high school in Littleton, Colorado. Because the situation, as I left to come out here, apparently is ongoing, I think it would be inappropriate for me to say anything other than I hope the American people will be praying for the students, the parents and the teachers and we'll wait for events to unfold and there will be more to say.'

14.38   Patrick Ireland, who was shot in the library, slowly climbs out a second-storey window. Camera crews broadcast his descent nationwide as SWAT team members drive an armored vehicle under him to catch him when he lets go.

14.42   The first SWAT team reaches the gravely wounded Dave Sanders. They evacuate sixty students from the science area.

15.12   Sanders dies in the arms of a SWAT officer thirty minutes after being found.

15.25   Littleton Fire Department reports finding several live bombs and gasoline containers in Eric's home. The bomb squad is called and the rest of the neighborhood is evacuated.

15.30   SWAT officers enter the library and report twelve dead bodies on the floor.

15.32   Harris and Klebold are identified. Police find four adults hiding around the library.

15.55   The third SWAT team identifies the cars belonging to the suspects. Officers discover the black BMW is wired with a bomb.

16.00   Bomb technicians remove an explosive device from Eric's home.

16.04   A Littleton fire captain enters the school and shuts off the fire alarms and the emergency sprinkler systems.

EQUAL OPPORTUNITY HATRED

'You know what I hate? Star Wars fans: get a friggin' life, you boring geeks. You know what I hate? People who mispronounce words, like "acrost", and "pacific" for "specific", and "expresso" instead of "espresso". You know what I hate? People who drive slow in the fast lane. God, these people do not know how to drive. You know what I hate? The WB network!!!! Oh Jesus, Mary Mother of God Almighty, I hate that channel with all my heart and soul.' – Eric Harris

Nothing was going to stop these two maniacs from letting their equal opportunity hatred spill all over the floors of Columbine High. As we've seen through this book, high school has a brutally cruel pecking order, and Eric and Dylan were squarely at the bottom of it.

'Our school is very status structured. People would yell comments to them, like "weirdo" or "outcast",' said Johanna Nelson, seventeen, a junior at Columbine. 'They'd blow it off, but over and over, it must have had an effect.'

The duo was particularly bitter over the treatment they endured from the 'jocks'. Traditionally, jocks are the more popular and well-adapted students in American high schools, but they can also be the most cruel and abusive toward their geekier classmates. In Columbine, the jocks zeroed in on the two rampagers with glee and abandon, making fun of their clothing and hair, and calling them fags and weirdos. 'They were constantly insulted and harassed by other students,' said sixteen-year-old Eric Veik. 'I guess they finally decided not to take any more crap.'

As usual, neighbors described the teenagers as quiet and unassuming, but obviously something darker was brooding inside. Some students at Littleton described Eric and Dylan as 'satanic individuals'. Others said they were Goths and Marilyn Manson freaks. 'I heard somebody saying they loved Marilyn Manson,' commented their friend Dustin Gorton. 'They both hated Marilyn Manson. The people who are saying things like that didn't know them.'

In any case, while they might have shown a passing interest in the occult and even Marilyn Manson, their true Dark Lord was Adolf Hitler, not Beelzebub. The two Hitler-loving youths enjoyed talking in German and sporting swastikas on their clothes. Eric was described by classmates as someone who would show up to school wearing steel-toed combat boots and a German cross, like he was going to war. When the two went bowling and one would do something good, he would shout, 'Heil Hitler!' and throw up his hand. Not coincidentally, the school rampage was timed to coincide with the 110th anniversary of Hitler's birth. Harris, in particular, fetishized anything German and of World War II vintage. Klebold, blond, Aryan-sized and imposing at 6-foot 4, fetishized BMWs and guns.

THE TRENCHCOAT MAFIA

'Killing enemies, blowing up stuff, killing cops!! My wrath for January's incident will be godlike. Not to mention our revenge in the commons.' – Dylan Klebold

Eric and Dylan liked wearing long black trench coats like the ones worn by Keanu Reeves and Laurence Fishburne in the sci-fi epic *The Matrix*. Their trench coats, in a strange spin of media-directed info overload, somehow became the focus of worldwide attention. It was as if the choice of wardrobe by Littleton's kings of infamy was directly responsible for the bloodshed they perpetrated. Or was the media looking for a catchy keyword to signify everything evil behind the murderous teenagers and their senseless killings?

Fellow student Bob Sapin said the gunmen were part of a school clique called the 'Trenchcoat Mafia'. Another student, Jason Greer, called the killers and their friends 'jerks' and said, 'they are really strange.' Sean Kelly, a sixteen-year-old junior, described the group as 'kind of gothic. They are wearing dusters. They wear them every day, all black clothing.' A female said: 'They talk about Hitler a lot. They take a real pride in him. It's creepy.' Thus, the stage was set for the lynch mob.

The media, in search of blood, alternately blamed the internet, the computer game 'Doom', Goth rock, Marilyn Manson, KMFDM, *The Basketball Diaries*, *Natural Born Killers*, the German industrial metal band Rammstein and, finally, the Trenchcoats. The press based the alleged Trench 'call for apocalypse' on an innocuous reference found under a picture of a group of friends remembering good times in the 1998 Columbine High yearbook:

'Who says we are different? Insanity's healthy! Remember rocking parties at Kristen's, foosball at Joe's and fencing at Christopher's! Stay alive, stay different, stay crazy. Oh, and stay away from CREAM SODA!!! Love always, the chicks.' – The Trenchcoat Mafia.

Soon, the Trench Mob was more feared than Al Capone, Jeffrey Dahmer and Adolf Hitler rolled into one. In less than 48 hours the Trenchcoaters were transformed from a loose group of misfits with a cute name who hung out at a particular spot in the school cafeteria, into an organized jock-hating, white-supremacist, ass-kicking, Goth-rockin', swastika-wearing, web-designing, bomb-making, confederate-flag-wearing, Marilyn-Manson-loving, vampire-role-playing, 'Doom'-addicted, wargame-freaking, Hitler-worshipping gang of suburban terrorist youths.

As the veritable (mis)information tsunami about the Trench-coats swept through online and traditional media, no one bothered to check the facts. Everyone – from CNN to MSNBC to Matt Drudge to Tom Brokaw – focused on half-truths and speculation to paint a picture of a killer 'gang' of alienated youth running roughshod through Columbine High.

London's *Telegraph* led their coverage of the massacre with a story about the 'gang affiliations' of Harris and Klebold, and their links to Satanism and neo-Nazi youth groups. The *Telegraph* then called the Trenchcoaters a 'terrifying gang of Goth rockers' and portrayed them as a twenty-first-century Manson-like 'family'.

Further fueling the 'mediatization' of the rampage, several fake Trenchcoat web sites popped out of nowhere, turning, once again, the 'Coats into the lead story in nightly news reports throughout the US. Eventually the furore died, and the 'Trenchcoat' became once again the 'trench coat' – a fashion statement for a group of kids at Columbine who didn't get along with jocks.

ICH BIN EIN AUSLANDER
Member name: Eric Harris
Hobbies: today is my last day on earth
Computers: be prepared
– Posted on an America Online chat room at 8.41 on the morning of the rampage.

More telling than any Trenchcoat conspiracy is Harris's AOL member profile: 'Quit whining. It's only a flesh wound. Kill em AALLLL!!!!' and his favorite chat room: *Ich Bin Ein Auslander*, meaning 'I am an outsider'.

Harris's web page, under the screen name Rebdomine, started with: 'REB's words of wisdom, if you don't like it, I'll kill you.' The site, which was quickly taken down by the AOL brass, was filled with drawings of devils, guns and skulls. It also had instructions on how to make a bomb and a collection of stories and poems entitled: 'The Written Works of the Trenchcoats.' One of the stories, 'The Trenchcoat Psychopath', is about an obsessed loner in a trench coat driven to cleanse the world by killing jocks and other undesirables.

The day before the carnage, Harris, ignoring the potential penalties stipulated by the 1998 Digital Millennium Copyright Act, posted a medley of lyrics from three KMFDM songs – 'Waste', 'Stray Bullet' and 'Son of a Gun' – on the front page of the Rebdomine site: '*APOCALYPSE NOW – WALLS OF FLAME – BILLOWING SMOKE – WHO'S TO BLAME*' – KMFDM

KMFDM stands for Kein Mitleid für die Mehrheit, meaning 'No Pity for the Majority'. Though they bill themselves as a German industrial metal band, in reality the shock rockers turned out to be from Seattle and the German affectation was merely a promotion gimmick. Coincidentally (or not) the day of the rampage, besides being Hitler's birthday, was also the release date of their CD titled *Adios*.

The infamous Rebdomine website became evidence in a lawsuit against the Jefferson County Sheriff's Office when it was revealed that, more than a year before the rampage, the parents of one of their friends called the Sheriff's office and complained about the content of the site. On 18 March 1998, Randy and Judy Brown reported that Harris had posted on his website death threats against their son and others. The parents also informed the Sheriffs that the young psychopath had detailed bomb-making instructions. The Sheriff's Department never investigated the allegations. Incidentally, Brooks Brown, the boy that was threatened, was the youngster whom Eric told to go home the morning of the attack.

DEAR DIARY

'It's my fault! Not my parents, not my brothers, not my friends, not my favorite bands, not computer games, not the media, it's mine.' – Eric Harris

The Lennon and McCartney of the teen killer set, Eric was the brains of the tandem, while Dylan was the muscle. Eric was the leader, Dylan was the gullible stooge. Eric, in his diary, on his website, in notes, essays, printouts, computer files and several videos, left a veritable trail of information explaining the motives behind the mayhem. Clearly, the high school assault was an act of revenge against Columbine High, its teachers, its abusive social order, and against the 1,870 students whom he considered inferior.

The diary, found in his room, was full of messages of across-the-board hate. In no uncertain terms, Eric chronicled how he and his friend were planning their massacre for over a year. 'I'll go on my killing spree against anyone I want,' he wrote two years before the rampage. Leaving nothing to chance, the killers made maps of the school and designed intricate hand signals to ensure a high bodycount.

Though the diary is still sealed by court order, enough flotsam and jetsam of his writing has been released to get a sense of Eric's vitriol and hatred against the world. In the diary, Eric wrote about how he, Reb (as in Rebel), and voDKa, Dylan, were different from their peers because they had self-awareness. For more than a year, he documented how much they wanted to extract revenge against those who he perceived had wronged them. 'I'm full of hate and I love it,' he proclaimed.

According to the diary, Eric and Dylan hatched the deadly plan for the school assault shortly after four popular athletes and another student from Columbine High were arrested for felony burglary. Eric was outraged when the boys were later let go with a mere slap on their wrists. This preferential treatment infuriated him and Dylan and, unlike their choice of music, movies or love for black trench coats, might have led to the massacre.

Through much of his writing, Eric talked about not fitting in and not being accepted. He reflected upon natural selection, self-awareness and his feelings of superiority. In page after page he plotted against jocks, the girls that ignored him, his fellow outcasts or anybody else who had somehow offended him. Anyone and anything he hated. But his writings and vitriol were contradictory. He hated 'niggers, spics, Jews, gays, fucking whites', but then, he also hated the concept of racism. 'You know what I hate? Racism. Anyone who hates Asians, Mexicans, or people of any race because they're different.'

Eric wrote they were hoping for a 'big kill' of at least 500 students. Then they would attack nearby homes, hijack a plane and – in an eerie anticipation of the events of 11 September 2001 – crash it into New York City.

'I suppose when you first hear it, you think that it's some horrible fantasy,' District Attorney Dave Thomas told NBC's *Today* show. 'But we now know that at least the first portion of those planned activities were in fact carried out . . . We also know that, had a couple of the devices in the school actually detonated as they had planned, the death toll could have been much higher than it was.'

'He was into combat more than anyone else I've ever seen,' said his friend Andrew Beard. In fact, he had applied to join the Marines. Five days before the massacre, Eric's application to the Marine Corps was rejected because had been taking the drug Luvox, an antidepressant. Luvox, which is often used to treat obsessive-compulsive disorder, is among the serotonin reuptake-inhibiting substances that have been associated with explosive teenage behavior.

However, the Columbine attack was in no way an impulsive action. Nor could it be called a 'cry for help' from a pair of depressed or confused teenagers. Eric and Dylan thoroughly and deliberately prepared for the attack, anticipated its consequences and followed a well-defined plan. 'Eric Harris went to war', wrote Wolf DeVoon in his 26 April 1999 article 'The Decision to Kill'. 'He gave his life to attack Columbine High School and everything it represented.'

Among all the finger-pointing that follows each schoolyard massacre, the relationship between serotonin-inhibiting antidepressants and teen rampagers has been practically ignored. But the fact is that Eric Harris had been taking Luvox, Kip Kinkel was taking Prozac, one of the two Jonesboro rampagers was also taking antidepressants. David Attias, Santa Barbara's Audi killer, was given both Ritalin and Lithium. The proof, as they say, is in the pudding.

Confirming the possible linkage between the medicating of youngsters and their propensity toward violence, Dr Peter Breggin, author of *Toxic Psychiatry*, said, 'I have no doubt that Prozac can contribute to violence and suicide. I've seen many cases. In a recent clinical trial, six per cent of the children [in the test] became psychotic on Prozac. And manic psychosis can lead to violence.'

SUICIDE VIDEOS

> *'I'm going to kill you all. You've been giving us shit for years . . . You're fucking going to pay for all the shit . . . We don't give a shit because we're going to die doing it.'* – Eric Harris

If the diary was indicative of what was in Eric and Dylan's minds, the suicide videos left no doubts. Clearly, the three videos, shot over a period of two months before the attack, were made to assure their rightful spot in the world catalogue of infamy. The youngsters – who repeatedly addressed the camera with 'All you fucking cops' – filmed the videos as a goodbye present for investigators. In a way, through the videos, Eric and Dylan returned from the grave to help police sort out the mounds of evidence and put together a clearer picture of their mindset. It was also their guarantee of fame and attention.

'Directors will be fighting over this story,' Klebold boasted. 'Steven Spielberg . . . Quentin Tarantino,' Harris added as potential directors.

'It is obvious that these guys wanted to become cult heroes of some kind,' Deputy District Attorney Steve Jensen told the *Denver Post.* 'They are making statements which they thought would facilitate that status.' Harris and Klebold were 'going to become superstars by getting rid of bad people,' said lead investigator Kate Battan during an interview with Dave Cullen of Salon.com. 'And you know, it worked. They're famous.'

The three videos were two hours, 22 minutes and forty minutes long respectively, and were shot over thirteen different occasions during March and April 1999. One tape shows the boys in Eric's room, laying out their weaponry. They also recorded each other doing dress rehearsals. Sounding a bit like the UFO-loving, Heaven's Gate freaks from San Diego, the two boys talked about how 'evolved' they were, and how they felt 'above human'. In a juvenile display of bravado, the youngsters claimed they had been planning their rampage way before the Jonesboro killings. 'Don't think we're trying to copy anyone,' said Eric to the camera. Clearly, they wanted everyone to know they had not been influenced by any other rampage before them.

One thing, though, they did love their families: 'My parents are the best fucking parents I have ever known,' Eric said. 'My dad is great. I wish I was a fucking sociopath so I didn't have any remorse, but I do . . . This is going to tear them apart . . . It fucking sucks to do this to them.' Then, in a heads-up to his teachers, he quoted Shakespeare's *The Tempest*: 'Good wombs hath borne bad sons.' Dylan, in his brutish way, also said his parents were great: 'They gave me my fucking life,' he said. 'I appreciate that.'

GUN SHOWS

'Fuck you, Brady. All I want is a couple of guns and thanks to your fucking bill I will probably not get any! Come on, I'll have a clean record and I only want them for personal protection. It's not like I'm some psycho who would go on a shooting spree.' – Eric Harris

Like other famous armed maniacs such as David Koresh and Timothy McVeigh, Dylan and Eric went shopping for weapons at the loophole-ridden world of gun shows. Planning for maximum bodycount, they wanted small, high-tech weapons with lots of firepower. Dylan liked the TEC-DC-9 semi-automatic pistol. Eric settled on the 9mm Hi-Point carbine rifle.

The boys obtained their weapons from two people: Mark Manes, a friend of a friend, and Robyn Anderson, Dylan's girlfriend. Manes, 22, met Harris and Klebold through Philip Duran, a co-worker at the Blackjack Pizza Parlor. Phil, also 22, knew that Eric and Dylan were looking for a piece. His friend Mark wanted to sell his TEC-DC-9. On 23 January, the two parties met, the boys gave Manes $500 in cash, and the happy seller sweetened the deal by throwing in a couple of 36-round clips. He and Duran also gave the rampagers three shooting lessons.

'I'd like to make a thank you to Mark and Phil,' Harris said in a shout-out in one of the infamous suicide tapes. 'I hope you don't get fucked.' Klebold, adding his two cents: 'We used them. They had no clue ... Don't blame them. And don't fucking arrest them ... Don't arrest any of our friends or family members or our co-workers. They had no fucking clue. Don't arrest anyone, because they didn't have a fucking clue.'

Strangely, the Colorado District Attorney's Office disagreed. Manes was arrested and charged with illegally selling Klebold the TEC-DC-9. He was sentenced to six years in prison. Duran was charged with assisting Manes with the gun sale.

A few months after the original purchase, Robyn Anderson, Dylan's girlfriend and an honors student at Columbine, went to the Tanner Gun Show to buy more steel for her boyfriend and his little friend. Anderson, eighteen, was able to legally buy two twenty-year-old shotguns: a Savage Arms Model 67 pump shotgun and a Model 31D double-barrel shotgun, as well as the 9mm Hi-Point carbine rifle. Strangely, it was also legal for her to give the weapons to Dylan and Eric, as long as she bought the guns from a private party and not a licensed gun dealer. This is called a straw purchase. This is what Charlton Heston and the rest of the NRA have been tirelessly fighting for, day in and day out, as if their lives depended on it. 'I don't support the notion that criminals are getting guns at shows,' said Wayne LaPierre, the NRA's executive vice-president. 'I don't believe more regulation is the answer.'

Heston, as president of the NRA, said in the wake of the killing: 'Our spirits must endure this terrible suffering together and so must the freedoms that bring us together.' Sounding more like Rambo than Moses, he continued: 'If there had been even one armed guard in the school he could have saved a lot of lives and perhaps ended the whole thing instantly.' Showing that he has a heart of gold next to his six-shooter, Heston announced that the NRA would reduce from three days to one their annual convention scheduled in Denver for the weekend following the shootings. In an even grander gesture, the NRA took down their promotional billboard of Charlton holding a gigantic gun, inviting people to 'join' him.

The day before the attack Harris convinced Manes to buy at the local Wal-Mart 100 rounds of 9mm ammunition and sell it to him for $25. After the sale, Manes asked Eric if he was planning to go shooting. Eric answered, 'Maybe tomorrow.' In the documentary *Bowling for Columbine*, filmmaker Michael Moore took two youngsters who still had bullets from the shooting lodged in their spine to the same Wal-Mart that sold the bullets to Manes. After the symbolic returning of the ammunition Wal-Mart announced they would stop carrying the guns and bullets used in the shooting.

THE COLUMBINE REPORT

'We don't blame anyone else for our action. This is the way we want to go out.' – Dylan Klebold

Nineteen months after the Columbine massacre, investigators, hoping to clarify all misconceptions about the killings, released the massive Columbine Report. The Report, with over 11,000 pages of material, audio clips, photographs, 4,500 witness interviews and 10,000 pieces of evidence, was put on CD-ROM and sold by the Sheriff's Department for $602, plus shipping charges. Interestingly, the report refuted several self-perpetuating myths stemming from the rampage.

One myth debunked was the often-reported concept that the attack was an assault on jocks, blacks and Christians. The report concluded that the actual attack was random and indiscriminate. Though Eric and Dylan had several hit lists, they did not specifically target their enemies on the day. In the library, they had something nasty to say about everyone they shot. Though the press focused on the racist and the 'death to jocks' statements they made, they also taunted one boy for being fat – 'Whatta we got here, a fat boy?' – and another for wearing glasses: 'You think those glasses look cool?' However, the press never said the carnage was directed against the fat and the optically challenged.

A second myth debunked was the still-prevalent belief of a third gunman involved in the attack. Like the phantom grassy knoll gunman in Dallas the day Kennedy was shot, this myth of a third and even a fourth Columbine gunman has had a life of its own. In one book, *Everything You Know Is Wrong: The Disinformation Guide to Secrets and Lies*, there's a chapter dedicated to the multiple gunmen theory. Russ Kick, the editor, lists a series of instances pointing at the possibility of extra shooters. One of the suspected 'extra gunmen' was repeatedly spotted on the roof of the school. The report identified the 'third gunman' on the roof as a freaked-out worker servicing an air-conditioner on top of the girls' locker room.

Another myth debunked was Cassie Bernall's supposed expression of faith when confronted with the cold steel of a TEC-DC-9 semi-automatic. The myth was that Dylan, holding the gun to Cassie's face, asked her if she believed in God. She said yes, and Dylan blew a hole through her neck. The story became an inspiration for Christian youth throughout the United States. Cassie's mom, Misty Bernall, even wrote a book about it, *She Said Yes: The Unlikely Martyrdom of Cassie Bernall*, which became an instant bestseller.

The press loved the story and ran with it for months, even though, as was later revealed by Salon.com, many reporters knew the alleged pronouncement of faith was factually untrue. Dylan, as it turned out, played a grotesque version of peek-a-boo with Cassie before shooting her in the neck. 'There was a girl crouched beneath a desk in the library, and the guy came over and said "Peek-a-boo" and shot her in the neck,' said fifteen-year-old Byron Kirkland. It was another little girl, Valeen Schnurr, who was asked if she believed in God. She said yes and Dylan spared her.

The Cassie myth seemed, at some point, to become a matter of economics. When the book was released, even though most reporters covering Columbine knew that the story was dubious, the newspapers they worked for ran glowing reviews about it. The Bernalls themselves appeared on the *Today* show, *20/20* and *Larry King Live* to promote the fictitious tale. And with the book landing on the *Publishers Weekly* bestseller list with 350,000 copies in print and more than 250,000 already sold, undoubtedly no reporter wanted to step in and stop the cash flow.

A fourth myth debunked by the report was the belief that student Daniel Rohrbough was not shot by the rampagers, but by the cops. The Rohrboughs were suspicious about who shot the fatal round after the Sheriff's Department adamantly blocked them from seeing any information about their son's autopsy. With growing criticism on the less-than-heroic performance of their three SWAT teams and how they could have saved the life of teacher Dave Sanders, the Sheriff's Office decided to clamp up.

Indeed, it seems a bit strange that the 'bravest of the brave' took three and a half hours to secure a crime scene in which the perpetrators were already dead, but second guessing a life and death situation is easy to do in retrospect. The Sheriff's Department, angry over the criticism and the subsequent lawsuits, became reluctant to release any other information that could be used against it. That, in effect, made their perceived guilt that much greater. But the report stated, in no uncertain terms, that no one other than Eric and Dylan killed anyone that ill-fated April morning.

COPYCATS

'We're going to kick-start a revolution' – Eric Harris

Following this unprecedented Columbine attack, schools throughout the nation experienced a rash of copycat situations leading to the closing of entire school districts. 'The wackos are coming out of the woodwork,' said Sheriff's spokesman Sergeant Jim Parr. 'A lot of sick people think this is something to emulate.' Other school districts banned students from wearing trench coats. At least sixty threats specifically mentioning Columbine were reported worldwide.

In one instance thirteen-year-old Seth Trickey shot and wounded five classmates at an Oklahoma middle school several days after telling a psychiatrist that he wanted to know what it was like to be in the shoes of the Columbine killers. Another youngster, fifteen-year-old Andy Williams, killed two students and wounded thirteen at his high school north of San Diego, California, after warning his friends that he was going to 'pull a Columbine'.

In Cupertino, California, home of Apple Computers, nineteen-year-old Al DeGuzman was arrested for stockpiling an arsenal of weapons and sixty homemade bombs and planning an assault or, in his words, a 'purification in the form of carnage' on DeAnza Junior College. DeGuzman, on his website, listed one of his hobbies as 'worshiping Eric Harris and Dylan Klebold'.

Websites, mailing lists and chatrooms like 'thechurchofdylananderic' and 'ElevenSeventeen' have popped up all over the internet, confirming that, indeed, Eric and Dylan did start a revolution for the disturbed and disenfranchised. Many boys and girls might log on to 'thechurchofdylananderic', but that doesn't mean they'll be killing anyone. 'There's a difference between wanting to do something like that and doing it,' said 22-year-old Seth Shatsnider, who started the 'ElevenSeventeen' chatroom. That difference might be – in contrast to what Charlton Heston would say – having access to a high-powered weapon.

10. ANGEL OF DEATH

Name: David Edward Attias
Born: May 1982
Age at time of rampage: 18
Date of attack: 24 February 2001
Number of victims: 4 dead, 1 wounded
Victim profile: students
Weapon: a black 1991 Saab 9000
Media keywords: Angel of Death, tweaker, rave culture, amphetamines
Early warning signs: was a virgin, thought God was speaking through him
Probable cause: needed to get laid, mental illness, bad driving
School: University of California Santa Barbara
Location: Isla Vista, Santa Barbara, California

'I was crazy. I don't know. People were walking in the middle of the street and I hit them . . . Whatever – it's all good. There were four people dead . . . They have not given me shit in writing yet . . . I didn't do anything wrong . . . My dad's on the way, with his lawyer – it's kinda funny, dude.' – David Attias

'I always hoped that everything was evolving and changing and that he could move through it. My goal was always for him to get better . . . I now know that he needs medication, and I know that more than ever now.' – Daniel Attias

WARM LEATHERETTE
Truth can sometimes be stranger than fiction. When British author J G Ballard wrote his seminal novel *Crash*, one could not think of anything more disturbing than a middle-aged, car-crash-obsessed yuppie couple who wanted nothing more than to make love on the leatherette seats of a smoldering highway wreckage. Nearly thirty years later, David Attias, a disturbed California teenager, upped the ante on the great

British author by plowing his car into five innocent bystanders in a twisted psycho-sexual quest to lose his virginity.

Authorities in Santa Barbara County, California, charged eighteen-year-old college freshman Attias with four counts of murder for intentionally ramming his black, turbocharged Saab into a crowd of University of California Santa Barbara students, killing four people and seriously crippling another. The victims of this so-called 'car Columbine' were UCSB sophomore Nicholas Shaw Bourdakis, 20, of Alamo; Santa Barbara City College student Ruth Dasha Golda Levy, 20, of San Francisco; her visiting brother's roommate, Elie Israel, 27, of San Francisco; and Christopher Edward Divis, 20, of San Diego County. Levy's brother, Albert Levy, was critically wounded by Attias's crushing Swedish luxury vehicle. The 27-year-old San Francisco resident suffered multiple fractures to both legs, extensive muscle damage to his left leg and a head injury. A year later, he was finally able to walk again after reconstructive surgery on both legs.

The 1991 Saab 9000, which rammed into the partying students at a speed of 60 mph, also banged into nine cars as it ground to a halt. Witnesses said that after the crash, the highly volatile Attias jumped out of the car and paced through the site, yelling, 'I am the Angel of Death.' According to 25-year-old Sevan Matossian who, by chance, filmed the mayhem, Attias was 'swinging at people and yelling and bouncing around like he was a boxer . . . It looked like he was on something.'

At his dormitory, the Francisco Torres Residence Hall, the suspect was referred to as 'Tweaker' and 'Crazy Dave'. His mother called him 'sickly', 'inconsolable' and plain old 'weirdo'. The night before the carnage, Attias allegedly burst into the room of a female student and said, 'God is speaking to me. Life is a game, and you only make it if you're beautiful and rich . . . I'm a virgin, and I need to have sex right now.' Obviously, he didn't get any that night. Consequently, the next night he left Francisco Torres because 'he thought he was going to die' if he didn't lose his virginity 'within five minutes'. Instead of sex, he found twisted steel and warm leatherette, leaving five people broken and bleeding on the pavement of

Sabado Tarde Road, and his name, David Attias, etched in popular culture as the tweaking, car-rampaging and self-proclaimed Angel of Death.

HOLLYWOOD HEARTBREAK

After the arrest, his father, Daniel Attias, read a statement on behalf of his wife and himself, expressing their extreme grief: 'We're both just struck by just how hopelessly inadequate any words could be. On behalf of my wife, I just want to say how devastated and heartbroken we are for everybody who's been affected by this.' His wife, Diana, sobbed quietly by his side as he continued, 'It's a very horrible tragedy and we know that it's affected not just the loved ones and the families of the victims, whose grief must be unspeakable, and we extend whatever compassion we're capable of. But we know it has also left a terrible, terrible gash in this whole community and we can't begin to tell you how saddened we are.'

Born into a privileged Southern California entertainment family residing in the city of Santa Monica, David was a bright and loving child, but he showed early warning signs that he was developmentally different from the rest of his peers. His father, Daniel Attias, was a top-rated TV director, whose work can be seen in the hit shows *Ally McBeal, The Sopranos* and *Six Feet Under*. His mother was a book editor who, after his birth, became a stay-at-home mom. David was born into a world only a few know: the privileged one percentile of the rich. A life of movie-star parties in luxurious homes, of lavish extravaganza, of decadent fun.

From the beginning, his mother, Diana, who was 52 at the time of the crash, knew something was hopelessly wrong. It wasn't long before doctors told her that her son was not like the other kids. He was a child who never learned to crawl. Instead he rolled around on the floor, flailing his arms. As a toddler he learned to walk months after his peers walked. And when he spoke, it was in garbled words only his mother could understand. Diana saw that the boy was prone to bizarre behavior. He was socially inept, physically awkward and had strange tics and unusual mannerisms.

David saw his first psychiatrist at age four. By age seven, he took a psychological test and was diagnosed as a slow learner who suffered from neurological problems and dyslexia. His parents were also told that he was borderline autistic. By age eight, he was diagnosed with attention-deficit hyperactivity disorder, and was prescribed Ritalin – the first in a series of anti-psychotics, anti-depressants and sedatives he's been prescribed over the course of his life. Ritalin, like other serotonin reuptake-inhibiting drugs, has been associated with explosions of anger and violence in children and teenagers. At his trial, his mother described David's early years: 'It never got easier . . . He would bite himself. Sometimes he would arch his back and stiffen his body suddenly. He didn't seem to connect with the other kids [in nursery school],' she said. 'There was awkwardness to his walking. I remember him walking in a jogathon with his arms out. He was trying really hard, but it was just an unnatural body position.'

It seemed that Diana could not accept the irreparable diagnosis of her son being mentally challenged. She could not accept the lifelong burden of having a child with 'special needs'. Daniel Attias, her husband, said he was hesitant about medication and diagnoses when David was a child because he was fearful 'a paper trail of labels' would stigmatize his only son for the rest of his life. 'I was always worried David would stop being seen as who he is,' he said. 'I didn't want people to see a label.'

As David became an adolescent, his behavior became more erratic and his angered outbursts more frequent. His estrangement from his family and friends was marked during this period by new and odd behaviors, including mood swings, giddiness and compulsive list-making. 'We kept all the lists he made,' said his mother. 'The intensity of the passion would shift from one thing to another . . . from cars to sports to quail to music to comic books. [With our cats] he was very loving . . . he had a fixation with them like he did with other things.'

MENTAL ILLNESS

David's mother believed his problems were her fault and attributed them to her own parental shortcomings. She connected more with David's younger sister, Rachel, whom, in a jealous rage, he tried to strangle. The attack led the then thirteen-year-old to an extended period of hospitalization at the UCLA Medical Center adolescent in-patient ward that lasted until he was sixteen. The youngster was kept in the psychiatric ward from early December 1995 until 26 January 1996. At the time his mother felt a strange sense of relief and felt it might be better if he didn't come home. 'I didn't want him to come home. I didn't think it was good for him or us,' she testified in court. 'But he came home and went the next two years at a regular high school. He did very well. He got good grades. He graduated. He was accepted at a number of schools. He held three different jobs.'

His lawyer, Jack Earley, said in opening statements that throughout his life, Attias had shown symptoms of Tourette's syndrome, Asberger's syndrome, autism, attention-deficit disorder, persuasive-development disorder, obsessive–compulsive disorder, bipolar mood disorder and schizophrenia. 'These are things,' Earley said, 'that were seen in David from the very beginning – well before this case ever came, before there was any motive to say he had a mental illness.'

Before the strangulating incident, the boy was accused of spreading sexual rumors and making 'homicidal' statements about a sixth-grade girl at his school. Attias boasted to classmates that he was going to kill the girl's parents as well as his own. Psychiatrist Matthew State, who treated David in the UCLA Medical Center adolescent in-patient ward, said David's psychosis was very difficult to label for various reasons and referred to him as a diagnostic challenge. 'He had a very serious problem with acting before he thought, he was impulsive. He would say something before he thought about it and then he would be remorseful,' the doctor testified in court.

'We were challenged to understand what was going wrong at the time,' said State, adding that, 'they were a lovely family, David was a very nice boy struggling mightily against . . . very difficult issues.' State eventually diagnosed David as bipolar and prescribed Lithium, a powerful anti-psychotic medication.

While Daniel Attias became more consumed by the demands of his career and tried not to work out of town on location, Diana Attias started cracking under the weight of David's emotional needs. According to Daniel, his wife would 'personalize things that were not personal – they went right into a wound of her own.' She withdrew from the family, often sullen or in tears, feeling hopeless and diminished under the strain, which got so bad that at some point she considered leaving the family and moving out on her own.

'As time went on I found I could not rely on her as an equal partner. I think having a child with special needs, and particularly the kinds of special needs that David has, was very difficult for the kinds of needs my wife had. I think there was a clash there – she's fragile in certain ways,' he said. '[Diana] loves David, but I think she tended to withdraw.'

In court, both parents took the stand to explain what went wrong. 'I love my wife, but it made me frustrated and stressed. I have my own stresses in my own occupation and I didn't always act admirably,' Daniel said. 'Part of the poignancy of our situation was that . . . everything was extremely easy for [our daughter Rachel] . . . It made for an extremely difficult situation to make up rules that would appear as equitable . . . David really needed extreme structure.'

CRIES AND WHISPERS

When he went to UCSB, David stopped taking his antipsychotic and anti-depressant medication and his behavior became increasingly more volatile. As Santa Barbara District Attorney Patrick McKinley said, when David got to college, 'The defendant used an incredible amount of illegal drugs almost all the time . . . When he got to UCSB, it was like turning a kid loose in a candy store – he stopped taking his meds, and deteriorated, until he came down the street, killed people.'

David told his father that he was unhappy at UCSB and wanted to attend Santa Monica City College, a school just minutes from his home. His father insisted he finish out the year in Santa Barbara. Daniel placed a strong emphasis on education, calling it a 'high priority', and believed that if his son 'fixed' his mental problems and stayed in college, he could become part of society and have a normal life.

'At Thanksgiving I talked to Daniel about it. I knew David was wanting to come home, but David was told to complete school where he was,' his mother said. 'I was never afraid David would hurt other people. I thought if anyone, he would hurt himself. I thought it was a momentary blip and he would get back on track.'

After an explosive argument during Christmas break, Daniel took away his son's keys to the family's Santa Monica home. He and his wife wanted David to abide by rules they had agreed upon, which included David's going back on medication and seeing a therapist once a week. Until that contract was fulfilled, the house was not open to him. 'Over the break he was going out to clubs and coming home very late and I was concerned. I told him while he was under our roof, I wanted him to come home at 2.30,' Daniel said. 'His reaction to that was unlike anything I've ever seen. It was full-blown, grandiose, bordering on megalomania, on how dare I tell him what to do . . . it was at this point the bipolar diagnosis became clear to me.'

Shortly after that, David totaled his car while driving back to school on 7 January 2001. Believing that safety was an issue, the parents responded by replacing the Saab he totaled with another one, a black one they purchased for $6,000. They also used the car as a bargaining chip, hoping that it might lure their son back to therapy. This was the same car that David would later transform into the 60 mph killing machine he used to strike down his fellow students on the crowded walkway at the 6500 block of Sabado Tarde Road. Daniel Attias would later lament in court that he wished he'd never bought that black Saab. 'It turned out to be a horrific, horrific mistake.'

THE FLOOR THAT NEVER SLEEPS
Santa Barbara, California, nestled between the Pacific Ocean and the Santa Ynez Mountain range, can only be described as

an idyllic location. When not at the beach, a freshman at UCSB knows the party is at the Francisco Torres Residence Hall, a spacious ten-storey dormitory building in the college community of Isla Vista, next to the University. With room for 1,300 students, the dorm includes two large cafeterias, a swimming pool, tennis courts, fitness center and a computer center with unlimited direct access to the Internet. All for the price tag of $9,125 a year.

Isla Vista, where Francisco Torres is located, is a student city of 20,000 jammed into less than a square mile. It is the most crowded place per square mile west of the Mississippi. Crimes there involving alcohol have skyrocketed in recent years. The 796 reports of public intoxication in 2001 were three times as high as in 1998, according to statistics supplied by the Sheriff's Department's IV Foot Patrol, which supplies law enforcement in Isla Vista. Loud party calls increased five times, and urinating in public more than doubled to 250 incidents a year. Those are just the garden variety nuisance crimes. In 2001 there were 18 rapes, 22 cases of resisting arrest and more than 100 cases of battery and spousal abuse. But no murders. That is until 11.08 p.m. on the fateful night of 23 February.

One student described the building where David Attias roomed on the seventh floor as pure 'sex and drugs and rock and roll'. Attias's attorney, Jack Earley, referring to the hall where David lived, said it was known as 'the floor that never sleeps'. The name alludes to its chaotic all-night party atmosphere and the legendary abuse of stimulants by its wild residents. Clearly, this new environment exacerbated Attias's well documented mental problems as well as joyfully indulged his taste for all kinds of drugs. In the hall, David had a reputation as a 'tweaker', that is, someone who takes meta-amphetamines all night long. According to his lawyer, Attias was christened with the nickname 'Crazy Dave' after he stopped taking the anti-psychotic drug Zprexa, which was designed to smooth out his twitchy, impulsive personality.

Crazy Dave had a habit of barging into other students' rooms uninvited and lecturing them on everything from world events to hallucinogenic drugs. Beyond the party atmosphere in Francisco Torres, Attias was considered so disruptive that his floor mates asked him to leave the floor. 'People would laugh or snicker whenever he left the room. Some would leave when he entered the room,' said Catherine Brownstein, a neighbor at the Francisco Torres dormitory. 'He wasn't treated the way a human being is supposed to be treated.'

DEATH DRIVES A SAAB

On 23 February 2001, David Attias was supposed to go to a rave in Los Angeles with his friend Richard Ramsey. But deciding he was in no condition to drive down from Santa Barbara he chose another way to spend the evening. That night his lawyer said Attias had a 'psychotic break' and didn't know what he was doing. According to testimony, the last thing he remembers is driving down nearby Del Playa Drive, rolling down the window, getting lost in the music blaring from one of the parties and accidentally stepping on the gas.

Witnesses indicate that the blaring music came in fact from his car. He had rapper Master P's 'Only God Can Judge Me' cranking in the stereo at ear-splitting decibels as he crashed into the crowd of partying youngsters. Witnesses said that after the collision, Attias was strutting like a prize fighter through the street saying 'I'm the angel of death' as well as screaming the lyrics to Master P's rap song, 'Ride or Die'. In court it became clear that the 'angel of death' statement was a reference to a Slayer song that Attias had told a friend contained 'hidden Nazi messages'.

Kelly Brandli, who lived at 6572 Sabado Tarde Road at the time of the incident, was one of the people on the witness stand who testified about Attias's actions after the crash. 'I remember him saying something like "This is a joke, don't believe this, it's the government's plan to teach society about something." ' Brian Glassco, who was at one of the parties on Sabado Tarde Road at the time of the incident, said Attias was picking a fight with everyone around him. 'I remember him taking off his hooded sweatshirt . . . and he was trying to egg people on – "Bring it on. What are you going to do?" He came swinging at another individual I was standing next to, and then he swung at me and I ducked out of the way. Then the first Highway Patrol showed up.'

James Alessi, a Caltrans representative who investigated the fatal incident, testified: 'Attias maintained his course by refusing to brake. He struck one of the cars parked on the side of Sabado Tarde Road with enough force to deploy the airbag.' When the victims were struck, they were hurled between 100 and 200 feet from the impact point. George Sterbenz, a forensic pathologist who performed the autopsies, said the victims were hit at highway speeds.

Attias's post-crash histrionics were captured by a TV crew filming the party scene on Sabado Tarde. For most of the tape we see drunken students hamming it up for the camera. Two guys tell raunchy jokes about bestiality as a woman shows her pin that says: 'I'm Hot! Take advantage of me!' Another woman pulls down her pants to show her thong underwear. The twenty-minute video was made by UCSB students Greg Shields and Sevan Matossian for their public access cable television show *IVTV*. The show is some sort of *Wayne's World* meets Santa Barbara party culture with Shields playing host and Matossian taping him as he hops from party to party.

The two videographers found themselves about a block away when they heard the crash. They ran to what they said resembled a 'war zone' and started filming. On the tape you see Crazy Dave jumping, screaming, running and throwing punches as the bodies lie still at his feet. People are heard screaming, while others are seen using cellphones to call for help. Then a group of bystanders tackle Attias and start angrily kicking and pummeling him into submission. The camera pans down to a shoe on the asphalt: the spot from where one of the victims was catapulted.

DRUG CULTURE
According to a sheriff's department spokesman, Attias showed signs of being drugged or intoxicated. But tests later proved that he had no hard drugs, just marijuana in his system. His

friends and acquaintances said that David enjoyed smoking pot, which he did regularly, but he also snorted coke, did Special K (also known as ketamine) and had, at least once, done Ecstasy. Special K and Ecstasy are drugs associated with the Southern California rave scene.

David was a regular raver in Los Angeles and enjoyed the music and its drug-saturated party lifestyle. Raves were described in court by Santa Barbara sheriff's deputy Sandra Brown as drug-fueled 'underground parties with DJs playing techno music on dual turntables'. Deputy Brown also explained that 'most of the drugs kids take at raves are hallucinogenic. To increase the experience of the drugs, people will do dances with the glowsticks in people's faces. Ecstasy is a hallucinogenic and a stimulant, so people will dance and sweat and grind their teeth and want to be touched.'

Attias's demeanor and taste in music changed in the months before the incident. His friend Richard Ramsey, who met Attias in a club in LA in December 2000, said that since January 2001, David had changed and was behaving 'paranoid'. He added that David started listening to violent rap, which previously he had referred to as 'stupid music'. Ramsey was supposed to meet with Attias the night of the crash and go to a rave in LA but David told him he couldn't go: 'He wanted to lose his virginity that day or that evening. I just figured he was obsessive with some things. I just took it as that.'

'When we first met, he listened to electronic music. Towards mid-January he started listening to a lot of rap,' Ramsey said. 'He really began idolizing the rap performers and he even began to talk like they did . . . he talked about how God picked DJs to spread good through the world and he was also picked to spread good.'

Another friend, Scott Ammann, who met Attias at a gym in LA, said he did not remember the conversation he had with Attias on the night of the collision. He recalled very few details from any of their interactions, but did admit that Attias called him the week of the incident at about 2 a.m. to tell him that 'he was very scared and knew the end was near'. Assistant

District Attorney Patrick McKinley asked Ammann if the call alarmed him, to which he answered, 'Not really.' Dave, apparently, said a lot of weird things on the phone and in person.

Hallie Johnston, a UCSB student who lived in Francisco Torres Residence Hall at the same time as Attias, testified that Crazy Dave exhibited a volatile temper and irregularly attended classes the quarter before the accident. 'His face was animated, his eyes were always wide open and he moved around a lot more than most people,' she said. 'He was usually by himself, but we were nice to him because he seemed like a nice guy and he didn't have other friends.'

Britni Saavedra, a former Francisco Torres resident and friend of the defendant, said she met Attias through a mutual friend in October 2000 and smoked pot with him on numerous occasions.

In court McKinley asked Saavedra if Attias ever told her he used drugs beside pot. 'PCP, cocaine and I don't really know the rest. He took Ecstasy one time and said he didn't enjoy it very much,' she said. 'The first time I met him he was on LSD.' Saavedra said she spoke to Attias almost every day over the 2000 winter break and also visited him in Los Angeles, although she never actually went into his parents' Santa Monica residence. She testified about the traffic accident in January 2001, in which Attias totaled a car on Highway 101. 'He told me he got in a car accident on the freeway. I remember he usually didn't use cocaine . . . but he said he had done a little bit that morning, before the accident occurred,' she said. 'He said he had in his car K, coke, marijuana, some sort of pills . . . and he threw them over a bridge or something.'

Britni saw Attias for the last time in her dorm room a few days before the crash. 'He wasn't the normal Dave. He was kind of relaxed, he looked kind of sad. When he left he gave me a hug, and that was the last I saw him until this day,' she said. 'The only unusual thing that stuck in my head was that he was so calm . . . that night he came in, kinda sweet. He looked kinda sad.'

ONLY GOD CAN JUDGE ME

Attias was charged with four counts of second-degree murder, four counts of vehicular manslaughter while driving under the influence of marijuana and one count of gross negligence resulting in great bodily injury while driving under the influence of marijuana. He pled guilty by reason of insanity. The trial, held at Santa Barbara Superior Courthouse in Santa Barbara, California, lasted from 24 April to 15 May.

Deputy District Attorney Patrick McKinley called over one hundred witnesses to paint a picture of a spoiled rich kid who 'didn't care about other people – he only cared about himself'. McKinley said that David was an unstable and irresponsible youngster who was immersed in the drug and rave culture and maliciously ran over a group of partying students on Sabado Tarde Road. Attias's defense team worked to represent him as an impressionable and mentally ill student who talked about drugs to fit in at UCSB, had a 'psychotic break' and did not understand his actions the night of the crash. 'He believed the world was a computer game and began to receive messages from music and TV shows.'

On 12 June 2002 the David Attias murder trial came to an emotional end when Judge Thomas Adams read the verdict to a packed courtroom: guilty to four second-degree charges. A jury of seven women and five men found Attias not guilty of the lesser charge of driving under the influence because toxicology tests determined that he had only 1.1 nanograms of marijuana in his system at the time of the wreck. The guilty verdict also rendered moot the additional four charges of vehicular manslaughter. Attias, probably zonked out on anti-psychotic drugs, showed little emotion over the jury's decision.

Eight days later, the same jury that found him guilty of murder, concluded that David Attias was insane and declared that he couldn't be held responsible for the crime. The shocking courtroom reversal by the jury outraged many of the relatives of the four people killed. For his part, the convicted killer was visibly animated and overjoyed by the unexpected turn of events. He hugged Nancy Haydt, one of his two high-powered lawyers and smiled at his mom. According to the American Psychiatric Association, the insanity defense is successful only 26 per cent of the times it is invoked.

Tony Bourdakis, the father of one victim, remarked that Attias and his lawyers manipulated the judicial system to 'get away with murder'. Assistant District Attorney Patrick McKinley bitterly concluded that David 'was either high or crazy. He wasn't high, so he must be crazy.' The sudden change of fortune for Crazy Dave can only be attributed to the fact that in the United States, if you have money, justice will always serve you. Hopefully justice will be served for the victims' families in the two federal suits filed against Dave and his parents.

11. THE VAMPIRE CLAN

'She just basically looked straight at me and said, what do you want? By that time, you know, it was pretty obvious, I had blood on me and a crowbar in my hand, I was fixing to say, yeah, I want to have coffee with you, son of a bitching smartass, but anyway then that's when she lunged at me, 'cause I was actually going to let her live, but after she lunged at me I just took the bottom of the crowbar, and kept stabbing it through her skull and whenever she fell down I just continually beat her until I saw her brains falling on the floor.' – Rod Ferrell

'It is our interpretation that heinous means extremely wicked or shockingly evil; that atrocious means outrageously wicked and vile; and, that cruel means designed to inflict a high degree of pain with utter indifference to, or even enjoyment of, the suffering of others . . . The factor of heinous, atrocious or cruel is proper only in torturous murders – those that evince extreme and outrageous depravity as exemplified either by the desire to inflict a high degree of pain or utter indifference to or enjoyment of the suffering of another.' – The Supreme Court of Florida

For years, the Baptist, semi-rural town of Murray, Kentucky, was best known as the home of the national Boy Scout museum. But the Vampire Clan forever changed that when sixteen-year-old Rod Ferrell – Murray's now most famous citizen – shocked the world with his dyed, shoulder-length black hair, his shaved temples, his makeup, his black fingernails, and his vampire leanings. Not what you'd expect from this Bible Belt community of 15,000 God-fearing folks. But there he was, defiantly wagging his tongue at the press, letting the world know that evil does lurk in the backwoods of Kentucky.

A 1997 study of local teenagers by the *Lexington Herald-Leader* in Kentucky revealed that 'there's a subculture at nearly every school that includes Anne Rice-influenced gothic kids, faux vampires and outcast kids who dabble in the occult.

After all, in the Bible Belt, what could be more shocking than experimenting with witchcraft, vampirism or satanism?' Lexington is not too far from Murray, which is not too far from West Paducah, another Southern farming community featured in this writing. What's up with Kentucky? *Deliverance*, anyone?

CROSSING OVER

On the afternoon of 25 November 1996, Rod Ferrell performed a blood-drinking ritual in a cemetery to induct, or 'cross over' as a fellow vampire, his old girlfriend, fifteen-year-old Heather Wendorf. 'The person that gets crossed over is like subject to whatever the sire wants,' according to Heather. 'Like the sire is boss basically. They have authority over you.'

The two wannabe vampires talked about their plans to leave town. Rod had come from Murray, Kentucky, to Eustis, Florida, to pick her up and go to New Orleans to participate in its flourishing vampire scene. Heather and Rod first met a year before when he attended Eustis High School. Two kindred spirits, they found solace in each other's company. 'I think she just felt she could talk to Rod, and then as they got to know each other, they started relating things,' her older sister Jennifer said. But by the end of ninth grade Rod, his mother and his grandparents moved back to Murray and Heather's best friend was gone.

After Rod left town, they remained in touch through letters and endless phone calls. Rod and his friend Stephen Murphy would call collect and chat for hours with Heather and sometimes with Jennifer. Their conversations were ringing up huge phone bills that led to Heather's upset parents putting a stop to the collect calls. One day, Heather told Rod that her parents were abusing her. She told him that she wanted to run away and wouldn't mind if her parents were dead. Little did she know that within a year, Rod would be back in town 'on some unfinished business' with a vampire crew in tow and trouble burning a hole in his head.

The events leading to the death of Heather's parents started three days before, when Rod and three other teenagers decided that they'd had enough with Murray and were ready for a road trip to New Orleans. The other kids were Scott Anderson, sixteen, whom Farrell had known since second grade, Dana Cooper, nineteen, whom he'd just met, and his new girlfriend, Charity Keesee, sixteen, whom Rod liked to call Shea. On the way to New Orleans they were going to stop in Eustis and pick up his old girlfriend, Heather. Then they would 'cross her over' and make her part of their little coven. Incredibly, they were all convinced they were vampires. And Rod Ferrell – who saw himself as the true Prince of Darkness and the Son of Satan – was their 'sire', their leader.

When they arrived in Eustis they visited Shannon Yohee, another of Rod's old girlfriends from his days in Eustis High. Then they visited Audrey Presson, yet another old girlfriend. Rod asked Audrey if she wanted to come with them to New Orleans, but she declined. The next day the Buick Skylark they were driving – which belonged to Scott's mother – had a flat tire. On top of that, the local cops stopped them and asked a bunch of questions. Obviously, it was time to leave town, but they needed a new car.

Ferrell decided he would go to Heather's parents' house, steal money and a car, then they would split. Their half-baked plan was to 'hog tie or something' Heather's parents and rob them. He mentioned he would 'take them out' if they tried to resist, but Heather told him not to hurt them and nothing else was said about it.

On the day of the killings Ferrell and the gang stopped near the Wendorf home and met Heather, whom he gave the vampire name of Zoey, down the road. The three girls, Zoey, Dana and Shea, left in the Skylark to visit Heather's boyfriend and pick up Jeanine LeClaire, Heather's best friend. Ferrell and Anderson stayed behind. Rod had never seen Heather's parents before that night. He even went to the wrong house first, but he didn't kill anybody because he looked in and saw little kids. Rod later told police, 'I don't kill anything that's little. Now adults, that's perfectly fine, sixteen and up.'

That night, Rod allegedly was flying on eight hits of acid, which might explain the senseless madness that followed. 'We never thought about it until about ten minutes before we did it,' he told detectives. '[We] didn't exactly plan on beating them to death.' The two vampires searched the outside of the Wendorf home, looking for some way to get inside. They entered through an unlocked door to the garage and searched for a weapon. Ferrell finally settled on a crowbar with a sharpened tip.

When they entered the home, Heather's mom, Naoma Queen, was showering in another part of the house. Her dad, Richard Wendorf, was asleep on the couch in front of a blaring television. As Anderson disconnected the phones from the wall, Ferrell walked up behind the sleeping father and 'smacked the fuck out of him' with the crowbar. Wendorf, 49, had no defensive wounds on his arms and hands confirming the fact that he never knew what hit him.

According to Rod, Wendorf took about twenty minutes to die completely, plenty of time to steal his Discover card and burn with a cigarette a 'V' sign surrounded by circular marks on his body. Police said the 'V' was the sign of the Vampire Clan and each circular mark represented one of its members. By the time he was done, 53-year-old Naoma had finished showering. She had towelled dry, put on a bathrobe and was in the kitchen pouring herself a hot cup of coffee.

That's when she saw Rod, blood on his clothes and the crowbar in his hands. Instinctively, she threw the scalding hot coffee on him, lunged at him, scratching his face and arms. Ferrell beat her down to the floor and bashed her brains in with the sharpened end of the crowbar in a frenzied attack. 'She clawed me, spilled fucking scalding hot coffee on me, pissed me off,' he said in his confession. 'So I made sure she was dead.' And so he did, by completely severing her brain stem.

Anderson, who had never seen anyone killed before, was in shock as he followed Rod around the house 'like a little puppy'. With Heather's parents dead, the two young men searched the house for money. They only found $4.75 in cash. They took Naoma's pearls, which were wrapped around a teddy bear, a hunting knife, and the keys to their 1994 powder-blue Ford Explorer. With nothing else left to take, they drove off in their new set of wheels.

Next stop was Jeanine's house, where they picked up the girls, Zoey, Dana, and Shea. Once they were inside the Explorer, Heather realized what had happened. Rod told detectives that she 'flipped for about a hundred miles or so' then accepted it. When questioned by investigators, Heather said the only reason she went with the group was because she had no place to go and feared she would be blamed for the murders.

Back in Eustis, Heather's seventeen-year-old sister Jennifer, was about to make the grisly discovery.

THERE'S BLOOD EVERYWHERE

Jennifer: I need two ambulances. My mother and father have just been killed. I just walked in the door. I don't know what happened. They're dead.

911: Both your mother and your father? They are not breathing at all?

Jennifer: I don't know. I didn't check. I can't get that close; they're my parents.

911: Is anybody there with you, ma'am?

Jennifer: I have no idea. I don't know who is in the house. I have no . . .

911: What makes you think that they have been killed?

Jennifer: There is blood everywhere. Please, as fast as you can . . .

911: We're on the way. We have law enforcement on the way also. Are you there alone?

Jennifer: I have no idea. There could be somebody in the house.

911: Nobody is there with you?

Jennifer: My sister is gone, though. I don't know where my sister is. She's gone.

911: What do you mean? She lives there with your parents?

Jennifer: She should be here. She's only fifteen years old. And she's gone.

Jennifer Wendorf, a cheerleader at Eustis High, was returning home from a date with her boyfriend when she found her parents' bodies, bloody and beaten, in the living room and the kitchen. At first, investigators feared Heather had been abducted by the ruthless assailants but it soon became clear that she was also a suspect, along with Rod, Dana, Scott, and Shea.

The group had dumped the old Buick they had driven down from Kentucky after switching the license plates, so that the stolen Explorer had the Buick's plates and the ditched Buick had the plates of the Explorer. They drove west along Interstate 10 through Tallahassee and towards New Orleans. Throughout the drive they were pulled over by police five times, but the cops – unaware that they had just killed two people – found a reason to arrest them. When they arrived in New Orleans, Shea freaked out. Apparently, she had never been in a metropolitan area as big as New Orleans and was terrified by the sight of 'black people carry(ing) around AK-47's in their back yards'.

On 29 November, four days after the murders, the Vampire Clan found themselves somewhere in the state of Louisiana, lost, hungry and broke. Shea called her grandmother in Rapid City, South Dakota, and told her she and her friends were in Louisiana and needed money. Grandma told her to call her mom. Her mother, who worked for the Sheriff's department, was already in contact with the Florida authorities that were looking for her daughter and the rest of the clan. She told the teen to go to a motel and have the clerk call her to arrange to pay for a room. Incredibly, the junior vampire sect fell for it. When the clerk called, the Baton Rouge police department was alerted. Officers quickly moved in and arrested the clan as they were driving from the motel in the Explorer.

INTERVIEW WITH THE VAMPIROID

'Kentucky, and the whole South, is more susceptible to vampirism. It's a breeding ground for bizarre behavior. These are bible-thumping people; kids are raised to believe in Christ

and the devil. It's a scary place, almost medieval in the way some Southerners believe there are real demons in every shadow.' – Gordon Welton, editor of *The Vampire Book: Encyclopedia of the Undead*

One must understand that when I talk about 'vampires', I'm not talking about the fictional creatures populating Bram Stoker novels. The vampires referred to in these pages would be more correctly called vampiroids. Though some vampiroids actually believe themselves to be real vampires, they are not reanimated corpses from beyond the grave.

Vampiroids are living and breathing human beings who pretend to be vampires. A vampiroid is a human who embraces and identifies with what he or she assumes is a vampiristic lifestyle based largely on what is depicted in films and literature. Vampiroids become totally seduced by the vampire mythology, having almost no regard for what is real and what is imaginary.

Within the vampiroid subculture, there are two groups of vampires: the metaphorical vampires who sleep in coffins, wear fangs, and keep nighttime employment; and the 'real' vampires who take it a step further – drink blood and tend towards being borderline psychotics.

Many cross from one group to the other, or exist somewhere in between. Almost all vampiroids are adults with marginal incomes who appear to be living outside reality and in a world of Anne Rice-inspired fantasy. The *Los Angeles Times* noted that for the second group of vampires, their 'lifestyle is beyond mere trend. They avoid the sun at all costs. Some drink blood and perform ritual magic. Most claim to possess psychic abilities. Some say they are tormented by wandering spirits.'

Many teen vampires in the United States win their 'fangs' through role-playing board games like 'Dungeons & Dragons' and 'Masquerade'. In the best-selling 'Masquerade', players physically act out the vampiric scenarios as if they were performing in a play. As dictated by the game's storyteller or 'sire', the players assume different vampire identities and go through a series of adventures. Greg Fountain, an executive with White Wolf, of Clarkson, Georgia, which markets 'Masquerade', said their game can be extremely realistic, but it's not a cult. 'It can be quite intense,' he said. 'The core premise is personal exploration.'

PRINCE OF THE CITY

Ferrell's vampire-playing antics eventually led him to meet a man called Stephen Murphy. The more experienced Murphy – who went by the vampire name of 'Jaden' – 'crossed over' Ferrell and turned him into a 'real' vampire. Murphy, or should we say Jaden, also gave him the vampire name of 'Vesago', which refers to a character from the Anne Rice novel *Interview with the Vampire*. Ferrell allegedly saw the movie on video over thirty times. April Doeden, another vampiroid, testified that on the night Murphy crossed Rod over he cried and shivered all night long like a scared little boy.

Now a fully fledged vampire, Rod started hanging out in cemeteries all night, cutting himself so others could drink his blood, and saying he was a 500-year-old vampire. Rod's appearance started changing drastically, physically transforming from a typical redneck teenager with a mullet to a demonic creature with dyed black hair and shaved temples wearing a long black coat and walking with a wooden cane. Jaden, being the local head-honcho vampire, also went by the name of 'Prince of the City', which is a powerful character in the 'Masquerade' game.

Local police believe there were a number of adults behind the rise of teenage vampiric activity in Murray. Some have mentioned two rival vampire gangs at war in the area. 'We have just scratched the surface of vampirism in Kentucky,' said Calloway County Sheriff Stan Scott. 'There are many more involved in the valley than just Ferrell's group. Right now, I think most of them are lying low.' According to the sheriff, there were over thirty youths from Murray involved in a county-wide 'Masquerade' game, with some taking their vampire identities more seriously than others. 'It's pretty easy to tell who's been a vampire for any length of time,' said

Sheriff Scott. 'Most of them are going to have self-inflicted razor cuts or knife cuts.'

Murphy and Ferrell's friendship ended in September 1996 when they had a power struggle over the control of their vampire minions. Murphy, whose six-foot frame and 194-pound body would clearly overpower the rail-thin Ferrell, threw the youngster against a wall and choked him until he fell unconscious. Apparently Ferrell wanted to challenge his Prince of the City title and was planning to form his own vampire group to 'take over the town'. Several days later Ferrell pressed charges against Murphy. His former friend pleaded guilty in court and was sentenced to seven days in the Calloway County Jail. He was also ordered to remain 100 feet away from Ferrell.

Shortly after the fight Sondra Gibson, Rod's mom, was charged with soliciting Murphy's fourteen-year-old brother, whom she tried to seduce with letters promising sex. 'I long to be near you, to become a vampire bride, a part of the family immortal and truly yours for ever,' she wrote in a letter found by the fourteen-year-old's mother. 'You will then come for me and cross me over and I will be your bride for eternity and you my sire.' Gibson was originally charged with solicitation to commit rape, but instead pleaded guilty to a felony charge of unlawful transaction with a minor. Though she faced five years in prison, she was given five years probation. Her attorney made a plea stipulation that said she was guilty of the crime but was mentally ill when she committed it.

Sondra went to a psychologist as part of her plea agreement. She told the psychologist that members of Ferrell's vampire group gathered at her house and, after doing drugs, they would rape her. Not one to hold back, Sondra said her son had no soul and was ruining her life. He and only he was responsible for all her miscarriages and for killing all of his unborn brothers and sisters. But after her appointments were over, she would return to their vampire lair and hung out with the rest of the coven.

MOMMY DEAREST

'I was not the Betty Crocker type. Not by a long shot.' – Sondra Gibson

Sondra Gibson was not your typical mother. She went out dancing and clubbing almost every night and would turn the occasional trick to make a little income. She was more like Rod's peer; a vampire queen for her son's coven. Her vampire name was 'Star'. When she signed her name, she would draw a star to the side. She too played the 'Masquerade' games. 'I played it with him. It's hard enough to find something you can do with your kids today, and the game was fun,' she told Associated Press. 'It was a thrill, sure, but it was still role playing. People pretended to do stuff, but didn't really do it.' When Rod decided to drop out of school, she didn't care. When her son stayed out all night doing drugs, she would join him. When Rod and his vampire gang hung out at the Vampyre Hotel for an initiation ritual or a bloodletting, she would be there.

She never disciplined him, not even as a child. Sondra had Rod when she was seventeen. His father, Rick Ferrell, was also a teen. The two youths were married nine days after Rod was born. Three weeks later, they separated and Rod's dad left Murray to join the Marines. Sondra was described by Rod's father as 'manipulating' and deceitful. Her temperamental nature made it nearly impossible for him to have a relationship with his son. Rick finally gave up and, until the vampire murders, he had not seen his child since the boy was eight.

For most of his life, Rod lived with his mother and her parents, Rosetta and Harold Gibson. Because of the nature of his work, the grandfather kept moving the family back and forth from Murray to central Florida. The first time they moved to Lake County, Florida, Rod fell ill with a near fatal case of encephalitis, which is swelling of the brain caused by a viral infection. Dr Wade Meyer, a psychiatrist specializing in the study of homicidal children and children involved in the occult, said the encephalitis might have acted as a mitigating circumstance in Rod's future lethal behavior.

Around the mid 80s, the family moved from Eustis back to Murray. During this time Rod said his grandfather, Harold Gibson, took him to several black mass rituals that involved, among other things, human sacrifice. In a taped confession after his arrest he explained that Harold was a member of a cult called the Black Mask. The group would meet in the woods outside Murray for their rituals. 'When I was five they chose me as the Guardian of the Black Mask and the Guardian has to become one with everybody,' he told detectives. 'In other words, they raped me. And they have to sacrifice a human to the Guardian so they sacrificed someone right in front of me.'

More plausibly, Ferrell's links to vampirism and the occult might stem from playing with his mother and father fantasy role games since he was a tot. These fantasy games, which undoubtedly shaped his early psyche, eventually became an enormous part of his everyday life.

When Roddy was around ten, he and Sondra moved back to Eustis, Florida and again began living with his grand-parents. Rod enrolled in Eustis Middle School, and later started his first year at Eustis High. Friends in Eustis described the youngster as a nice and quiet 'laid back kind of guy'. In middle school he met Audrey Presson. At Eustis High he dated Shannon Yohee until he met Heather Wendorf and Jeanine LeClaire. Once he'd hooked up with Heather and Jeanine, they all started obsessing over vampires. Sondra first realized something could be amiss with Rod and his friends when in December 1995 she walked into his room and found Jeanine, Rod and another boy with the lights off, their arms sliced open and blood all over the place.

Sondra didn't make too much of their juvenile bloodletting. She had just married a drug dealer by the name of Darren Vraven and couldn't have been happier. Once again, the whole family, including Vraven, relocated back to Murray. There Rod enrolled in Calloway County High School. Mean-while Vraven started dealing drugs to Rod and his friends, which didn't seem to bother Sondra. Vraven, by all accounts, was not a model citizen. As well as making a living selling drugs, he was physically and mentally abusive towards Sondra and the boy. Reportedly, Vraven was also involved in satanic worship rituals.

Darren and Sondra moved to Michigan leaving Rod behind. Darren, now Rod's stepfather, had no love for the boy. When they left town he told Rod that his mother was never coming back, so he might as well get used to it. When Sondra found out, she was furious. She returned to Murray to be with her Roddy and served her drug-dealing husband with divorce papers.

THE VAMPYRE HOTEL

With Mom back in Murray, Rod's vampire world expanded as he started engaging in serious occult activity. Calloway County authorities said Ferrell and his vampire groupies hung out at an abandoned building known as the Vampyre Hotel. The so-called 'hotel' was a twenty-year-old concrete shell of a six-bedroom house whose building permit expired before it was ever completed. The building was covered with graffiti, pentagrams and messages like 'Follow me to death' and 'Please deposit dead bodies here.'

Meanwhile, Rod's school work slipped into never never land. He began flagrantly violating the school's policies by skipping class, smoking on campus and generally defying teachers and school officials. In September 1996 Ferrell was suspended from school, after which he never returned. Instead, he stayed at home sleeping all day and having bloodletting rituals and group sex parties at night.

At Calloway County High, the assistant principal tried to get Rod to see the school counselor. Rod attended six sessions with Marianne O'Rourke, the counselor, before he was expelled. O'Rourke said the problem was that Sondra, as Rod's mother, did not care about the obvious signs of her son's budding psychopathy. She knew he was self-mutilating, doing drugs all night, bagging all his school work, and yet she did not try to steer him toward a productive life.

In May 1996 Sondra took her son to an evaluation with the Kentucky Mental Health and Retardation Board. Rod, who showed up to the session wearing all black with black nail polish, makeup and a wooden cane, told social worker Debra Mooney that he felt threatened and persecuted by society. But neither mother nor son showed up for another therapy session. Next, Sondra engaged the assistance of the Division of Child Services and had Rod declared an uncontrollable minor. However, once again, she minimized his need for counseling and lied about her son so that he could avoid getting a job, going to counseling, and participating in the real world.

As Rod became more disassociated from reality, the Vampire Clan moved beyond role playing to real-life violence. In October, one month before the killings, Ferrell and Anderson were charged with breaking into the county humane society, beating up forty dogs and mutilating two puppies. 'They had stomped one of them to death and one of them, they pulled the legs off,' said Sheriff Stan Scott of Calloway County. 'The animal shelter thing was the first visible sign he had gone beyond game-playing,' added Calloway County prosecutor David Harrington.

John Goodman, a fellow vampire friend who didn't travel with them to Florida, told police that, prior to the killings, Ferrell had become possessed with the idea of opening the Gates to Hell, 'which meant he would have to kill a large, large number of people in order to consume their souls. By doing this, Ferrell believed he would obtain super powers.' Perhaps the Wendorf murders were the beginning of the opening.

GENUINE EVIL

'This is just like a big fucking joke. My life seems like a dream. My childhood was taken away at five, I don't know whether I'm asleep or dreaming anymore so whatever, for all I know I could wake up in five minutes.' – Rod Ferrell

But no, Rod, your life is not a dream, it's an ugly reality of madness, chaos and self-hatred. Three mental-health experts – Dr Wade Meyer, Dr Harry Krop and Dr Elizabeth McMahon

– concurred that Rod Ferrell was mentally ill. Their diagnoses were varied, but all agreed that Rod suffered from a schizotypal personality disorder.

All three doctors stated that, although Ferrell could appreciate the criminality of his conduct at the time of the crimes, his ability to conform that conduct to the requirements of the law was substantially impaired. This shortcoming was the result of Ferrell's significant childhood abuse, his schizotypal personality disorder, his bizarre thought processes, his lack of responsible adult role models in his life, and his excessive use of drugs and hallucinogenics.

On 12 February 1998, as the state offered its opening arguments, Ferrell pled guilty to the four charges against him: armed burglary, armed robbery, and two counts of first-degree murder. Defense attorneys tried to persuade jurors against the death penalty, saying that Ferrell was forced to live in a fantasy world created by a sexually abusive family obsessed with the occult. But on 23 February the jury voted unanimously to give Rod Ferrell the death sentence. 'There is no comfort except that we as a society hold people accountable for what they do,' said prosecutor Brad King.

Before the judge accepted the decision, Ferrell's lawyers argued that his client's young age, his emotional age – which psychiatrists placed at three years – and his extreme emotional and mental disturbance should be considered as mitigating factors in his sentencing. But the meting out of justice in Florida knows no age constraints.

After five days of additional testimony from both sides, Judge Jerry Lockett accepted the jury recommendation and officially sentenced the youngster to the electric chair. 'I think you are a disturbed young man,' the judge said. Lockett also urged prosecutors to charge Heather Wendorf as an accessory to the murder of her parents. 'It is the strong suggestion of this court that the grand jury be reconvened,' Lockett said. 'There is genuine evil in the world. There is dark side and light side competing in each of us.' Rod, who was nineteen when he when he was sentenced, became the youngest person on Florida's death row.

A year later, Florida's Supreme Court ruled that the state cannot execute killers who committed their crimes before the age of seventeen. The court said that the July 1999 death sentence would be cruel and unusual and therefore unconstitutional. Rod's sentence was commuted to life in prison.

A year before Rod's trial, Heather Wendorf was cleared by a grand jury of all charges and walked out of jail a free woman. She immediately went into seclusion while she tried to rebuild her life with the help of a court-appointed guardian. God only knows where she is today. Sondra Gibson said she felt her son did not deserve the death penalty, but endorsed the judge's suggestion about little Heather. 'There's one person walking around who's just as guilty as he is,' she said after the sentencing.

The others, Shea, Dana and Scott, were tried separately for their roles in the killings. Charity Lynn Keesee (Shea), Ferrell's girlfriend, was slapped with a ten-and-a-half year sentence. Dana Cooper was sentenced to seventeen years in prison. Scott Anderson got life in prison for his role in the murders. As for Heather, less than one week after Rod was sentenced to death, she sold the rights to her story to a writer for $1,000. The writer, Aphrodite Jones, said the money was a good faith payment toward a possible $50,000 Hollywood movie deal for the book, *The Embrace*. As of writing, no one in Hollywood has embraced the idea.

12. POST COLUMBINE

Name: Robert Steinhaeuser
Age at time of rampage: 19
Date of attack: 26 April 2002
Number of victims: 16 people, himself, and four wounded
Victim profile: 13 teachers, 2 students, 1 policewoman
Arsenal: 9mm Glock pistol, 20-gauge pump action shotgun
Dress code: black ninja outfit, black ski-mask
Media keywords: gore films, violent video games, Slipknot, crumbling Old World values
Early warning signs: joined a gun club, stockpiled ammunition
Probable cause: revenge. Angry at being expelled from school. Wanted to be famous. Definitely not the Slipknot song 'School Wars'
School: Johann Gutenberg Gymnasium
Location: Erfurt, Germany
Outcome: death by self-inflicted gunshot to the head immediately following the rampage. Tighter gun laws in Germany

'I thought this must be a bad film. I thought this kind of thing only happened in America.' – Thomas Rethfeldt

THE AMERICAN CONDITION

Until 26 April 2002, high school rampages were considered exclusively an 'American condition'. That's when Robert Steinhaeuser, an expelled nineteen-year-old student, donned the customary black and, with an Austrian-made Glock 9mm in one hand and a 20-gauge shotgun in another, went hunting for teachers through the halls of the Johann Gutenberg Gymnasium in Erfurt, in eastern Germany.

An expert marksman, Steinhaeuser was bent on killing as many teachers as possible in revenge for being expelled from school for forging medical excuses. With typical German efficiency, he managed to kill thirteen teachers, two students and a police officer in a twenty-minute blood-soaked frenzy of revenge. The rampage was brought to an end by a heroic History and Art teacher who confronted the shooter and locked him in a classroom. Moments later, Steinhaeuser pumped a bullet through his own brain. When the smoke settled, this pleasantly plump youngster had perpetrated the worst shooting violence seen in Germany since the end of World War II.

'The so-called "American conditions" have reached us. We cannot let these excesses of violence become a part of our daily life,' said Konrad Freiberg, the head of Germany's police union. 'This happens a lot in America, but it's not just an American thing any more,' said Robert Kippel, seventeen, a student from another school. 'America is so far away and it never seemed real to me before,' said sixteen-year-old Christin Beinlich.

Hours before the deadly rampage, Steinhaeuser told his mother he was going to school to take a math exam. As he left the house, she wished him good luck. Incredibly, the youngster had been expelled from the school two months before and never told her or his father about it. 'The parents thought he was going to school every day and was successfully moving toward his high school diploma,' Police Chief Rainer Grube said.

A little before 11 a.m., Steinhaeuser walked into the school building – a six-storey structure featuring early twentieth-century Jugendstil architecture – and headed to the bathroom where he changed into a Ninja outfit and stashed 500 rounds of ammunition. Then he slipped on his ski-mask, cocked the Glock and pumped his shotgun, and headed to where his classmates were taking a math exam.

The shooting started around 11.00, when he charged into a class and announced, 'I'm not going to write anything,' and started firing. 'The pupils ran out of the classroom and he came after us and shot a teacher next to me,' one female student told German radio. Another student told *Der Spiegel* how a teacher tapped her index finger on her forehead as if to say he was insane, to which Steinhaeuser answered by putting a gun to her head and pulling the trigger.

By all accounts, he stalked through the school searching out teachers and killing them with point-blank shots from the Glock to their heads. 'There were dead bodies lying everywhere in the corridors,' said Thomas Rethfeldt, eighteen. In all, the lethal teenager shot forty rounds and killed almost a quarter of the school's teaching staff. 'I thought it was fireworks. Then the door opened, and a masked man came through the door. The teacher was standing there, and he shot her through the head, through her glasses,' said student Dominik Ulbricht.

Dubbed the 'Erfurt Terminator', Steinhaeuser killed pretty much everyone he aimed at. 'Many of the victims were killed with headshots, he clearly was a trained marksman,' said Bernhard Vogel, premier of the state of Thuringia, where Erfurt is located. Only one person was wounded on the leg from a gunshot. The other three wounded were hospitalized from shock.

During the morning rampage, 180 of the 700 students in the Gymnasium locked themselves inside classrooms. One group of students held a handwritten sign pasted to a window reading 'HILFE' – Help. 'It was chilling,' a witness said, 'I saw this big placard with the word "Help" on it, and people moving around behind it but I couldn't tell if they were children or attackers.'

The two teenagers killed, a fourteen-year-old girl and a fifteen-year-old boy, were hit when Steinhaeuser fired through a closed door. It is believed that he killed them by accident, considering the meticulousness with which he hunted down his other victims.

Police were called by the school janitor at 11:05. The first squad car took five minutes. By then Steinhaeuser had made it out to the school parking lot and was chasing down a teacher. 'She was running for her car and she tripped, and he shot her in the leg,' said nineteen-year-old Christian Becker, who saw the cold-blooded murder through his classroom window. 'He ran over and shot her three times in the head with his pistol.'

Steinhaeuser was then confronted by the arriving officers. The rampager exchanged fire with them, killing one police-woman, before fleeing back inside the building. No more shots were heard until . . .

THE HERO OF ERFURT

'I opened the door from the art classroom and saw a masked man in a black Ninja warrior-style outfit. He held a pistol up to my chest. Suddenly he pulled off his mask. His hair was plastered to his head with sweat.' – Reiner Heise

The bloodbath was brought to an end by Art and History teacher Reiner Heise. Proclaimed by the German press 'the hero of Erfurt,' Heise, sixty, encountered the shooter when he opened his classroom door looking for students. Instead, he encountered the business end of an Austrian-made Glock pointing at his chest. The rampager, for reasons unknown, decided to take off his mask in front of Heise.

Heise recognized Steinhaeuser and instinctively started talking. 'Robert,' Heise said. 'Pull the trigger. If you shoot me now, then look in my eyes.' Steinhaeuser looked at him, lowered the pistol, and replied, 'No. That's enough for today, Mr Heise.' Heise then told him they should talk and motioned as if to lead him into the classroom. As Steinhaeuser momentarily let down his guard, the teacher quickly shoved the nineteen-year-old into the room, closed the door, locked it and ran to the principal's office. 'I didn't have time to be afraid.' In hindsight, the teacher doesn't know why he survived while his peers were murdered. 'Perhaps he just liked me. Perhaps he didn't think I was bad,' Heise said.

Soon afterward, police commandos swarmed through the building and closed in on the killer. Steinhaeuser, perhaps tired of indiscriminate murder, put the Glock to his head and blew his brain out. Officers securing the building described the school hallways as covered in blood and littered with bodies. In fact there were bodies everywhere; in classrooms, in hallways and in bathrooms. Police spokesman Manfred Etzel said it was 'horrible'.

Twelve hours later, police discovered that what they thought was Steinhaeuser's personal website had been updated. At first, police believed Robert might have had an accomplice, but soon concluded that the alteration was done by hackers trying to bring attention to themselves. Eventually, Erfurt police chief Rainer Grube brought to question the actual authenticity of the site, noting that the youngster's home computer did not have Internet access.

The alleged *www.robert-steinhaeuser.de* homepage turned out to be a prank. The top of the page contained a banner reading 'Teachers and other low life forbidden.' The first link on the site was to the Gutenberg Gymnasium. The bottom of the web page had a line from Pink Floyd's 1979 hit, 'Just Another Brick in the Wall': 'Hey, teacher, leave those kids alone.'

THE CITY IS WEEPING

The night after the shooting, all of Erfurt's church bells rang in mourning. Erfurt's historical St Mary's Cathedral was filled with mourners who prayed and wept inconsolably. Psychiatrists moved in to help the students cope with the mounting horror of the massacre. An impromptu memorial of flowers spilled down from the school's front steps to the street as crowds of shocked citizens gathered around it in a candlelit vigil under the steady rain. 'Why?' was the question on everyone's lips as the city, and all of Germany, wept.

'We cannot find words for what we feel in Germany right now,' German President Johannes Rau said. 'Germany is in mourning in the face of these incomprehensible events.' The government ordered flags flown at half-staff, and Chancellor Gerhard Schroeder's party canceled an election rally that was planned for that weekend. 'We are stunned in the face of this horrible crime,' a grim-faced Schroeder told reporters. 'All explanations we could give right now don't go far enough.'

Erfurt is a medieval city of 197,000 people in the former communist East Germany. The capital of the eastern state of

Thuringia, Erfurt dates back to 1250, when it was a crossroads for medieval trade routes. Its rich history includes being the birthplace of nineteenth-century sociologist Max Weber, and the home of theologian Martin Luther in the sixteenth century. But the Nazis, World War II bombings and the ruinous communist regime have taken a toll on the buildings of its historic core. 'It's a terrible shame that Erfurt is now known around the world for this crime,' said Erfurt resident Jens Probst, 'I only wish the town could have become famous for other reasons.'

School administrators said classes would be canceled for at least a week to give students time to mourn the loss of their teachers and schoolmates. Erfurt Mayor Manfred Ruge said that after meeting the school's parents, teachers and students, they had resolved to clean up and reopen the building as soon as possible, to 'seize the chance to make a new beginning'.

The school remained sealed for three days as police searched for clues to piece together the horrific chain of events. Once investigators finished, work crews moved in to remove all traces of blood-soaked mayhem. 'It will take years to get over this,' said senior Michaela Seidel in a news conference following the meeting with the Mayor. 'At this time, none of us understands anything.'

Seidel, who had finished her final math exam and had left the building ten minutes before the shooting began, said that they had discussed putting a memorial outside the school, but decided it would be inappropriate. 'We don't want a huge plaque in front of it that reminds us of what happened every time we pass by.'

The Monday after the shooting, all of Germany paused for a minute of silence to honor the victims of the school suicide attack. Also, all schools in the city were closed in honor of the fallen Gutenberg Gymnasium students and teachers. Christiane Alt, director of the Gutenberg Gymnasium, told Germany's public TV channel, 'We are traumatized, but we have to do our jobs so that students can, with time, return to their normal life.'

THE ERFURT TERMINATOR

All evidence suggests that the unprecedented attack by the 'Erfurt Terminator' can best be described as an act of revenge against the teachers who had failed him, the institution that expelled him, and perhaps even the whole German education system. Some have interpreted the attack as an assault on authority figures.

The trouble started the year before the rampage when Steinhaeuser failed a rigorous end-of-school examination and was forced to repeat his final year. The exam, called the Abitur, is critical for a student's career, just like the A Levels in Britain or the SATs in the United States. To enter college a student must pass the Abitur. Without it a student would only receive an intermediary diploma for completing the ninth grade. In effect, the student would be blocked from getting a decent job or furthering his or her education.

In February, when Steinhaeuser was expelled from school for having forged a medical excuse, he lost his opportunity of ever taking the Abitur exam again. 'He desperately needed his high school diploma for status, but when that failed his world collapsed around him,' the weekly news magazine *Der Spiegel* wrote. 'It was a death sentence for the young man. It was a disgrace that he kept secret from everyone, even his own family. That's what led him to seek revenge on Friday with the executions and punishment.' Not coincidentally, Steinhaeuser launched his attack as his classmates were taking the math portion of the test.

After failing the Abitur exam for the first time, Robert joined a shooting club, which gave him access to the weapons he ultimately used in the attack. 'Everything points to the same conclusion – that he was sure he would fail again and was planning his revenge for when that time came,' Police Chief Grube said.

Authorities believe Steinhaeuser had been carefully preparing for the attack for months. He stockpiled around a thousand rounds of ammunition for his Glock 9 pistol. 'It is impossible to buy this amount of munitions even with a license,' the chief speculated. 'Steinhaeuser must have bought the cartridges time and time again off the black market.'

The youngster had, in total, four gun licenses: two for the guns he used in the rampage and two others for the ones he had at home. 'He seemed to have devoted a lot of time and energy to weapons,' said Rainer Gruge, the detective in charge of the investigation. 'He was a very good marksman.' He was a member in good standing of the German Shooting Federation and frequented two local rifle clubs where, in effect, he had been practicing his lethal marksmanship for over a year.

Eager to distance their activities from their most infamous member, Josef Ambacher, president of the German Shooting Federation, said: 'This was a case of an individual, someone who should not be connected with recreational shooting. What happened in Erfurt has nothing to do with marksmanship.'

I WANT TO BE FAMOUS

Those who knew Robert Steinhaeuser said he was shy, ordinary, a loner, unassuming, timid and lazy. He did not have a good relationship with his parents – but what teenager has? At school he had a reputation for being a problem student and had been disciplined repeatedly by his teachers. He had a problem with authority and truancy. But no one suspected the chubby prankster, nicknamed 'Steini', would turn into Germany's most savage rampage killer.

Isabell Hartung, a friend of his from school, described Steini as 'jolly', adding that he was the type of person who was always telling jokes and trying to be the center of attention. He once told her, 'One day, I want everyone to know my name and I want to be famous.' In retrospect, Isabell said, 'It's macabre but he seems to have made his dream come true.'

During a class field trip to Berlin two years before the attack, Steinhaeuser pointed his fingers gun-style at a teacher after he was chastised for smoking. 'He pretended to make a pistol out of his hand and was full of hatred as he took aim at the teacher,' said classmate Cassandra Mehlhorn. 'The teacher was extremely angry. Robert got a reprimand for that. He said he was just fooling around.'

Police Chief Grube said that Steinhaeuser, while still attending school, proposed to make a film with his classmates in which a man takes revenge on a gang for killing his girlfriend. The man kills each gangster execution style with a gunshot to the head. In a chilling parallel to the carnage he inflicted on his former school, the avenger ends the film by killing himself.

Searching Steinhaeuser's home, police found two more guns, 500 rounds of ammunition, violent comic books, videos containing 'dark, blood-dripping and violence-worshipping' images and a number of computer games with 'intensive weapons usage'. His favorite game, 'Counter-strike', is an award-wining first-person shooter game featuring terrorist and counter-terrorist units wearing masks and hunting down each other. In its official website, its makers hope 'you will be immersed in the frightening and intense world of Counter-Terrorism'. In his computer, they found articles about Harris and Klebold and the Columbine killings, which might be a little more indicative of what he had in mind.

Steinhaeuser lived in a tidy, middle-class apartment a block from the Gymnasium with his mother – a nurse – and his grandparents. His parents were separated, but his father would come over on weekends, and the whole family would have a barbecue in the garden. 'The Steinhaeusers were always friendly people,' said his neighbor Lisa Engelhardt. 'He [Robert] seemed very normal.'

In a signed letter published in local newspapers, Robert Steinhaeuser's parents and older brother apologized for the killings and said they were filled with grief and torment over the events. Horrified by the massacre perpetrated by their son and brother, they were at a loss to explain his pent-up 'hate and desperation' that led to the senseless rampage. 'Until this brutal, crazed act, we were an absolutely normal family and we knew a different Robert,' the letter said. 'We are infinitely sorry that our son and brother brought such terrible suffering upon the victims and their relatives, the people of Erfurt and Thuringia states, and all of Germany.'

Peter, his older brother, was quoted in the *Thueringer Allgemeine* newspaper saying that the family knew Robert had trouble in school and had joined a local gun club, but that they had no clue he had bought four weapons and had been expelled from school.

SCHOOL WARS

With the usual finger-pointing, pundits and politicians were quick to blame violent computer games, dark metal music, and horror movies for the carnage. Conservatives throughout Germany called for an across-the-line crackdown on offensive entertainment. Edmund Stoiber, the conservative challenger to Chancellor Gerhard Schroeder's Social Democrat party, accused the government of a 'scandalous' failure to 'take a tougher line against those who peddle these sorts of killer games'. Calling the shootings 'an alarm signal for our society', Stoiber said Schroeder was doing nothing to stem the rising tide of violence.

Calling the attack from the conservatives 'shameless and indecent', Interior Minister Otto Schily said, 'We now must also ask ourselves the deeper question of what actually is going on in our society when a young person causes such disaster in such a way.'

Investigators reported that the youngster's favorite band was Slipknot, a gore metal band from Iowa whose members all wear horror masks. First the UK's biggest-selling daily newspaper the *Sun* published a story stating that 'A song named "School Wars" by heavy metal band Slipknot may have prompted this massacre fiend to go on his rampage.' The article went on to quote a provocative line from the alleged song: 'Shoot your naughty teachers with a pump gun.'

Soon, the story gathered steam with several other European newspapers blaming Slipknot and their song 'School Wars' for the horrifying school killings. Viva and Viva Plus, Germany's biggest music television channels, announced they had pulled the Slipknot videos out of rotation. The UK's MTV followed suit. As lynch mobs gathered throughout Europe preparing to bring the masked musicians to justice, it became clear that Slipknot had never recorded a track called 'School Wars'.

In a statement issued on their website, Slipknot – blowing the credibility of the mainstream media covering the rampage

– responded to the apparent conspiracy against them by the European press:

> 'It is ludicrous to place the blame on our band or any other form of music. SLIPKNOT does not have a song called "School Wars", we have never written a song called "School Wars", and we certainly would never encourage people to kill others. We are a blanket of hope for our kids, not a scapegoat for attacks like this, and while we send our most sincere condolences to those affected by this, we will not take responsibility.'

A writer for the Metal Hammer website noted that Steinhaeuser also had a poster of Posh Spice in his bedroom, which prompts the question, why didn't the Spice Girls shoulder part of the blame?

THE 'LAWLESSNESS' OF GUN CONTROL

Like most European countries, Germany has tight gun-control laws. In Germany, there are about 10 million legal weapons among its population of 82 million. Mostly the weapons are kept for hunting, sport, or as collectibles. Germans, like other Europeans, do not have an obsessive relationship with their right to bear arms.

And, unlike the United States, there's no politically powerful gun lobby like the NRA that invariably puts guns before humans. Germany's tough gun-control laws require applicants to pass a rigorous test and put up with a lengthy waiting period before obtaining their weapon. 'In America, you can buy a gun. Here, it's not so easy,' said Romy Willart, a friend of Steinhaeuser's brother. 'But this shows you can just go to a club and learn to shoot, and one year later you can come back and do this.'

Ironically, while Steinhaeuser was stalking the corridors of Gutenberg shooting his former teachers in the head, the German lower house of parliament passed a law lowering the age at which children can use air guns from twelve from ten. But two hours after the attack, Germany's parliament jumped into action and immediately tightened the nation's weapons laws. The proposed new amendments called for licensing of all air guns, banning several types of knives, and forcing gun owners to store pistols in steel cabinets and bullets separately. Members of parliament said they would also tack on to the bill a provision to raise the minimum age of gun ownership from 18 to 21.

A week before the Erfurt massacre, and on the other side of the world, Michael Barnes, the president of the Brady Center to Prevent Gun Violence, gave testimony to a special US Senate subcommittee about the Bill H.R., which is designed to put the US gun industry above the law.

> 'The Bill is a misguided, unjust attempt to provide special legal protection for the gun industry at the expense of innocent Americans who have been harmed by the dangerous and irresponsible actions of firearms manufacturers and sellers. At the behest of the National Rifle Association and the gun industry, this bill would carve out special exemptions and protections for companies that make and sell deadly firearms in an irresponsible manner.'

The Bill, which would repeal any legislation that would force gun manufacturers to implement safety measures such as trigger locks or childproof guns, would also protect the same manufacturers from suits stemming from unintended deaths or injuries sustained by children or other innocent victims who might accidentally handle a weapon. 'It would immunize an irresponsible industry that is already grossly under-regulated. In short, this bill would be a perversion of the basic principles that underlie our justice system.'

In their standard take-no-prisoners attitude, loudmouth American gun pundits used the Erfurt tragedy to point out that the deadliest school rampage to date happened in a nation with strict gun-control laws, showing that 'the best defense is armed defense'. Sure, if every teacher at the Gymnasium was 'packing heat' perhaps someone would have stopped Steinhaeuser. But is that the type of society we want to live in? Perhaps the NRA and their lackeys should refrain from speaking when someone kills sixteen people with the very product they champion and worship.

'The expelled student-turned-gunman knew that his path would be virtually unobstructed,' wrote Tim Richmond for the gun-centric Objectivist Center. 'A society that recognized the individual's right to protect himself might have permitted a brave teacher or student the means of self-defense against the determined assassin.' The Objectivist Center, coincidentally, describes itself as a national not-for-profit think tank promoting the values of reason, individualism, freedom and achievement in American culture, which, in the real world, means gun-culture freaks.

Other NRA wannabes, like John K. Bates of the Conservative Truth, enjoyed a little Europe-bashing over the events, pointing out that 'anti-gun arguments are flawed'. With a final kick in the face to all the dead and wounded in Erfurt, Bates concluded his 12 May article with: 'One has to wonder how many of the faculty in Erfurt wish they would have had some outlawed guns on that tragic afternoon.'

PULLING A COLUMBINE

There have been many possible explanations given for the Erfurt shooting, ranging from his love of guns to his obsession with violent computer games to his thirst for revenge against the teachers who failed him, but none adequately explains the level of mayhem Steinhaeuser brought to his assault. The same could be said for the other school shootings featured in this book.

It seems that the level of violence in every new school attack is upping the magnitude of the one preceding it. Author Malcolm Gladwell, in his book *The Tipping Point*, examined how certain 'behavioral epidemics' follow mysterious 'adolescent imitative rules' in a way that may or may not make sense. Gladwell states that when trends reach a 'tipping point' they become epidemic and will follow their own rules. 'These are epidemics in isolation: They follow a mysterious, internal script that makes sense only in the closed world that teenagers inhabit.

'The post-Columbine outbreak of school shootings is . . . happening because Columbine happened, and because ritualized, dramatic, self-destructive behavior among teenagers – whether it involves suicide, smoking, taking a gun to school, or fainting after drinking a harmless can of Coke – has extraordinary contagious power.'

The author stated that he expects more kids to 'pull a Columbine' because teenagers are becoming increasingly 'isolated'. As a consequence, they have created their own world 'ruled by the logic of word of mouth, by the contagious messages that teens pass among themselves . . . Columbine is now the most prominent epidemic of isolation among teenagers. It will not be the last.'

RIPPLE EFFECT

Three days after the Erfurt massacre, in a perfect example of the tipping point, a seventeen-year-old student in the Bosnian city of Vlasenica, thirty miles northeast of Sarajevo, shot a teacher, wounded another and then committed suicide. Using his father's 7.65mm handgun, Dragoslav Petkovic shot and killed his history teacher, Stanimir Reljic, 53, outside his high school, then walked into a classroom where – in front of thirty students – he shot his fifty-year-old math teacher, Saveta Mojsilovic, wounding her in the neck. Seconds later, the eleventh grader put the gun to his head and splattered his brains against the blackboard.

The day before the shooting, while playing basketball, Petkovic told his best friend, seventeen-year-old Ognjen Markovic, that Reljic, the murdered teacher, disliked him and was going to fail him. Witnesses said Petkovic approached Reljic outside the school and asked him for another chance to improve his grades. When the teacher refused, he opened fire.

'According to the teachers of the school and other residents who knew him, the student who committed this murder was never perceived as a person who was capable of doing such a thing,' said Ostoja Dragutinovic, the mayor of Vlasenica. 'He was quiet and not such a bad student.' Dragomir Zugic, the school principal, described Petkovic as 'quiet and sensitive', and said the boy might have been influenced by the Erfurt shooting.

'I'm begging my mother to forgive me, and I'm thankful to her for everything she has given me. I'm thankful to my father for all the good advice and to my older brother for the help he always gave me,' the suicidal teen wrote in a letter he left behind in his room. In it, he asked for his belongings to be given to his six best friends. The letter concluded by saying, ominously: 'People learn from their mistakes.'

13. JAPAN'S TEEN TERROR WAVE

> 'This may seem extreme, but I fear that many young people today are mentally dysfunctional and unless measures are taken immediately, this country will be confronted with a serious situation this century.' – Toshiyuki Sawaguchi, from the Daily Yomiuri

A NATION IN AGONY

Though considered the safest industrialized nation in the world, Japan has endured an unprecedented rise in teenage crime and violence. Since 1997, when the severed head of an eleven-year-old boy was found outside the gates of a junior high school in Kobe, this once tranquil nation has been shocked into submission by a generation of teen sociopaths bent on murder and destruction

Statistics show that juvenile crime in Japan has hit a ten-year high. Murder rates have doubled. Weird teen crime sprees have occurred throughout the nation with unnerving frequency. Once seen as a Western phenomenon, teen violence has now become the tragic norm.

As in the West, the Japanese media have been gobbling up shocking accounts of teen mayhem with wall-to-wall sensationalist coverage as they point accusing fingers at the usual suspects – graphic video games, the Internet, violent movies and pornography. Nevertheless, Japan, as a nation, is hurting because of the wanton betrayal of tradition by its youth. The country itself is struggling through a period of introspection, agonizing in a solipsistic cycle of soul-searching analysis and diagnosis, trying to find the reasons behind its lost generation of disillusioned youths.

Presently, the minimum age at which an offender can be tried as an adult in Japan is twenty, regardless of the offense. A minor accused of committing a crime is initially sent to a family court, which decides whether to send him or her to reform school or to face criminal proceedings. If the youngster is found guilty he or she is sent to a correctional facility. No matter what their crime, whether it's murder or petty theft, the juvenile has to be released on his or her twentieth birthday. No wonder people say that in Japan a teenager can get away with everything, even murder.

The mass media have defined the phenomenon of normal kids who suddenly lose their temper and commit serious crimes as *kireru*. Experts and pundits have been unable to explain the causes behind these sudden bursts of inexplicable anger. In the United States it has been called, among other things, Intermittent Explosive Disorder. In the United States, when these kids snap, they bring in as much firepower as possible. In Japan the weapon of choice among its rampaging teens has been the butterfly knife.

In 1997 a survey by a municipal education institute showed that more than a third of elementary and junior high students believed 'they should never have been born'. Needless to say, there's a wave of juvenile depression sweeping the nation. This mental anguish, coupled with the economic depression of the late 90s, is one of the reasons behind the rise of juvenile crime.

According to Iwao Sumiko of Keio University, the rise in crime is a consequence of lower birth rates. Youngsters grow up with few or no siblings, creating a generation of selfish individuals that has never known what it is to compromise. 'Parents should rethink their approach to discipline beginning when their children are toddlers,' Sumiko wrote in a 1998 article in the *Japan Echo*. 'Measures should be put in place to increase the number of births.'

Sumiko stated that the rise of juvenile crime comes from the excessive value placed on individuality and personal freedom in the giddy 90s. He and others have called for a return to traditional values, with the reduction of individual freedoms for the sake of the common good. But once the Pandora's box of individuality is opened, there's no way to close it again.

Japan's high-pressure school system and the societal pressures stemming from it have also been called to task. Its intense after-school preparatory programs, endless study hours and rigorous testing are allowing the children little or no time for family life. With parents and children working so hard, individual interaction has become non-existent. Such constant pressure undoubtedly leads to heavy stress and eventual loss of interest in such a rigorous way of life.

'There is so much pressure,' said Yasuhiro Watanabe of the Police Juvenile Crime Division, 'and the value system is very confusing for them. They don't see anything good about working hard, getting to university and going to "good" enterprises. They don't see much hope in their future.'

Over the past years, an entire generation has seemingly forgotten the traditions of the past and has gone insane, committing murders, stranglings, rapes, decapitations and random acts of senseless violence. Former FBI profiler and serial killer expert Robert Ressler said that since 1997, there has been a wave of 'weird crimes' in Japan. Starting with the Kobe decapitation murder and ending with the bloody knife attack on a elementary school in Osaka, crime in Japan is starting to read like the evening news in Los Angeles or Miami.

Unlike in the 1950s, the new wave of perpetrators in Japan are not poor, orphaned or abused. Instead, they are the spoiled children of the middle class. Ninety per cent of the young lawbreakers come from well-to-do, two-parent homes. And it's no longer limited to the major urban areas. Teen crime is spreading throughout the country. The intensity of the crimes has also changed. Before, there were a few natural 'harmless' killers walking the streets, now it seems there's a whole generation of potential Dylan Klebolds and Rod Ferrells.

THE KOBE SCHOOL KILLER

'A demon is in my heart, crying out at aggression from outside, stirring fear. It is as though he is controlling me, like a skilled puppeteer controls his puppet by pulling strings as the music plays.' – The Kobe School Killer

On 27 May 1997, moments before students started arriving at the Tomogaoka Junior High School, a janitor made a grisly discovery: the decapitated head of an eleven-year-old retarded boy stuck on the school gate. Stuffed in his mouth, police found a note written in red ink and signed with a combination of six Japanese characters which when read together mean *Seito Sakakibara* (Apostle Sake Devil Rose). Jun Hase, the victim, had been missing for three days. Later that day the boy's headless body was found under a house in the woods near the school. Hase's killing was the second in that area in less than two months.

In the note the killer warned: 'This is the beginning of the game . . . You police guys stop me if you can . . . I desperately want to see people die, it is a thrill for me to commit murder. A bloody judgment is needed for my years of great bitterness.' It ended with words in English: 'shooll [sic] kill' and was signed by the mysterious 'Apostle Sake Devil Rose'.

On 16 March an elementary schoolgirl had been bludgeoned to death by an unidentified assailant. About an hour later, a second girl was attacked with a hammer and knife and seriously wounded. Previously, two more elementary school girls were assaulted with a hammer; one of the two was injured, though not seriously.

In the note he left behind, Hase's killer used a cross-like symbol reminiscent of the one used by San Francisco's infamous 'Zodiac' killer. Similar crosses were found painted on walls near the junior high where the head was found. Two mutilated cats were also found outside the school's main gate days before little Jun Hase vanished. Police sources said that mutilated cat carcasses were also found near the two other crime scenes.

A week after the terrifying discovery outside Tomogaoka Junior High, the killer sent a letter to the local daily newspaper, the *Kobe Shimbun*, claiming responsibility for the Hase murder and threatening to kill three people a week. 'I am putting my life at stake for the sake of this game,' said the rambling 1,400-word document, 'If I'm caught, I'll probably be hanged . . . police should be angrier and more tenacious in pursuing me ... It's only when I kill that I am liberated from the constant hatred that I suffer and that I am able to attain peace. It is only when I give pain to people that I can ease my own pain.' In broad strokes the letter lashed out at, among other things, the police and Japan's 'compulsory education which formed me, an invisible person'.

Like the note found in Hase's mouth, the three-page letter was written with a red ballpoint pen. It was sent in a brown envelope postmarked 3 June and signed with the now familiar six-character name *Seito Sakakibara* (Apostle Sake Devil Rose). The rambling note taunted police and the media, threatening to kill three people a week unless TV talk-show hosts pronounced his 'name' – Seito Sakakibara – correctly. 'From now on, if you misread my name or spoil my mood I will kill three dirty vegetables a week ... If you think I can only kill children you are greatly mistaken.'

In a desperate search for leads, police said they were investigating whether horror movies inspired the gruesome killing of Jun Hase. Detectives asked video stores in the area of the murder for lists of customers who rented specific horror films with mutilation scenes similar to the gruesome killing. 'We have narrowed it down to about ten horror movies that may have inspired the culprit,' a police spokesman told reporters. Taking it a step further, Japanese authorities decided to cancel the release of Wes Craven's immensely popular movie *Scream*, because it was deemed too similar to circumstances surrounding the beheading of the Kobe youngster.

Leaving no stone unturned, the tabloid newspaper *Tokyo Sports* reported that authorities were also investigating links between the killing and a local rock band called 'Killer and Rose'. One of their albums, *Devil Rose*, released several years earlier (and, strangely, considered a secret soundtrack for *The Wizard of Oz*), has a song called 'Rotten Vegetables', which sounds like the 'dirty vegetables' reference in the killer's letter to the press.

Investigators even pinpointed the maker of the word processor believed used by the 'School Killer' to write the message he sent to the *Kobe Shimbun* newspaper. Although the message was handwritten, it seemed that the author based it on one originally typed with a word processor. Police studied certain kanji characters in the message and discovered that only word processors manufactured by Sharp Corporation can convert the characters *kyo* (emptiness) and *ra* for *bara* (rose) into the particular types of kanji characters used by the killer.

THE BAD SEED

On 28 June all of Japan was shocked to learn that an ordinary fourteen-year-old boy was the feared School Killer. The youngster confessed to beheading his eleven-year-old neighbor because he hated his school. The killer, who under Japanese law cannot be identified because of his age, also confessed to the hammer and knife attacks of four elementary school girls in February and March. One girl, ten-year-old Ayaka Yamashita, died a week after being brained by the youngster.

The fourteen-year-old killer – who turned fifteen two weeks after his arrest – had recently stopped attending school and was undergoing psychiatric treatment. A true bad seed, the boy was apparently set on a violent path from the get go. He began carrying cutting weapons while still in elementary school. 'I can ease my irritation when I'm holding a survival knife or spinning scissors like a pistol.' At age twelve he exhibited extreme cruelty to animals, lining up a row of frogs in a street and riding over them with his bicycle. He was also fond of mutilating cats and decapitating pigeons.

The experimental type, on 16 March – after attacking two girls with a hammer – he wrote in his diary: 'I carried out sacred experiments today to confirm how fragile human beings are ... I brought the hammer down, when the girl turned to face me. I think I hit her a few times but I was too excited to remember.' On 23 March he noted: 'This morning my mom told me, "Poor girl. The girl attacked seems to have died." There is no sign of my being caught ... I thank you, God Bamoidooki, for this ... Please continue to protect me.'

The diaries, confiscated by police shortly after the arrest, allegedly detailed the two murders and multiple assaults. They also describe his Dahmer-like obsession with mutilating cats and other small animals. In the bits and pieces leaked to the press, the killer wrote about his crimes as 'holy experiments' done to appease the mysterious Bamoidooki. The imaginary deity, as described in his diary, was a floating head of Buddha with a swastika-like symbol.

In April, when he was still in school, he wrote an essay entitled 'My Thirteen-Year Imprisonment.' In the narrative, he claimed he was possessed by an evil spirit that forced him into the dark side. 'In the middle of life's journey, I have strayed from the straight path,' he wrote. 'I am lost in a dark forest.' Towards the end of the essay he quoted Friedrich Nietzsche:

'Whoever fights monsters must see to it that in the process he does not become a monster. And he who looks into the abyss must realize that the abyss also looks into him.' – Thus Spake Zarathustra

The quote might indicate that, instead of reading Nietzsche, the young killer was reading the classic serial killer study *Whoever Fights Monsters* by famed FBI profiler Robert Ressler. His friends and classmates told the Japanese press that the killer was obsessed with horror movies, the occult and serial killers.

Not surprisingly, one of his teachers strongly suspected the youngster after the March attacks on the two girls. It is unclear why he didn't tell anyone. Jun Hase's father said he held the school and the boy's parents responsible for the death of his son. 'The school and police should have dealt with this boy,' Hase's father was quoted as saying. 'His killing and assaults would not have happened if they did the right thing.'

After killing Jun, the boy kept his head in his room for several days and played with it as if it were a toy. The killer told police the head 'spoke' to him. He also drank Jun's blood. When the head started stinking up his room, he left it pinned to the school gates. When the teenager was arrested, Robert Ressler, who's profiled everyone from Ed Kemper to Sacramento's vampire killer Richard Chase, said he wouldn't consider releasing the boy until he turned fifty.

When police searched the youngster's room they found an extensive collection of violent comic books, lots of pornography and twelve gore films. In a Western-style backlash, Japanese Construction Minister Shizuka Kamei blamed the entertainment industry and called for the regulation of violent and pornographic videos: 'Movies lacking any literary or educational merit made for just showing cruel scenes ... Adults should be blamed for this.'

Under Japanese law, fourteen-years-old killers cannot be sent to jail. Juveniles can be held responsible for a crime, but they must be at least sixteen to be sentenced as criminals. The unnamed killer, at worst, could be sent to a reformatory school.

On 26 July, during a closed-door hearing at a family court in Kobe, the teenager admitted to murdering and decapitating Jun Hase and to the hammer murder of Ayaka Yamashita. Three months later, the decapitating teen was convicted of two murders and three assaults, and was sentenced to an indefinite detention at the Kanto Juvenile Medical Training School in suburban Tokyo. In the medical reformatory, the youth received psychiatric treatment and counseling under an initial rehabilitation plan that called for a total of five and a half years of treatment. In 2000, after showing marked psychological improvement, the youth was transferred to a normal reformatory where he's expected to stay until his twentieth birthday.

Giving this story an even more surreal twist, the killer requested permission to graduate from the Tomogaoka Junior High School with his class despite having been expelled for leaving the head of a youngster pinned to the gate. Should the school accept the request, the killer's name and picture will appear in the yearbook along with his classmates. The *Yomiuri Shimbun* newspaper quoted Yoshihiro Yamaguchi, a Kobe Municipal Board of Education official, saying that the boy has been doing well in classes at the reformatory and should be allowed to graduate.

THE YEAR OF THE BUTTERFLY KNIFE

The year 1998 saw the highest number of youth crimes in Japan since 1975. Though teenagers in Japan comprise only 9 per cent of the population, they accounted for 45 per cent of violent crimes. Butterfly knives have become a cool accessory in Japanese classrooms, resulting in an alarming rise in the number of knife attacks. Police noted that knife sales have taken off since Takuya Kimura, Japan's answer to Leonardo DiCaprio, used a butterfly knife in the wildly popular television series *Gift*.

The following chronology is merely a sample of the crime wave besetting this once crime-free nation. Though this list of crimes could be read as a relatively calm weekend in Los Angeles, in Japan this year-long spree was unprecedented:

18 JANUARY

A thirteen-year-old boy in the Tochigi Prefecture was arrested for stabbing to death his junior high school English teacher. The boy attacked the 26-year-old teacher with a butterfly knife after she scolded him for being late to class. The attack occurred at the Kuroiso Kita Junior High School, 93 miles north of Tokyo.

30 JANUARY

A sixteen-year-old high school boy was arrested after attacking and seriously injuring a female classmate with a kitchen knife. The boy allegedly attacked his classmate because she and her friend were blocking his way to class. After they ignored his request to get out of the way, he snapped and lunged at the girl with the knife, injuring her on the head.

2 FEBRUARY

A fifteen-year-old punk was arrested for attacking a police officer and trying to take his gun. The teenager attempted to stab 54-year-old Yoshinari Yasuda in the chest. Fortunately the officer was wearing a bullet-proof Kevlar vest which stopped the blade from injuring him. After being arrested the impulsive youngster said he 'wanted to try shooting a gun – really, really bad'.

9 MARCH
Two fourteen-year-old twin brothers stabbed to death a 58-year-old woman to 'cause a commotion' so they 'wouldn't have to go to school'.

10 MARCH
A thirteen-year-old boy stabbed a classmate from behind at a junior high school in revenge for a practical joke. The classmate was injured in the head and hand.

17 MARCH
Two junior high school girls attacked a 69-year-old man who they said 'would not return several thousand yen' they had loaned him.

15 APRIL
A 41-year-old man was stabbed to death by his son and a friend.

14 MAY
A sixteen-year-old boy attacked a 37-year-old housewife with an ice pick in a shopping mall, gravely injuring her.

10 JUNE
A fifteen-year-old student at the National Defense Medical College took a class hostage for five hours. The teenager, armed with a knife, pipe bombs and tear gas, was arrested after his hostages managed to escape. In custody, the boy said he did it to bring attention to his conviction that the Japanese Constitution should be shredded.

16 JUNE

Police arrested a sixteen-year-old girl and her fifteen-year-old brother for killing their grandfather. The youngsters admitted to killing their 69-year-old grandfather because he had repeatedly reprimanded them and had tried to kick their friends out of the house an hour before the murder.

24 AUGUST

Two sixteen-year-old boys clubbed to death a fourteen-year-old junior high school student.

2 OCTOBER

A nineteen-year-old boy killed a six-year-old elementary school student by throwing him out a sixth-floor apartment window.

THE BUS HIJACKER

Teen madness in Japan reached new heights in the year 2000 with several highly publicized incidents involving bus hijackings, baseball-bat rampages, matricide and homemade bomb attacks. The new wave of violence culminated with a frightening knife assault on an Osaka elementary school that left eight youngsters dead.

On 3 May 2000, a seventeen-year-old boy armed with a kitchen knife hijacked a bus and stabbed three women in their necks. The incident, played out live in front of millions on national TV, ended when riot police stormed the bus and arrested the hijacker. Nine passengers and the driver were unharmed. Police said the busjacker released the three women he stabbed earlier in the chase. One 69-year-old victim later died in the hospital.

The drama unfolded in the early afternoon in the south-western island of Kyushu where the bus, carrying about twenty passengers, left the city of Saga on a one-hour trip to Fukuoka. The youth commandeered the vehicle near the town of Dazaifu, said Yamaguchi Prefecture police spokesman Junichi Takezaki. News of the busjacking emerged only when a female passenger was allowed off the bus to go to the bathroom. Instead, she called authorities.

Police chased the forty-seater bus along the Sanyo Expressway, in Yamaguchi Prefecture, as it headed towards Hiroshima. The chase was broadcast live, like daily car chases in Los Angeles, as it was filmed from the sky by Japanese TV helicopters. Throughout the chase, the teenager kept his twelve-inch kitchen knife blade on the driver's throat. At one point two passengers – a woman and a man – leaped out of the moving bus and escaped.

In custody, the terror teen said he did it because he 'wanted to know what it was like to kill someone'. He added that he wanted to get back at his parents and society as a whole. Shockingly, at the time of the attack, the youngster was under psychiatric care. His mother had been fully aware of her son's violent nature, which she blamed on many years of bullying at school, but was unable to keep him hospitalized.

When he was at junior high school, school bullies forced him to jump off a sixteen-foot ledge, injuring his back and spending two months in hospital. The mother said she complained to the school, but got no response. Her son lost faith in the school system and dropped out shortly after beginning high school. His temper and violent outbursts at home soon escalated from chopping his younger sister's school uniform into pieces to torturing and killing his pets.

At a loss about what to do, his parents consulted several psychiatrists and educational experts. The boy, however, refused to see a doctor. Two months before the busjacking, the mother discovered several knives, hammers, and a stun gun in his room. She also found a note saying: 'There is someone else inside of me, who orders me to kill others' and 'I will hole up in a school building and kill people.' Alarmed, she called police to help her hospitalize the boy. At first, authorities refused to help, but after she contacted a psychiatrist she had heard on a radio talk show, the police helped her intern her son.

After 51 days of hospitalization, the boy was allowed an overnight stay at home. The doctors, thinking the youngster was improving, allowed him several more nights' visits until the day of the busjacking. After the crime, one of the psychiatrists treating him said they had difficulty identifying his condition because 'It is not a matter of personal pathology. Rather, he is the product of his living environment. There will be further cases like his unless we establish a new social system that goes beyond psychiatry.'

BASEBALL BATS & NAIL BOMBS

About a month after the busjacking, another shocking crime rocked the very foundation of Japanese society. In a horrifying act of matricide, a seventeen-year-old boy – described as 'timid' by his teachers – beat his 42-year-old mother to death with a baseball bat. Apparently, before the attack, his friends made fun of his haircut during baseball practice. Furious, he went back home and assaulted his mother after she refused to give him money for a new haircut. Following the assault the alienated youngster fled his hometown of Osafunecho and was arrested 700 miles away. In custody he told police that he had killed his mother because she would have disapproved of his fight with his schoolmates.

On 5 December, a seventeen-year-old youth was arrested for a nail-bomb attack on a video shop in the Kabukicho entertainment district of Shinjuku Ward in Tokyo. In the shocking attack, the high school bomber from the Tochigi Prefecture rolled a handmade nail bomb into a video store, burning the walls and ceiling and blowing out the windows. Fortunately, no one was injured. Fifteen minutes later, the suspect was arrested with 39 shotgun shells in his pocket – which he had stolen from his grandfather – and another softball-sized nail bomb.

'I wanted to destroy people,' he told investigators at the Shinjuku Police Station. The youth was described by school officials as one of the top students of his class. Classmates said he was quiet and had few friends. And, obviously, was obsessed with bombs. 'I lit the bomb and rolled it into the shop,' said the nail-bomber. 'I didn't care where it exploded.' The youngster made the bomb using a metal mug filled with gunpowder from fireworks and nails and wrapped everything with plastic tape. He also taped a fuse on the side to detonate it.

One of the most publicized cases of out of control teenagers was a baseball-bat rampage attack through Tokyo. Less than two weeks after the nail-bomb attack, a seventeen-year-old boy injured eight strangers with a baseball bat in a Tokyo subway station and the streets above. After having a fight with his father, the out-of-control teenager headed to the Tokyo subway to extract revenge.

The high school student first attacked a 32-year-old man in a public toilet at the Shibuya railway station. Then he moved to the streets where he assaulted seven other people. A 68-year-old housewife was severely wounded in the head, while the other victims suffered minor injuries. The Jiji Press news agency quoted the boy saying: 'As I had a quarrel with my father, I wanted to put him to shame. Anyone would have been fine.'

The bat attack occurred as youngsters flocked to see *Battle Royale*, a controversial and violent film about juvenile crime. The film, directed by the legendary Kinji Fukasaku of *Tora! Tora! Tora!* fame, had generated national controversy over its indictment of Japan's competitive education system and its depiction of teen mayhem. The film chronicles a class of school children who are supposed to kill each other until one remains alive. Imagine *Lord of the Flies* meets *Survivor*. While it was almost banned by the government, it naturally became a massive domestic hit.

'Teenage violence has become a major social problem in Japan in recent years, but the phenomenon is confusing to adults,' said the famed director in an interview with the *Guardian*. 'In the past there was still violence but there were always reasons behind it, like poverty. These days it is more difficult to understand, and so they don't know what to do about it.'

THE JAPANESE COLUMBINE

'There is no doubt that I entered Ikeda Elementary School and stabbed the children. I would like to atone for my deeds with my life.' – Mamoru Takuma

On 8 June 2001 Mamoru Takuma burst into an elementary school in Osaka, Japan, and slashed eight children to death with a kitchen knife. Takuma, 37, wounded eighteen other children and three adults before being subdued by the Ikeda Elementary School vice principal and a teacher. The attack, dubbed 'the Japanese Columbine', sent chills down the spine of every Japanese parent.

The rampager was arrested at the scene, but was taken to a hospital with self-inflicted knife wounds. The victims – six girls and two boys – were first- and second-grade students, ranging in age from six to eight. Two children died at the scene, six died at the hospital after the attack.

Police said the suspect, who had a long history of mental illness and was taking anti-depressants, had previously been hospitalized three times. Two years before the attack, Takuma had worked as a janitor at a nearby elementary school but was fired for spiking four teachers' tea with tranquilizers. He was arrested at the time but was never prosecuted because he was diagnosed as a schizophrenic and was sent to a mental hospital. Shortly afterwards, he was released.

The bloodthirsty killer told police he had taken ten times his daily dose of an unspecified anti-depressant before heading out to the school. He allegedly said he was 'sick of everything' and 'wanted to be caught and executed'.

The stabbings occurred after classes began at the elementary school. Takuma climbed into a first-grade classroom during the morning recess and began slashing children in the back of the room. Then he moved into a hallway and to another classroom. Within minutes of the attack, a cashier at a nearby grocery store said a group of terrified, bloodied children ran into the store. 'I saw one of them, a boy, with blood all over his body,' said Ikiyo Iriye, 23. 'He had been stabbed in the back.'

In court, prosecutors said Takuma set out to kill anyone to vent his anger at his former wife and his father who had disowned him. Takuma himself blamed the attack on his ex-wife: 'I would not have had to go through all that if I had never known her in the first place.' Before the attack, he considered committing suicide, but decided that it would only make his ex-wife and other people happy. He also thought about mowing people down with a dump truck, but decided it was too complicated and a school knife attack would be easier.

The savagery of the crime stunned Japan, making everyone feel uncertain at the future. Such school slayings are, as seen in this book, not uncommon in the United States. But a crime of this savagery has never been seen in Japan. Though not a teen killer per se, Takuma's school rampage stands as the apotheosis of everything that's gone wrong in Japanese society.

The absence of one clear answer to the rise of teen crime does not bode well for the future. Youth in Japan feel isolated and deadened by the pressures of modern life and by their alienation from their parents' world of tradition. Perhaps the rise in crime is a perverse way for a generation to feel alive. But the cherished safety of Japan has now become a distant memory from the recent past.

14. THE COLOMBIAN SICARIOS

'The price of a crime varies according to the fluctuations of supply and demand; in September of 1999, a human life in Medellín is worth $2,400.' – Mario Vargas Llosa

'No Dumping Corpses' – street sign in Medellín

While affluent white America reels in shock when its young people become involved in violence and murder, in the streets of Medellín – the heart and soul of the Colombian drug trade – death is more than routine. Children indifferently step over corpses on their way to school and everyone knows someone that has killed or been killed. Born out of this subculture of poverty, death and violence are the Sicarios, teenage assassins recruited from Medellín's shanty towns to do the drug cartels' dirty work.

Police claim that there are as many as 2,000 of these pubescent killers roaming the streets of Medellín. Independent sources say that between 5,000 and 7,000 young people in the city have committed at least one murder for money. Reports indicate that some of these teen assassins have been hired for contract killings in Europe and other Latin American nations.

The Sicarios were an invention of the godfather of cocaine trafficking, Pablo Escobar. Don Pablo, as he was known, was the first person to recruit gangs of young assassins to work for his drug cartel. Though he made millions trafficking cocaine, Escobar became the patron saint of the poor and disenfranchised by building housing projects and soccer stadiums in Medellín's poorest slums and employing legions of youngsters as foot soldiers in his drug war. When Escobar died, the violent culture that grew out of his empire did not. Instead it spread its wings throughout Colombia giving the deadly teenage gangs of Sicarios money, power and respect.

BULLETS AND HOLY WATER

Their motto is to 'live fast and die young' and they abide by it. They come with a folklore of bullets boiled in holy water and a mythology paralleling that of the American western outlaw. They are the Sicarios – the weapon of choice of the Colombian narco-lords. Though only teenagers, they are heroes to many; objects of admiration, with a patron saint to their own special craft – assassination.

'La Virgen de los Sicarios' sits in the main square of Sabaneta in the mountains surrounding Medellín. The Catholic icon's tunic is red, her cape blue. In the holy mother's arms rests a crowned baby Jesus. She is the one they pray to before launching their next contract hit.

The virgin is revered in the hope is that she will watch over the teenage Sicarios on their deadly missions of murder and revenge. Whether she actually helps the teenagers hit their target is a question of faith, but the visibility of these teenage assassins in Colombian society at large is significant. Mario Vargas Llosa, the noted Peruvian novelist and Latin American observer, said the Sicarios are an emblem of 'an unspeakable violence, highlighted by misery, unemployment, desperation, drugs, and corruption without end'.

The Sicario culture is an invention of the godfather of cocaine trafficking, Pablo Escobar. Since their first appearance in the front lines of the drug wars the Sicario culture has had a life of its own. The recruitment of child and teen killers has spread to the worlds of political assassination, family feuds, random kidnapping and other criminal enterprises needing the willing hands of a ruthless killer. These battered kids – without conscience, without hope – know only how to live and die by the gun. And if they make it to 21, they retire as old souls having dealt with death for as long as they could hold a gun.

THE ATROCITY EXHIBITION

Sicarios, in the historically fickle Colombian political landscape, have also proven useful scapegoats. They have been tied to everything from right-wing paramilitary squads to leftist guerrillas, government security agencies and any of the other fractious warring parties leading the beleaguered country down a path straight into hell.

In 1983, an experienced sixteen-year-old youngster pulled out a sub-machine gun and let it loose on Colombia's Minister of Justice. In 1990, an adolescent assailant ended the presidential aspirations of Carlos Pizzaro Leon Gomez of the M-19 party with the assistance of an Uzi. Leon Gomez was a former leftist-guerrilla who had renounced violence for a place at the electoral table. Violence, it seemed, had not renounced him.

In the most infamous case of Sicario violence, Andres 'El Bueno' Escobar, a star on the Colombian national soccer team, was murdered in 1994 shortly after having scored an accidental own goal that eliminated the Colombians from the World Cup tournament. The horrifying tale of senseless murder traveled the globe as a shocking and extreme example of the violence that had engulfed and still engulfs the Andean nation.

Sicarios were again to blame when the Catholic Archbishop of Cali was assassinated in March 2002. In an absurdist twist of the blame game, Orlando Marīn Pellicer wrote in the Cuban counter-revolutionary magazine *Siglo XXI* that 'It's a secret to no one that thousands of bosses and delinquents in the pay of narco-guerrilla cadres have been trained and indoctrinated by the worldwide subversion apparatus directed by Fidel Castro with the money of the Cuban people.'

Pellicer, blinded by his hatred of Castro and oblivious to rampant violence sweeping the streets of Colombia, unwittingly alluded to the fact that Sicario culture, following the cocaine trade routes, was being exported throughout the world. Perhaps some day these teenage assassins could become Colombia's second leading export.

HAVE GUN WILL TRAVEL

Linguistically and physically, the term 'Sicario' has already permeated the Spanish language and Latin American culture. Sicarios are blamed for killings in the Nicaraguan press. And, for what it's worth, the Venezuelan Defense Minister, Jose Vicente Rangel, claimed to possess intelligence linking a certain gang of Sicarios to a plan to assassinate President Hugo Chavez. Buoyed by a common language, low overheads, and some legal protection as minors, the long shadow of the Sicario has been felt as far as Spain.

There, in 2001, Governance Minister Francisco Javier Ansettegui informed the press that a 'group of teenage hit-men' had arrived in Spain with a plan to square accounts in a group of rogue drug dealers. At the time of the minister's announcement, seven men had been killed by the suspected Sicarios in two separate occurrences and the minister had asked Colombian authorities to apply the most stringent controls on the emigration of Colombians with criminal records.

The long shadow of the Sicario is but the edge of a larger shadow left by Colombian cocaine king Pablo Escobar, who was murdered by security forces in December 1993. 'Los Sicarios' were a primary expression of his reign as both international thug and benefactor to the poor in his hometown district of Antioquia, in the blood-soaked city of Medellín. Their continued existence not only stands as evidence of Escobar's institutional clout in the 1980s and 1990s, but also secures his place in the Violence Innovation Hall of Fame.

Escobar, who is also credited with the invention of crack cocaine in the early 80s, raised the employment of Sicarios to both a terrible art form and an industry. With time their use permeated downward and upward as both the political elite and neighborhood gangs have enjoyed their deadly services. 'Especially among the young, the yearning to have things – a motorcycle, imported basketball shoes, a gold chain – is tantalized by the proliferation of sumptuous goods spawned by the drug trade,' observed a Human Rights Watch/Americas study on Sicarios in Medellín.

Escobar's Medellín cartel cultivated a network of business fronts – real estate offices and car dealerships – from which dead-end youths were seduced with money and the cool stuff they desired into joining the region's most equal opportunity employer – the cocaine industry.

THE TRADE OF INNOCENTS

One does not simply become a Sicario – one has to earn the privilege. Most begin as children with the title of *chichipato*, committing petty crimes and running errands for neighborhood gangs. Surviving this apprenticeship means one is ready for the man's job of Sicario, which means one has to be ready to die to be an effective killing machine. It is mostly young teenagers who opt for the Sicario life because of their willingness to kill and their inability to grasp the finality of death. For them, taking someone's life or losing your own is like a game of chance. To become a Sicario, luck and fearlessness are tools of the trade. It's what keeps you alive in drug wars. Killing is the only way to stay in the game. Only a few make it to retirement at 21.

Colombia's Department of Criminological Studies and Identification, DECYPOL, estimated that 14 per cent of the 35,000 murders that have taken place in Colombia between 1986 and 1993 were of children. 'Here, grandparents bury their grandchildren,' a human rights activist in Colombia told Human Rights Watch.

The point is, promotion to full Sicario status in most countries would not be cause for celebration but, in a subculture where such behavior finds admiration from the neighborhood folk, healthy financial backing, even cultural status, things are different. Mothers, while disapproving of their sons' choice to live by the gun, are grateful for the financial rewards that come with their Sicario status, and in many cases stand by them until the bloody end.

'To become a Sicario you have to overcome certain challenges,' wrote Vargas Llosa. 'It's like being a knight in the Middle Ages.' Eventually the chichipato's cold blood is tested when they're asked to kill someone close to them, or some poor innocent waiting on a street corner. Devoid of any socialization, any respect for themselves or others, they comply in exchange for security, luxury, and validation of themselves as men in a macho society. Sometimes their reward is just a color TV, a Gameboy console or a pair of Nikes.

Having met the challenge of the first kill, the Sicario is handed the tools of his trade: a motorcycle, a mask and a .38. In fact, the classic Sicario hit is executed with two youths on the motorcycle – one drives and the other shoots. Before setting out, the kids get blasted smoking pot and basuco (a smokable form of cocaine paste), and/or snorting lines of cocaine and dropping 'rochitas', a powerful narcotic pharmaceutical from the good people at Roche Laboratories. With their heads in the right place and feeling all tingly, the young assassins are ready for the blessing that will assure them that their job is well done.

Then the boys ask the 'Virgin of the Assassins' to bless three scapulars they wear on their bodies during the hit: one on the wrist to steady the pulse; one on the heart for protection; and another on the ankle. The ankle detail, Vargas Llosa reports, has a twofold purpose: 'To escape in time, and so the motorcycle's chain doesn't hurt them. When shooting from a cycle on the run, the Sicario keeps his balance by pressing his lower legs against the engine – like a rider in the stirrups of their mount – and they are injured with frequency.'

And the fun doesn't stop after a hard day's carnage. There are legendary stories of Sicario gangs entering a local discotheque after cashing in from a particularly successful hit, ordering the management to close the place down, and partying until dawn before their horrified hostages. All this rather unhealthy social activity is made permissible by Colombia's many years of descent into perpetual violence and disorder and the rise of its virulent cocaine industry.

THE POLITICS OF PAIN
Since gaining its independence from Spain in 1810, Colombia has been locked in a recurrent civil war between Conservative and Liberal parties and the ancillary classes that congealed to them in the name of common interest. The incessant, almost dreamlike quality of this endless cycle of violence is captured in Nobel Prize-winning Colombian author Gabriel Garcia Marquez's novel *One Hundred Years of Solitude*.

Uprooting the rural populace, the conflicts precipitated a massive influx of peasant farmers to the urban areas of the country. In a pattern repeated throughout Latin America, the displaced peasants constructed haphazard shanty towns on the hillsides outside cities like Bogotá and Medellín. In Brazil these breeding grounds for exploitation, violence and murder are known as *favelas*. In Colombia, they have been dubbed *las comunas*. These volatile and dangerous neighborhoods, raked by poverty, disease and despair, are considered by some to be the most dangerous spots in the planet. It's not surprising that, in the comunas surrounding Medellín, there are more deaths per square mile than in many war-torn nations.

Bred in a corroding environment of overworked mothers, absent fathers, dissolving family units, abject poverty, and open sewers, it is not surprising that many of these children grow up to be teen assassins. 'Once in a displacement camp or shanty town, the external force on a displaced family can be tremendous,' stated the study *Colombia: No Safe Haven*, financed by the Canadian government and written by researchers Jimmy Briggs, Frank Smyth, Laura Barnitz, and Rachel Stohl.

'In single-parent homes, children and adolescents are often left alone for long periods of time,' the study noted. 'Approximately 20 per cent of Colombian children between the ages of 6 and 11 are not in school and, according to UNICEF, over 75 per cent of displaced youths who previously attended school do not go back after leaving their original homes.'

Unable to form a reliable estimate of how many small arms circulate in Colombian society, researchers cited their 'widespread availability and use'.

More specifically, the weapons of choice in Colombian crime subculture are the lethally effective Galil automatic (the standard issue in the Colombian army), the Russian-made AK-47, and the US-made M-16.

In fact, the study states that small automatic weapons are devastating the lives of children in Colombia. The raging conflict in what is the longest-running democracy in Latin America has placed adolescents on both ends of the weapons, both as perpetrators and victims of violence. In the year 2000, according to the Colombian Defense Ministry, over 200 children were murdered in Colombia. UNICEF said another 460 had been killed in the four years prior.

Though Colombia has been at war since it gained independence, the current situation, which is known as *La Violencia* (The Violence), started in 1948 with the murder of the then populist presidential candidate Jorge Eliecer Gaitán, and has claimed over 200,000 lives. In 1964 the conflict took a new turn with the emergence of the Revolutionary Armed Forces of Colombia (FARC) and the National Liberation Army (ELN), two rebel armies with ties to Moscow and Havana. To confront this wave of Marxist guerrillas, rich cattle ranchers organized rightist paramilitary groups that allied themselves to the armed forces.

Since the 1980s the entire conflict mushroomed as drug armies started factoring into the conflict. With the vast financial resources of the drug lords, all factions have become better armed and more powerful. Today, nearly forty years later, the violence rages on as the latest round of peace talks have collapsed and Ernesto Samper, Colombia's new president, has launched an offensive against the rebel-controlled areas.

NO CHILD IS SAFE

Politics and corruption are not the sole sources of violence suffered by youth. The problem has a domestic component as well. The Colombian Institute of Family Welfare estimates that as many as 100,000 instances of child abuse in Colombia occur annually. 'The loss of distinction between armed violence carried out in the context of political conflict and armed violence carried out for personal or criminal reasons has directly impacted children and is shaping their perceptions of society,' observed the *No Safe Haven* team.

The upshot for a country imbibing this heady brew is a culture of violence in which, the report concluded, 'no child is safe'. Writer Alonzo Salazar – a Colombian social worker and author of the 1990 book *Born to Die in Medellin* – explains: 'The actions of these young people questioned the meaning of life and death. We are talking of a generation that found its strength in a territory in which all limits were dissolved.'

The absence of a political response to las comunas and a population explosion within them, has led to a 'youthification' of poverty: a generation of young men without father figures, absent mothers working in humiliating and degrading jobs, sickly siblings, no constructive role models to identify with other than drug dealers and a bleak outlook for even their most immediate future. Add to this a total lack of public education, no sense of self-esteem and a 'do unto others' morality of revenge and aggression, and you have the perfect recipe for a merciless killer. Born in the sewer, live by the gun, die young, leave your mom a color TV. Either that or become a successful drug dealer.

WAR WITH NO BOUNDARIES

Fausto, a Sicario interviewed by Human Rights Watch, killed a man with a knife when he was sixteen. He spent two years in jail and then came out as a gang leader. 'I was famous because of the killing,' he told researchers. 'During adolescence, young people are inspired by great ideas of one kind or another,' wrote Salazar in an article entitled 'Young Assassins of the Drug Trade'. 'They look for paradigms and heroes. The youth gangs became an expression of the drug-dealing subculture in which ideals and heroes could be found. Drug dealers, and in some cases Sicarios, were idealized in just this way.'

In this hopeless spiral of death, drugs and poverty, Medellín has become the deadliest place in the world. The number of murders in Medellín surged from 730 in 1980 to 5,500 in 1990. In 1993 the city's population climbed to 1.7 million and its per capita murder rate became the highest for any urban center on the planet.

Territorial gangs, tightly held one-man dictatorships of death, have carved up the slums of Medellín into a mosaic of warring factions that would make Sarajevo during the Balkan conflict look like Disneyland. Lucky neighborhoods received protections in exchange for accepting the gangsters in their midst. Unlucky ones lived in perpetual fear, repressed by an invading army. Armies whose names echoed those of their leaders: 'Chucho's Boys', 'Nacho's Gang'. Some, like 'La Terraza', adopted the geographic appellation for their homeyhood.

With cocaine assuming its position as the country's number-one cash crop and a Marxist rebellion effectively fracturing the country, the long-running class dispute in Colombia has become even more desperate.

Rebel groups and cocaine traders found a common business interest. Paramilitary groups acting with impunity in the fight with both rebels and the cocaine-cultivating peasantry were financed by ranchers and large landowners; then, the paramilitaries and peasants formed alliances of convenience. In the cities, cartels battled over turf and markets both nationally and overseas. Boundaries between 'sides' grew more fluid and order became a chimera of the past as old points of reference dissolved and, depending upon where one stood, the good guys became the bad guys and the bad guys the good.

While everybody was fighting with everybody in an economy of ever-growing fear, the Sicario game expanded a thousandfold. With hits being called in from all sides, the Sicario business opportunity multiplied to the extent that a young assassin could find himself employed by any one of the warring factions or, for that matter, hunted by any of them.

With Escobar dead and defeated in his daring attempt to take on the combined military establishments of Colombia and the United States, a good portion of the terror infrastructure was appropriated by right-wing paramilitary leader Carlos Castaño – probably because his backers could provide the cash needed to pay the rank-and-file hit-boys.

DON PABLO

The use of the term 'terror' when discussing Sicarios is not necessarily misapplied or overstated. Like the left-wing guerrilla forces in Colombia – the FARC and the ELN – Pablo

Escobar conducted 'low-intensity' warfare designed to undermine confidence in the existing social structure and weaken its bulwarks in civil society. Unable to match the military might of a nation-state, rebel forces have relentlessly worked on a slow, purposeful and always violent assault from within. The destruction of roads, bridges, electrical and hydro-infrastructures impoverished the nation, darkened the countryside and, at times, the major cities of the country.

But Don Pablo brought the mayhem up to an uncharted level. Though generous and grateful to those who helped him, Escobar was ruthless when dealing with his enemies. And he spared no money to mete out revenge. Political figures, snooping reporters and anyone who got in Escobar's way were fair game, and he set his Sicarios upon them with the studied ferocity of an invading general.

In 1983 he was elected as an alternative to Colombia's Congress. In 1984 he started an all-out war with the state as government forces began cracking down on his drug empire. His campaign of murder, kidnapping, bombing and bribery forced a constitutional crisis in Colombia as the government banned extradition. His murderous campaign against judges and prosecutors forced the Andean nation to abandon trial by jury and begin appointing anonymous 'faceless' judges to prosecute drug criminals. Simultaneously his wealth grew at a stratospheric rate. In 1989 *Forbes* magazine listed Escobar as the seventh richest man in the world. That same year he offered to stop the violence and pay Colombia's national debt in exchange for amnesty for past crimes and the decriminalization of the cocaine trade.

At the height of his reign, Escobar and his Medellín drug cartel controlled as much as 80 per cent of the cocaine exported to the United States. In 1986 he instigated a takeover of the Palace of Justice in Bogotá that left more than ninety people dead, including eleven Supreme Court justices. In 1989, his army of teenage assassins killed three of the five candidates for the Colombian presidency. That same year, he blew up an Avianca Airliner outside Bogotá, killing 111 people.

The death in 1993 of the 44-year-old Colombian drug titan culminated a sixteen-month search that began when Escobar fled a luxurious prison built especially for him by Colombian authorities on a hillside near Medellín. 'It's the triumph of law over crime,' said Andres Pastrana, who, several years later, became president of Colombia. 'Escobar ended up being a symbol of violence and narco-terrorism. Now the country can begin to live more peacefully.' Ironically, Colombia's trafficking of cocaine and heroin has grown exponentially since the death of Don Pablo.

Throughout the 80s, the effectiveness of Escobar and his adolescent minions in taking advantage of a porous and corrupt state security system created a sense of vulnerability in Colombians that essentially paralyzed the country and its leaders. The government, it became clear, could not even guarantee the safety of its own. In fact, some say, Escobar had the government on the run.

Salazar cites a poll taken in the Antioquia province, wherein Medellín lies. When asked to identify the most important person in Colombia, 21 per cent of students said it was Don Pablo. The then president of the nation, Cesar Gaviria, ran two percentage points behind him. Rene Higuita, a goalkeeper for the Colombian national team – tainted by rumors of drug trade connections – came in third at 12.6 per cent.

Human Rights Watch reported: 'Although many of the *paisas*, as those from Antioquia are known, may have disapproved of Pablo Escobar's use of terror and murder, others admired his business acumen and philanthropic largesse, and may agree with Escobar's own assessment that he was "the most decisive, most energetic, most audacious Antioquian leader of the 80s".'

MURDERING THE MURDERERS

In an effort to address the situation of accelerating social mayhem following the murder of Liberal Party presidential candidate Luis Carlos Galan in 1990, the 'cleansings' of 'the criminal element' within las comunas began to occur with what some human rights groups claim was the connivance of right-wing paramilitary groups and the Colombian state.

Human Rights Watch said the picture of Sicario violence 'would be incomplete without a final element that provides not only another murderous force, but also part of the context in which murders occur: the role of state agents as murderers who go unpunished, observers who let murders occur without stepping in to stop them, and authorities who fail to ensure that the rights of the children are protected.'

Teofilo, a gang member and confessed killer interviewed by a human rights group, described his gang's dealings with the police. 'Sometimes they would sell us pistols. Other times it was threats of a *paseo* (stroll) to Santa Elena (a dumpsite for corpses). If they thought I was involved in a crime, they would take me to the station. There, they called me "gonorrhea". They would force a plastic bag over my head until I told them things. Other times, they threatened to put needles under my fingernails or give me electric shocks. Once, I was in [jail] thirteen days for murder. The police kill you alive with torture. Rival gangs just shoot you, and that's better.'

Organized and armed, these paramilitary cadres went first for the chichipatos, the least protected of the street children. They targeted Sicarios, too. But mostly, they targeted the young poor without discretion or distinction. The shootings were often public so as to set an example to anyone else doubting the resolve of those planning to establish the 'rule of law'.

During these raids, Fausto was arrested on four separate occasions. According to Human Rights Watch, police 'beat and tortured him with near suffocation.' By Fausto's own account, at least 200 youths and children were killed in his neighborhood during the cleansings. The cleansings themselves could take all night long. 'On those nights, it's best to stay indoors, since anyone on the street as is is at risk,' noted Human Rights Watch.

Dumped in a world without trash pick-up, patrolling police, or civic organization, the corpses often lay unmoved for days as people walked around them and went about their desperate struggle to survive. The cleansings came under scrutiny when a Christian children's construction guild, the Walking Builders of the Future, were shot dead. In all, eight children – the youngest an eight-year-old girl – and an adult were killed in what became known as 'the Villantina Massacre'.

'At one point,' the Human Rights Watch report recounts, 'the men apparently considered sparing the life of Johanna Mazo (the eight-year old) who several children attempted to defend. However, one of the killers disagreed, saying: "How can we leave this bunch of sons of bitches alive if they are the ones who kill us." He killed her.' Their blatant innocence is all that kept the child builders from joining hundreds of others in one of Medellín's twelve known corpse dumpsites, like the one at 'Devils' Curve' on the outskirts of town.

Accusations concerning this massacre have been made at the highest levels of Colombian government but no one has ever been punished or even found accountable for the tragedy. 'The investigation has been transferred to the capital,' says Human Rights Watch, 'to protect the investigators from frequent death threats. The man accused of giving the order to kill the children, Colonel Hernandez, continues to be the head of Medellín's F-2 (intelligence) and is appealing a procurator's order that he be dismissed.'

There are those who feel the cleansings strategy backfired, and that instead of exterminating the problem it further radicalized and alienated the same fourteen-, fifteen- and sixteen-year-old boys who were the prime targets for recruitment to the Sicario lifestyle. The militia groups which, at times, filled the power vacuum in neighborhoods also took to meting out vigilante justice upon any youngster they identified as a criminal. A militia typically warned a petty criminal of the need to halt his activities. Failing this, 'execution sentences' were signed, sometimes hundreds, during 'war councils' convened by the power-hungry vigilante forces.

MEDELLÍN IS FOR LOVERS

Murder, in general, goes largely unreported and unpunished in the streets of Medellín. Ivan Velasquez Gomez, a district attorney, told Human Rights Watch that 'in Medellín, criminal investigation does not exist. There are no measures to slow down this reality whether deaths occur at the hands of security forces or private individuals.' He confirmed that 98 per cent of the city's homicides go uninvestigated.

The lawlessness and the violence, and the cyclical tragedies and ironies this destructive behavior brings, make for good storytelling. Like the cowboys in the wild west and the Samurai warriors of feudal Japan, the Sicarios have found a place in the Colombian collective unconscious. Movies, novels, documentaries, riveting journalistic exposés – all have exploited the mythic tales of these young assassins.

Studied by international aid agencies, demonized by the forces of order, documented by the scale and daring of their own unorganized and desperate efforts, the atrocities carried by word of mouth through the poor sections of Medellín are then metastasized into Technicolor cinematic dreams and sweeping nightmarish novels. Two of the most notable novels dealing with the Sicarios are Fernando Vallejo's *La Virgen de los Sicarios* and Jorge Franco Ramos's *Rosario Tijeras*. These are stories of mindless violence, senseless death, cruel lives that never took off, and trapped people in a social order that provides no protection and no meaning. Their heroes and anti-heroes are young men with guns determined to address their invisibility, to leave a footprint in history, no matter how shallow the indentation.

Colombian director Victor Gaviria's film *Rodrigo D: No Hope* depicts the 'aimless brutality suffered by, and inflicted by, people in the slums of Medellín'. Gaviria, a Medellín native, used actual street urchins and Sicarios in the casting of his film. Since the release of his film, nine of his actors have been murdered. One Sicario actor, Gaviria told the *New York Times*, was killed on his way to the set by another Sicario who was hired by the film's producer that very same day.

The latest installment of the Sicario dream factory comes from acclaimed German director Barbet Schroeder. *Our Lady of the Assassins* is based on the above-mentioned Fernando Vallejo novel. The film, released in 2001, is a brutal tale of a washed-up writer who returns to Medellín to die but instead falls in love with a juvenile teenage assassin. Shot on location, the film contrasts the shocking everyday aspect of murder in Medellín with the strikingly beautiful vistas of the city. As one reviewer said, 'It's *Death in Venice* with 9mm Berettas.'

15. ANARCHY IN THE UK

'The gang culture has developed because these children don't feel they can trust adults. They turn to each other for support, and in Peckham the only currency they have is violence and anger.'
– Camilla Batmanghelidjh, of the charity group Kids' Company.

WELCOME TO THE TERRORDOME

As crack cocaine and the proliferation of deadly assault weapons in Britain's inner cities become commonplace, the UK's disenfranchised and alienated youth become ever more lawless, carrying out drug turf wars, chilling teen-on-teen homicides, armed mobile phone jackings and gangster-style executions. This era of vengeful sidewalk tragedies, which began at the turn of the twenty-first century, has spread throughout Europe and instilled fear in the minds of Middle Englanders. Teenage crime has become – along with international terrorism – *the* talking point of the first decade of the new millennium.

Termed by many the 'American condition', this worrying phenomenon shows no signs of abating. Ordinary citizens feel powerless as common courtesies seem to be dying out, replaced by arrogant aggression and a 'me first' attitude. The relatively harmless swagger that characterized previous generations of youth cultures seems to have morphed into something far more sinister: a genuine nihilism on the part of kids who put no faith in politics to change anything, and who are afraid of no one. We are seeing the emergence of a ruthless – and even murderous – new breed of super-predators not unlike the ultraviolent juveniles depicted in Stanley Kubrick's prescient film *A Clockwork Orange*.

A recent UK survey found that forty per cent of street crime is committed by ten- to sixteen-year-olds. The crimes are often committed while they play truant from school and an amazing quarter of all fifteen- and sixteen-year-old boys admit to carrying a knife or other weapon. There are also new types of crime adding urgency to the debate. Car-jackings, for instance, are a new threat, with 1200 incidents in one year alone. Meanwhile, mobile phone theft is soaring. An amazing 700,000 were stolen in Britain in the period 2001–2002 – that's one for every minute. In some urban areas, mobile phone thefts account for forty per cent of violent crime.

Last year, in London alone, there were 21 gangster-style gun murders and 67 attempted murders, which is a trifle in comparison to any major city in the United States, but remains a horrible new reality for the vastly more restrained London. The price of guns is tumbling in the UK, too – changing hands for just £200.

Imagine if you will a comparison with Los Angeles, California, where, through the first five months of 2002, there have already been 158 gang-related killings. And that's with a gang truce in effect. Say 'hi' to the future, Britons. Welcome to the Terrordome.

Some wonder if this lethal cocktail of brutality and drugs will challenge the very texture of British society, mimicking the institutionalized violence that defines American culture. Authorities are quick to fault everything from the influx of immigrants and the influence of rap to gun-powered movies and the 'yob' lifestyle of drinking and after-hours rebel-rousing. Much hot air can be generated debating the root causes of escalating violence among teenagers. But the real challenge facing us is how we stop young people embarking on violent criminal careers, where another person's life is seen as disposable. We have to act now, before another school-kid is seen sprawled in a pool of blood across the headlines of tomorrow's news.

LEFT TO DIE

On 27 November 2000, ten-year-old Damilola Taylor, a Nigerian-born schoolboy, was brutally attacked by a gang of youths and died as result of a stab wound to his femoral artery caused by a broken bottle. Damilola was murdered shortly before 5 p.m. on a Monday afternoon as he walked home from the local library to his dilapidated apartment in a sprawling North Peckham council estate. Poor Damilola bled to death after he collapsed on the urine-stained concrete stairs in between the first and second floors of his bleak council block. There, the child watched helplessly as blood poured from the wound. Adding to the horror, six different people stopped to try to control the bleeding, but were unsuccessful. Instead of calling for help, they moved on. Finally, when someone did call for the emergency services, it was too late for the paramedics to revive him, and he died on the way to hospital.

At school, three boys had been bullying Damilola, calling him 'gay', and taunting him with words he barely understood. He had told his mother, Gloria Taylor, about the bullying, and she tried in vain to talk with school authorities, but no one seemed to care. When Damilola's murder sparked a nation-wide debate on youth crime and bullying, the school officials quickly changed their tune.

Bola Ogun, of the Oliver Goldsmith Primary School, said action had been taken following Gloria Taylor's complaints. 'The school has a very robust attitude towards any form of bullying and any complaints which are brought before the school are taken extremely seriously,' he told BBC News 24. 'That's why in situations such as that the head would be keen to meet the parents.' Gloria said no one met with her and the school seemed to have forgotten her calls of complaint.

As it turned out, the school bullies had nothing to do with his death, but the bullying itself was indicative of the greater social ill that led to Damilola's senseless death. The youngster fell victim to the endemic youth violence of the council estate where he and his family moved in search of 'a better life'.

Four teenagers – two sixteen-year-old twin brothers, a seventeen-year-old and a fifteen-year-old boy – came to trial for his murder in March 2002. One of the two brothers allegedly told another delinquent – who had been held on the same wing of the detention center as him – that they killed the youngster 'for a laugh'.

Prison officer Darren De'ath said in court that the brothers began talking about the murder while they were at Feltham Young Offenders Institute in 2001, on remand for unrelated offences. Mr De'ath said he had asked the group if any of them were expecting long sentences. 'One of the brothers said, "possibly murder" and then laughed,' said Mr De'ath. 'One of the other boys asked, "Who did you murder?" and the other brother replied "Damilola Taylor, but we didn't kill him. We just stabbed him in the legs. It was not our fault that he died."'

Despite this, no one has been convicted of Damilola's murder. Halfway into the trial, a key witness – a fourteen-year-old girl named as 'witness Bromley', the only person to come forward as a witness to the attack – was deemed unreliable, and the judge acquitted two of the defendants due to the lack of evidence against them. The case against the twins continued but on 25 April 2002 the jury finally came to the verdict of 'not guilty'. The judge said the teenage girl's description of where the attack took place was contradicted by the evidence, and much of the detail she provided was already known to the public.

In a shocking reminder of the new set of values of inner-city youth culture, detectives investigating the case encountered a new breed of teenagers – a feral gang of youths with no fear of authority, complete disregard for the law and a sophisticated understanding of what they could get away with. Clearly, the youngsters that murdered Damilola knew that they would get away with murder if no one who witnessed the killing talked. And no one broke the 'wall of silence' because, in the North Peckham estate, no one talks to police, unless they too also want to end up in a pool of blood.

'They [local kids] just don't care what happens to them any more. The law and adults mean nothing to them – they have never had positive experiences of either,' said Camilla Batmanghelidjh of the group Kids' Company, a charity that works with teenagers from impoverished areas, including Peckham, trying to steer them away from a life of crime. 'They have shut down their capacity to feel. That makes them incredibly powerful.'

FERAL GANGS OF TEENAGE THUGS

'When they arrive they are just babies. By the time they are fourteen they are all carrying knives and calling the police Danish bacon. They believe the police are against them. There is no respect.' – A teacher at an inner-city secondary school

The sprawling housing estates like those in Peckham are ruled by roaming packs of feral teen thugs who go by the names of Ruff Riders, the Ghetto Boys, the Firehouse Crew and the Peckham Boys. In Peckham, people of Caribbean and African origin are the majority. Social inequality and institutionalized racism have created pockets of depravity where gangs, drugs and crime are the preferred career paths. 'What we are seeing is more extremes of violence among teenagers and young kids. We are seeing extreme lifestyles and a willingness to use weapons. There is a thing among young people to use violence at the moment,' said one black police officer who works with families in the area.

A former Peckham gangster told the *Guardian* newspaper: 'It's lawless out there on the street, but the laws are our laws, right. We want respect and we make sure we get it.' The gang subculture also comes with its own ready-made economy: drugs. 'It's easy money. I started selling puff to kids on their way to school. I was good at it,' said another former gang member, now in Feltham Young Offenders Institute.

A new generation of baby gangsters is being bred on gangster rap and the trappings of the 'cris life' – money, Nikes, gold chains and Cristal champagne. 'I tell my sons that they have to go to school and study hard so they can make something of themselves, but they just laugh in my face,' a Peckham clothing manager told the *Guardian*. 'They say, "Why should we study? So we can end up like you? No thanks." There are kids on the estate of twelve and thirteen who are going out stealing every day, and they are making more money than their parents earn. How are you supposed to convince people like that you know what's best? It's impossible.'

Instead, the gangsters and the drug dealers are the neighborhood heroes. They are the only ones with money, with the fancy clothes, with the opportunity to leave the bleakness surrounding them. In the twenty-first century, gang culture has become synonymous with hope. 'The kids just want to prove themselves. They want to be good at something, to be someone,' said 24-year-old Khadar Ahmed about the baby gangsters that live in North Peckham. 'They don't realize that what they do is bad. All the kids know that the law says you can't touch them.'

Unemployment around Peckham is twice the national average. Fathers are pretty much non-existent and mothers cannot control their children. As crack is gaining a foothold on the estate, a bleaker future is in the crosshairs: 'There is always a lot of crack around, and that makes people more violent,' said Ahmed. 'They need more crack so they commit more crimes to get money.'

Camilla Batmanghelidjh, who works with the young gangsters of Peckham, said the kids are 'socially lethal' and 'emotionally cold'. She thinks they are the products of the absence of meaningful adult relationships as they grow up. 'Peckham is just the beginning,' she said ominously. 'If the Government does not act, this sort of culture will develop in all our inner cities.'

Darren, a twenty-year-old drug dealer from Peckham, left school to fully dedicate himself to the job. 'If I go out to get a job I take home basic wages, but I have to take a load of shit with that,' he said, cynically. 'People say I'm a criminal: they put me in with those people who rob and beat people, but I'm not like that. I've got morals. I'm the good guy, but life is fucked. The only time I feel good is when I buy new clothes or go to a party. Otherwise it's just grim.'

ANTI-SOCIAL BEHAVIOR ORDERS

Anti-social behavior orders (ASBOs) were introduced as part of the 1998 Crime and Disorder Act to clamp down on out-of-control youngsters who repeatedly committed crimes. ASBOs work like a restraining order, forcing offenders to behave for two years or face a possible term in prison for up to five years. 'Tackling anti-social behavior on housing estates and on the streets of the most difficult areas is key to addressing the fear of crime and reinforcing the task of communities to build securer and safer neighborhoods,' Home Secretary David Blunkett said.

Hoping to stem the tide of younger and younger offenders getting away with murder – literally, as in the case of Damilola Taylor – Blunkett said that twelve- to sixteen-year-olds would be held on remand if they had a criminal record. Until then, young thugs who were picked up by an officer for serious offenses were able to return to the streets a day or two later. Giving the current crime wave a Dickensian dimension, Metropolitan Police Commissioner Sir John Stevens said officers were now arresting children as young as eight for serious crimes.

Another tactic invoked to crack down on wayward youths has been the recent trend by magistrates of 'name and shame'. Previously, juvenile offenders could not be named, but now, repeat offenders can be named after they've violated an Anti-Social Behavior Order.

One interesting lot of 'name and shame' youngsters are the infamous 'terror triplets'. The triplets, Shane, Natalie and Sarah Morris, all thirteen, had an Anti-Social Behavior Order imposed on them after a seven-month intimidation campaign in the Gillingham town center. Identified by the *News of the World* as part of its rogues' gallery of the 'worst child thugs in Britain', the triplets had their names made public by the authorities when they repeatedly violated their ASBOs.

One source close to their case said: 'They have been depicted as monsters. They are not that but the fear is that being notorious now could send them on a downward spiral. They are, to some extent, victims of politics.' Perhaps explaining their anti-social behavior, the triplets have all been diagnosed with attention deficit hyperactivity disorder (ADHD). Sarah and Shane also suffer from epilepsy and Natalie has a speech impediment.

Police, trying to control the spiraling crime statistics, have resorted to electronically tagging teen delinquents while they are out on bail. When the measure was announced in February 2002, there were 1,800 youngsters between the ages of twelve to sixteen out on bail. With all the kids tagged, officers would be able to enforce their ordered curfews and track their movements while they await trial.

There's been an alarming 39 per cent increase in robbery between April 2001 to February 2002. London police, in particular, complained of twenty to thirty 'untouchable' teen muggers operating in each borough who would be out on the street committing crimes the minute they were released on bail. One mugger was arrested eleven times only to be released, pending his next court appearance.

MOBILE PHONE JACKING

The recent skyrocketing growth in street crime has been attributed to a surge in incidents of cell phone jacking. This horrifying new trend became headline news when a nineteen-year-old London woman was shot in the head on New Year's Day 2002. The woman was on her way back from visiting her family in Walthamstow, East London, when she was attacked. 'This lady was walking down the road when she was approached by a man who asked her for her mobile phone. She struggled with him briefly and the phone was taken from her,' said a Metropolitan police spokesperson. 'It looks at this stage as though she was shot after he already had the phone.'

No one has been arrested in connection with this horrific crime. Remarkably, the woman survived the attack, despite suffering a fractured skull. This case is notable as the injuries sustained by the victim are out of all proportion to the value of the goods seized. It shows the lengths ordinary street robbers are now prepared to go to obtain the trappings of conspicuous consumption. Previously, such injuries would only be found in crimes such as bank robberies, where millions of pounds were at stake. Not any more.

Muggings in London alone have risen by 31 per cent in 2001 and the numbers are still moving up. The two worst boroughs in London – and in the whole of the UK for that matter – are Lambeth and Hackney. 'This increase has matched the increase in mobile phone ownership,' a police spokesperson told BBC News Online. 'Some areas have as high as fifty per cent of robberies involving mobile phones.' In London, in fact, more than a third of all street robberies involve cell phones.

A lot of street robberies are carried out by schoolchildren preying on other schoolchildren. This phenomenon has been explained by the fact the nowadays youngsters carry much more valuable items with them. In the past, one could only rob school children of their lunch money. Now they have cell phones, hand-held gaming devices, CD players and some are even going to school with laptop computers.

According to figures quoted by BBC News Online, the number of gun murders in London has increased by 88 per cent. From April to November 2001 there were thirty gun murders, compared with sixteen in the same period last year. Armed robberies have gone up by 53 per cent, from 435 to 667, meaning at least two people a day were robbed at gunpoint. Though front-page headlines like 'CRIME UK' blaring from the tabloids might suggest complete lawlessness in the UK, these numbers seem like a joke to anyone familiar with crime in the US. In 2001 there were about 4,000 armed incidents throughout England and Wales and 42 people died from gun violence. In the US about 30,000 people die a year from gun violence and 90,000 more are injured.

GANGSTA-RAP

'Young nigger in a warpath, when I'm thru, it's gonna be a bloodbath' – NWA

The toxic relationship of guns and rap music is one that many are quick to blame for a rise in gun-related deaths in and around London nightclubs. Though in the US rappers like NWA, Ice Cube and TuPac Shakur are identified with a bad boy image that includes 'pimpin' bitches' and 'packing heat', the UK is at odds with this recent Americana import. At the center of a burgeoning controversy lies the So Solid Crew, a collective of more than twenty DJs, producers, singers and rappers, considered among the brightest stars of the British garage scene.

As pointed out in an article by Joseph Harker titled 'Rap Culture Has Hijacked Our Identity', ten years ago police were the most threatening force in the inner city. Nowadays, it's the gangsta-rapping groups of aggressive black youths. According to Harker, the profanity-laden, misogynistic imagery of rap videos have been given free rein to hijack black culture. Being black is all about music, sex, guns, drugs and living on the street. This, in turn, affects impressionable youngsters who think that they can achieve more respect and 'street cred' from 'packing weapons' and serving a stint in prison than from graduating from college and scoring a good job.

Youngsters, buying into the gang lifestyle portrayed by the lyrics of So Solid Crew and their US counterparts, place more value on the conspicuous consumption depicted by gold Rolexes and Cristal champagne than in the reality of honest work for an honest day's pay. The truth is that if you're in the ghetto, the good life, in short-term, comes from joining a gang, gaining street respect and making money selling crack. 'To carry a gun is hip,' said convicted armed felon Danny Thomas. 'They are carrying a gun with their Reebok trainers, with their Moschino jeans, with their Gucci tops.'

'It does look as though a significant number of young black men in some areas are beginning to admire as role models some people who are quite heavily involved in crime,' Ellie Roy, London's crime reduction director, told the *Guardian* after a shooting incident during a So Solid Crew concert. 'But blaming the band for street violence, she added, 'confuses the messenger with the message.'

GUNS IN NOTTINGHAM
While Britain has some of the toughest firearms laws in the world, there's a disturbing growth in armed crime throughout its streets. And armed teens are not only a problem in London. Birmingham, Manchester and Nottingham are also experiencing a new wave of gun crime. On the one hand,

police believe most armed youngsters are involved in the lucrative and violent crack market. On the other, some believe the recent growth of street violence is due to inner city police officers being reassigned to protect terrorist targets in the wake of the 11 September terrorist attacks.

In response to the increased gun violence in the tough inner-city neighborhoods of Nottingham, police patrolling these areas have resorted to packing some heat of their own. Are these armed units precursors of a future armed police force? Traditionally, 'bobbies' have resorted to wielding their clubs to enforce the law. The image of armed-to-kill new centurions walking into war zones has come from the streets of New York or Los Angeles, but not the UK. British civility has always chafed at the idea of arming their cops. But now, perhaps, British civility itself is at stake.

The police insist this new strategy will not become the norm for all bobbies. It is meant as a specific response to send a message to young criminals not to use guns. But it could also be interpreted as a racist police force upping the ante when dealing with black and immigrant thugs.

Handguns in the UK were banned in 1997 following the Dunblane massacre in Scotland. On 13 March 1996, disgraced scoutmaster Thomas Hamilton opened fire inside the gym of the Dunblane Primary School, killing 16 children and one teacher before putting a final bullet through his head. Since then, more than 160,000 handguns have been handed voluntarily to the government.

'The vast majority of handguns surrendered to the police have been destroyed, or will be, when the relevant compensation claims have been settled and disposal instructions issued by the Firearms Compensation Section,' said Lord Williams, who implemented the 1997 Firearms Act in Parliament.

MAYHEM ROCKS MANCHESTER

The city of Manchester is another area in England that has lost neighborhoods to gangs and street crime. In response, police have stepped up patrols after several officers were threatened at gunpoint during violent gang turf wars in April and May of 2002. Machine-gun-toting police patrols are now a part of daily life in Manchester, which is something you would expect in Kosovo, Medellín or Kabul, but not in the birthplace of the rave scene.

Threats to police are compounded by three shootings, including one fatality, in the area during April 2002. Aeon Shirley, eighteen, died after he was shot in Longsight, which has often been a focus for recent gun incidents. Two other people, including a heavily pregnant teenager, were also shot and injured. A senior police officer warned that in the Longsight and Moss Side neighborhoods, guns were becoming 'almost a fashion accessory'.

With the help of anti-gang measures such as Operation Goodwood, launched by police in May 2002, armed officers will accompany their unarmed colleagues on foot patrols. Officers will be using stop and search powers under section 60 of the 1994 Criminal and Public Order Act to disarm youngsters throughout the city. Police said they have recovered more than 623 firearms, air weapons, replica guns, stun guns and ammunition in Greater Manchester in the first four months of 2002.

In March 2002, gangland killer Thomas Pitt was jailed for life for the murder of a rival gang member and three other attempted murders. Pitt, 24, was convicted of shooting Longsight Crew member Marcus Greenridge in September 2000. Boys in his gang, some as young as fourteen, would deliver, on their bicycles, pot, heroin and coke. Under their hoodies, the youngsters wore Kevlar vests and packed serious firepower just in case someone tried to rip them off.

One former resident of the Longsight area sums it up: 'It's the "have it all" culture. These are kids who don't aspire to proper jobs that they know they won't get. But they want trainers that cost over £100, a nice lifestyle, and they don't think you have to work for it. They'll get it by any means necessary.'

BABIES WITH GUNS

'It's not about turf wars over drugs any more, it's just the way they operate day to day. Kids of 14 are carrying guns, they're just babies.' – Sheila Eccleston

Despite protests in Manchester's most notorious suburbs by a group called Mothers Against Violence (MAV), more than fourteen youngsters have been gunned down at the hands of local drug-trafficking gangs. Though MAV's members have buried sons, relatives and friends as a result of the violence, they are a committed group of community activists determined to take back their neighborhoods, one child at a time.

In the summer of 1999, three young men were shot dead within a two-mile stretch of south Manchester in the space of two weeks. Patsy McKie's youngest son, Dorrie, aged twenty, was one of them. Three youngsters on bikes, wearing bandanas, chased Dorrie, whom the family called Junior, until three bullets stopped him forever by the side of the road.

'Junior loved basketball, riding his bike, hanging out with his friends, listening to his music, all that rap stuff I don't understand,' said his mother. 'He had never been in trouble with the police, and I'd never had to worry about him. Whenever I went to bed, I rested. I didn't lie there thinking he's going to be shot. Never entered my head. But it happened,' she said.

After attending two more funerals that month, McKie and two other women formed MAV. 'People were touched, but it also stirred them into doing something,' she said. 'We're here to support each other, our families, anyone in the community who needs us.' The three-year-old group now has twenty members. McKie said she doesn't want to perpetuate the gangland hatred by speaking out for revenge. Instead, she hopes the community will take action to heal itself. 'I've forgiven them, whoever they are,' she said. Thus far, no one has been arrested for Junior's murder, but two men are behind bars, serving extended sentences for possession of the gun that killed him.

Sheila Eccleston, another founding member of MAV, said that the older boys draw younger ones into gangs; they want the money they are paid for small jobs, and are too frightened to refuse. 'The only thing they know is fighting and killing each other. It's who is going to be the big man, who kills the most. The boy who murdered my son is bragging that he's the main man now.'

'One day I'll be sitting here next to the woman whose son killed mine,' said Eccleston. 'I'll have to listen to her talking about her wonderful son, how worried she is for him. But we should be here for them too. It's not their fault. And we all want to stop the violence.'

Along with routine police patrols, the community also has to take responsibility for the violence. 'Values and morals have to be built in children from a young age,' McKie told the *Guardian*. 'But we have young mothers who are inexperienced and we have a society that is reluctant to intervene, to take action when we see children misbehave. We need to look at the family, to be good role models ourselves, and police our community.'

McKie sums up the climate in Manchester: 'Confronting the gangs isn't about "us and them". It's not a case of feeling vulnerable if we take a stand. We are the community, and it's close. We know these boys. And we've had enough.'

THE BATTLE FOR BRIXTON

'The centre of Brixton is a 24-hour crack supermarket.' – Chief Superintendent Brian Moore.

As the gang wars litter the streets of Manchester with fresh trails of bodies cut down in their prime, tough neighborhoods are under siege from another front: crack. The distribution of crack cocaine has reached epidemic proportions in the UK. Officials say the use of crack has risen over two hundred per cent in the past three years. In response, police are asking for new detainment powers, allowing them to hold suspected dealers indefinitely.

'Crack cocaine has had a negative impact on the lives of many Londoners, causes most harm to the capital's communities and is behind much of the gun-related violence,' said Deputy Assistant Commissioner Mike Fuller, head of Scotland Yard's drugs directorate. Fuller acknowledged that crack is fast reaching critical mass, particularly in London, Liverpool and Manchester.

In London's Brixton market, crack is becoming a burgeoning economy. Brian Moore, Acting Borough Commander for Lambeth, told the *Observer*: 'We have fifteen dealers during the day and up to twenty throughout the night. They each sell a hundred rocks per week at ten pounds a time. It means the centre of Brixton alone is a crack market worth twelve million pounds each year. The level of demand means that even if we arrested a thousand dealers, they'd be replaced by a thousand new ones the next day.'

To counteract the rise of hard drugs in the streets, Brixton police has decided to relax the enforcement of cannabis-related offences. The program, referred to as the 'softly-softly' approach, is hugely controversial. The cannabis experiment was launched by the outspoken Metropolitan Police Commander Brian Paddick and has found critics even in the Drug Enforcement Agency of the United States. But then again, the DEA with its failed Drug War has been pumping money and weapons into Colombia for twenty years as cocaine consumption in the United States remains at record levels.

Since the Brixton cannabis experiment began in July 2001, there has been a thirteen per cent increase in the number of marijuana dealers on the street. Drug offenses in the borough have risen by eleven per cent and recorded cases of cannabis possession by 34 per cent Statistically, one must say that the experiment seems to be failing. 'They have abandoned the streets to the dealers,' Reverend Ivelaw Bowman of St Andrew's Church told the *Guardian*. 'You cannot use the bus stop at the top of Coldharbour Lane or the nearby telephone boxes because they have been taken over by the dealers. They sell drugs openly and without fear . . . The law is not being enforced and the question everyone in the community wants an answer to is this: if we can see it, why can't the police?'

Critics have forgotten the reasoning behind Commander Paddick's plan. When he took over the Lambeth patch, an independent Home Office inquiry concluded that clamping down on soft drugs was an inefficient way of allocating resources. The idea was to effectively manage the dwindling police resources. According to the *Observer*, 'Britain has the highest number of drug-related deaths in Europe.' Paddick's plan, in effect was to put more men fighting the real killers, like crack and heroin, while allowing a bunch of middle-class white people to enjoy their joints without fearing the strong arm of the law.

The South London borough of Lambeth, which incorporates Brixton, holds the distinction of having the highest crack abuse in Britain. There are currently 74 crack houses in the Brixton area, most of them in buildings housing vulnerable members of the community. Dealers, as a rule, prey on the vulnerable and mentally ill, taking over their homes to set up their drug dens. With budget cutbacks removing a hundred officers from the street, Paddick needed to design a drastic new approach. Arresting and charging someone with possessing a few joints would keep officers busy for up to eight hours. Under Paddick's plan, the community needs were better served as police would focus on hard drug issues instead.

But it all went south when the same dealers selling pot also started selling crack. Adding insult to injury, the street dealers would steer their customers toward crack, even when they asked for weed. To top it off, the use of heroin in Brixton has also rocketed to an all-time high. With so many needles, syringes and crack pipes littering the sidewalks of Brixton, Faith Bowman, Chief Executive of Lambeth Council, announced a plan to implement Britain's first drug paraphernalia cleaning team.

LITTLE SAVAGES

'In the past five years, we have noticed the rise of a new form of violence which manifests itself as a kind of "nationalism of the neighborhood"' – Lucienne Bui Trong

The UK is not the only part of the continent under siege from marauding and uncontrollable teen street gangs. It's hard to imagine one of Paris's most exclusive shopping centers, La Défense, turned into a war zone. But that's exactly what happened in February 2001 when two teen gangs, armed with baseball bats, knives, hammers and axes, chose the luxurious shopping center to settle past scores.

Sixteen-year-old Sofiane said he and a hundred fellow hoodlums went by train from Chanteloup-les-Vigne, their rundown suburb outside Paris, to the fashionable city center to fight a rival gang, the Grags, from the Val-Fourre estate in Mantes-la-Jolie. The site of the rumble, the chic and strategically neutral La Défense shopping center, was decided after a series of mobile phone calls by the leaders of both gangs.

When Sofiane and his boys arrived for battle, the two-hundred-strong Grags were already harassing shoppers and making a nuisance of themselves. What followed was a two-hour brawl that was eventually brought under control by two hundred police officers and a battalion of the CRS riot squad. As the smoke settled and the Louis Vuitton shopping bags were returned to their rightful place, the whole of France recoiled at the site of its future nightmare taking over their bastions of liberty, fraternity and equality.

Sofiane and three of his friends, dressed in shockingly preppy Lacoste shirts, boasted about their roles in the riots. One youngster pointed out that the French only care if the white middle-class is involved in this burgeoning social upheaval. 'If the battle had taken place in Chanteloup-les-Vignes, you wouldn't be here. Everybody – press, TV, intellectuals – only get interested in our problems when the white bourgeois are embroiled. If it's just a matter of us kids stabbing each other, it's not even news. But when we get into a brawl where all the nice families are shopping, suddenly it's international news.'

But, then again, it's the same everywhere else in the world. One need only look at Columbine, Paducah, Jonesboro. White boys get the media saturation coverage. If the school rampagers in the US were ghetto kids, would there be more than a quarter million returns on a Google search for the word

Columbine? On 23 February 2002, a sixteen-year-old boy killed six adults with a baseball bat in Camden County, New Jersey. Has anyone heard the name Llewelyn James? Google returns 69 hits on a search for his name. Is it, perhaps, because he and his victims were all black? Yes, the world is an ugly place, and the media focus is by and large racist.

That's why, until they rampaged through La Defénse, no one cared about the gangs of kids running roughshod through the dilapidated high-rise housing projects of Chanteloup. It comes as no surprise that most of the neighbors in Chanteloup are from North Africa or Sub-Saharan Africa. Just like the twenty other suburbs ringing Paris and housing France's eleven million minorities. In this urban sprawl, black and Arabic 'guests' live in squalid conditions. In these 'immigrant cities' school attendance is a joke, employment is a dream, everybody hates the police and Law and Order is a show on TV. Drugs and violence rule, and teen gangsters are the kings of the street.

NATIONALISM OF THE 'HOOD

In the outskirts of Paris, nine new police stations have been opened in railway stations after thousands of public transport workers went on strike to protest the repeated attacks on them by youth gangs. 'Senseless gang violence is a fast-growing phenomenon in several suburbs,' said a police spokesman. 'It is an extremely worrying development.' Burgeoning gang violence is reportedly also on the rise in the poor suburbs of Marseille, Grenoble and Strasbourg.

Explanations for the rise in French youth crime abound, from institutionalized racism and poverty to the absence of parental control and the influence of drugs. But no one explanation convincingly accounts for the spate of violent gang feuds and revenge killings of the young throughout the Gallic nation. Between 1993 and 1999, the number of thirteen- to eighteen-year-olds in jail doubled from 2,247 to 4,326. In 1998, some 3,825 teenagers were jailed for committing violent crimes, nearly three times the number of violent teens in 1994.

The Paris sprawl has become balkanized. Neighborhood nationalism is rampant. Gangs have become the armies defending the local underclass. Like their counterparts in South Central L.A., violence is about your territory, about defending your 'hood. The only difference is that in Mantes-la-Jolie and in Chanteloup-les-Vignes, it's done with knives and baseball bats. In South Central's Nickerson Gardens and Watts, it's AK-47s and TEC-9s.

Romuald, fourteen, was killed in November 2001, in a battle between the Aunettes at Evry and the Canal at Cour gangs in a housing estate south of Paris. After a youngster from the Aunettes was attacked by fifteen gangsters from Canal, the Aunette kids decided it was time for payback. Taking a page from the South Central Gangster handbook, they went for the always terrifying drive-by, or in its French version, the park-by. Parked in a car, the three kids waited for someone to kill. When Romuald and another boy walked by, the driver called them. When they turned, they were met with the double-barreled 'hello' from a shotgun. The first blast blew out Romuald's left lung. The second killed him. Tragically, Romuald had no gang affiliation.

Look out for other compelling, all-new True Crime titles from Virgin Books

MY BLOODY VALENTINE – Couples Whose Sick Crimes Shocked the World
Edited by Patrick Blackden

Good-looking Canadian couple Paul Bernardo and Karla Homolka looked the epitome of young, wholesome success. No one could have guessed that they drugged, raped and murdered young women to satisfy Bernardo's deviant lusts. Nothing inspires more horror and fascination than couples possessed of a single impulse – to kill for thrills. Obsessed by and sucked into their own sick and private madness, their attraction is always fatal, their actions always desperate. The book covers a variety of notorious killer couples: from desperados Starkweather and Fugate, on whom the film *Natural Born Killers* was based, right through to Fred and Rose West, who committed unspeakable horrors in their semi-detached house in Gloucester, England. With contributions from a variety of leading true crime journalists, *My Bloody Valentine* covers both the world-famous cases and also lesser-known but equally horrifying crimes.
£7.99 ISBN: 0-7535-0647-5

DEATH CULTS – Murder, Mayhem and Mind Control
Edited by Jack Sargeant

Throughout history thousands of people have joined cults and even committed acts of atrocity in the belief they would attain power and everlasting life. From Charles Manson's 'family' of the late 1960s to the horrific Ten Commandments of God killings in Uganda in March 2000, deluded and brainwashed followers of cults and their charismatic megalomaniac leaders have been responsible for history's most shocking and bizarre killings. Jack Sargeant has compiled twelve essays featuring cults about whom very little has previously been written, such as the Russian castration sect and the bizarre Japanese Aum doomsday cult that leaked sarin gas into Tokyo's subways.
£7.99 ISBN: 0-7535-0644-0

DANGER DOWN UNDER – The Dark Side of the Australian Dream
Patrick Blackden

Australia is one of the most popular long-haul tourist destinations, but its image of a carefree, 'no worries' culture set in a landscape of stunning natural beauty tells only one side of the story. *Danger Down Under* lets you know what the tourist board won't – the dark side of the Australian dream. With a landscape that can be extremely hostile to those unfamiliar to its size and extremes, and an undying macho culture – not to mention the occasional psychotic who murders backpackers, or crazed gangs of bikers and cultists – there is much to be cautious of when venturing down under.
£7.99 ISBN 0-7535-0649-1

DIRTY CASH – Organised Crime in the Twenty First Century
David Southwell

There was once only one Mafia: now every country seems to have its own. Until fairly recently gangsters kept to their territories, but crime – like every other business – has been quick to take advantage of the new global economy. Business, it seems, is good, with over $150 billion laundered each year in Europe alone. As links are formed between the Mafia, the Triads, the Yardies, the Yakuza, the Russian Mafiya and the South American cartels, a tide of misery spreads throughout the world. The book looks in detail at the specific groups involved, the horrifying crimes they commit, and the everyday lives of their members.
£7.99 ISBN: 07535 0702 1

December 2002

FEMALE TERROR – Scary Women, Modern Crimes
Ann Magma

Statistics show that female crime and female violence is on the rise, particularly in America where, in 1999, over two million violent female offenders were recorded and the rise was cited as 137 per cent. Women are becoming an ever-growing presence in crime statistics, becoming a major force in both organised crime and terrorism. In the last ten years they have also come to the fore as homicidal leaders of religious sects and gun-toting leaders of Los Angeles street gangs, whose members are every bit as tough and violent as their male 'gangsta' counterparts. From Ulrike Meinhof to Wafa Idris; from IRA terrorists to Mafia godmothers, this book will look at the rise and rise of female terror.
£7.99 ISBN: 07535 0718 8

January 2003

MONSTERS OF DEATH ROW – Dead Men and Women Walking
Christopher Berry-Dee and Tony Brown

From the cells of Death Row come the chilling, true-life accounts of the most heinous, cruel and depraved killers of modern times. At the time of writing, there are 3,702 inmates on Death Row across the USA, many of who have caused their victims to consciously suffer agonising physical pain and tortuous mental anguish before death. These are not normal human beings. They have carried out serial murder, mass-murder, spree killing, necrophilia, and dismemberment of bodies – both dead and alive. In these pages are to be found fiends who have stabbed, hacked, set fire to, and even filleted their victims. So meet the 'dead men and women walking' in the most terrifying true crime read ever.
£7.99 ISBN 07535 0722 6